Planners
and
Public Expectations

Planners
and
Public Expectations

by

Howell S. Baum

SCHENKMAN PUBLISHING COMPANY, INC.
Cambridge, Massachusetts

Portions of the book originally appeared elsewhere and are included here in modified form with permission:
— Portions of Chapters 2, 3, and 8 are reprinted from "Sensitizing Planners to Organization," in Pierre Clavel, John F. Forester, and William W. Goldsmith, eds., *Urban and Regional Planning in an Age of Austerity*, New York: Pergamon Press, 1980, pp. 279-307, © 1982 by Pergamon Press, with permission.
— Part of Chapter 5 is reprinted from "The Uncertain Consciousness of Planners and the Professional Enterprise," *Plan Canada, 20*, 1 (March, 1980), pp. 39-53, © 1980 by the Canadian Institute of Planners, with permission of the publisher and editors of the journal.
— Part of Chapter 6 is reprinted from "Analysts and Planners Must Think Organizationally," *Policy Analysis, 6*, 4 (Fall, 1980), pp. 479-494, © 1980 by The Regents of the University of California, by permission of The Regents.
— Portions of Chapters 6 and 8 are reprinted from "Policy Analysis: Special Cognitive Style Needed," *Administration and Society, 14*, 2 (August, 1982), pp. 213–236, © 1982 by Sage Publications, Inc., with permission.

Schenkman Publishing Company, Inc.
Cambridge, Massachusetts 02139

Library of Congress Cataloging in Publication Data

Baum, Howell S.
  Planners and public expectations

  Includes index.
  1. City planning—Decision making.   2. City planners—Attitudes. I. Title.
HT166.B387   1983   307'.12   82-16961
ISBN 0-87073-634-5
ISBN 0-87073-635-3 (pbk.)

Printed in the United States of America.

To Irving Baum, Ruth Klein Baum,
and Madelyn Siegel Baum

CONTENTS

TABLES

ACKNOWLEDGMENTS

This book has been written with the intellectual and emotional support of a number of people. Leonard Duhl first encouraged me to become more sensitive to psychological issues in planning. He insisted that personal biography influences professional practice. As I have studied planners, he has provided provocative ideas and an urging to look still deeper into the ways in which planners attempt to make sense of their work.

John Forester has provided a wealth of ideas, including many clear thoughts about the ways in which planning involves organizing. He carefully read and commented on earlier drafts of the book, and he continually offered encouragement to think and write further about what the interviews with planners might mean. Ralph Hummel persistently supported the way of thinking about planners represented in the book and offered thoughtful suggestions to improve the manuscript. Jerome Kaufman, Melvin Levin, and Barry Checkoway read the manuscript and offered innumerable helpful criticisms on the basis of their years of planning experience.

Throughout work on the study and the book I have benefited from the ideas and assistance of others who have thought about planners, organization, research and education. These contributors include Amrit Baruah, Robert Beauregard, Paul Ephross, Donald Gelfand, John Holland, Donald Klein, Charles Levine, Arnold Meltsner, Donald Michael, Beryl Radin, Donald Schon, John Seeley, Hans Spiegel, Robert Tennenbaum, and Stanley Wenocur.

The gentle prodding of Seymour Sarason led me to initiate the research which is described in this book. In an early speculative discussion about planners, he suggested quite simply that talking with planners would be the best way to understand them.

This book would not have been in any way possible if planners in Maryland had not generously agreed to talk with me or if they had been less candid. Their efforts to struggle with me to make sense of what they do had contributed to the understanding of their work and careers expressed in the book.

My wife, Madelyn, has taken a continuing interest in my work on the book. She introduced a number of ideas that have found their way into the book. She asked many questions that improved the clarity of the manuscript. And she faithfully insisted that the study and the writing were worth the effort.

INTRODUCTION

This book examines the ways in which experts provide advice for public decision-making at a time when many people feel that "government doesn't work." Citizens and social critics increasingly contend that an elite of experts have taken decision-making power out of the public arena. Politicians themselves often complain that they are the victims of unelected specialists who surround them: planners, policy analysts, social workers, lawyers, engineers, and management scientists. Many of these experts consider themselves "planners." This group has recently come under especial attack as "bureaucrats" who promulgate and unthinkingly enforce regulations which impede reasonable independent choice by individuals and organizations.

The study presented here looks at planners and these charges against them in an unusual way: planners themselves were interviewed about their work, their influence, their satisfactions, and their problems. What planners say is noteworthy. In the context of complaints about technocratic displacement of public decision-making, planners themselves complain about their power-lessness. Thus the central question raised in this book is why planners are relatively powerless. What is planners' expertise, and why does it bring them only limited influence? How do planners experience and make sense of the gap between their expectations of influence and their actual power?

In analyzing the reasons for the limited influence of planners, the study makes a significant finding which may be generalized to a wide range of experts who render advice. The research shows that planners exercise limited power in decision-making because they misunderstand the ways in which decisions are made in bureaucratic organizations and in the political process. The analysis presents a conceptual framework for clearing up this misunderstanding. The study examines the "cognitive maps" of planners—their mental images of the world in which they work—and finds that *a majority of planners do not see bureaucratic structures or the ways in which organizational decisions are made.* As a result, they have little chance of influencing these decisions.

In examining why planners do not recognize organizational decision-making processes, the research explores planners' feelings about power. Many planners appear to misunderstand decision-making because they have mixed feelings about exercising power—which is the essence of decision-making.

Members of the public make yet another criticism of planners. Citizens and elected officials complain that these experts, for all that they may know, do not offer useful advice on how to solve important problems. Not only do citizens suffer from poor housing, bad health, limited education, and low incomes, but public decision-making about these problems is stalemated by complex conflicts of interest among groups each of which claims to have answers for these problems. There is no means of sorting out these competing claims or resolving the conflicts which hinder an examination of the claims. If experts want to be useful in public decision-making, these critics argue, then the experts must demonstrate that they can help to deal with these underlying problems of societal governance.

In analyzing the reasons for the apparent weakness of planners in responding to problems of governance, the study finds a serious discrepancy between public expectations of experts and the expertise which planners develop. Many citizens expect planners to develop new ground rules for public decisions, so that government will "work" again. However, the study indicates that, *while members of the public expect planners to solve broad procedural problems of governance, most planners have developed expertise as purely intellectual problem-solvers who work on narrowly defined substantive problems*, such as housing, health, and transportation. This finding may be applied to a wide range of experts who give advice. Here is a second reason why planners have limited influence: their expertise is not matched to public expectations.

The finding that planners exercise limited influence over public decisions may provide comfort to critics who are concerned that experts are assuming unwarranted power. At the same time, this finding is likely to disturb those citizens who believe that public decisions should be based on the best expertise available, wherever it may reside and however it may be formulated. In addition, the finding is likely to trouble those planners who have been working for professional status and influence for planners in the larger society.

In the context of planners' concerns about professional status the study makes another significant finding which may be generalized to many experts who render advice. In seeking prestige and influence, *planners have followed a traditional model of a profession which is inappropriate to the work which planners do.* Pursuing the model enjoyed by physicians and lawyers, planners have attempted to set themselves off as experts who have independence from and power over their clients and constituents. This effort has contributed to hostility toward planners and the perception that they exercise significant but illegitimate power. This effort has led to successful measures to limit the influence of planners, who describe their powerlessness in this study.

Because most planners do not understand the organizational context in which they work, they do not understand that their work is social and inherently political. Their proposals concern the distribution of valued goods and services among groups with different political interests. These groups expect to participate in making decisions about the allocation of these goods and services. While they may want the advice of planners, they do not want planners to dominate the process of making decisions. For these groups, planners' legitimacy as experts depends on their responsiveness to group interests.

The book presents a new model of a profession which is appropriate to the work of experts like planners. In the traditional model of a profession, practitioners claim autonomy as essential to their practical effectiveness and then assert that their apparent effectiveness provides legitimacy for their autonomy. In contrast, in the practice of planning, autonomy is inimical to both legitimacy and effectiveness. Planning is part of a process of social decision-making in which *planners' accountability to public groups is necessary for planners' legitimacy to practice and, consequently, their effectiveness in influencing decisions about social problems.*

The study identifies the ways in which many planners have pursued an inappropriate model of expertise in a self-defeating way. Planners' misunderstanding of organizational decision-making has encouraged them to develop an expertise which is primarily intellectual and which ignores the political context of decisions.

Planners' selection of an anachronistic traditional model of a profession has encouraged them to disregard the concerns and expectations of their clients and constituents. The book, which assumes that planners have useful expertise to contribute to decision-making, suggests ways in which planners may increase their influence by responding to public expectations of experts. The book makes recommendations for the reform of planners' practice and their education.

The study described in this book looks at the activities of one group of experts engaged in planning. This is a group who have traditionally called themselves "planners" and have, at least in their antecedents, been linked with the architectural, engineering, and public administrative activities of "city planning." The study examines the ways in which they have defined planning and the ways in which they have thought about planning as a profession. In a limited sense, this book provides an intensive view of a single group of practitioners comprising only part of a broad planning movement. However, the thinking and actions of this group are remarkably similar to those of others who are involved in planning. It would appear that the nature of planning work and the organizations in which it is conducted attract people with similar predispositions and skills and guide and constrain their thinking and actions in similar ways. Hence this study should be read as a representative example of the ways in which a broad range of experts are attempting to define their work in planning and the ways in which they respond to the attractions of a profession.

ORGANIZATION OF THE BOOK

The focal questions explored in the book are these: How do planners perceive and respond to the changing conditions under which practitioners acquire professional status? Do planners conceptualize their practice in a way which is likely to lead to effectiveness vis-à-vis important problems of planning?

Part One provides an introduction to the issues with which the book is concerned. Chapter One discusses the nature of planning and professions and presents a model of a profession which is appropriate to present public expectations of planners.

Part Two presents findings from the study. Chapter Two examines planners' motivations to enter planning and their perceptions of their expertise as planners. Chapter Three describes planners' views of their autonomy in their work and their responses to limitations in autonomy. Chapter Four analyzes planners' preferences regarding their relationships with their clients and public constituents. Chapter Five brings together material to articulate planners' consciousness of themselves as professional practitioners. Chapter Six provides an interpretation of planners' perceptions in terms of their cognitive maps of organizations and their feelings about power.

Part Three presents conclusions and implications from the study in the context of the issues raised in the first part of the book. Chapter Seven assesses the present likelihood that planners will acquire professional status. Chapter Eight recommends reforms in planners' practice and education that will increase planners' public legitimacy in decision-making.

The Appendix discusses the design of the study, methodological issues, data analysis, and characteristics of the sample. The following information is offered to the reader who does not look at the Appendix before reading the study findings.

The planners interviewed comprised a random sample of 50 members of the Maryland Chapter of the American Institute of Planners. Although the AIP is most closely linked historically to "city planning," the practitioners interviewed work in planning physical facilities, social services, and economic development. Both the diversity of these planners' activities and their similarities to other practitioners suggest that the findings should be interpreted as representative of the broad range of practitioners who work in planning and who weigh the attractions of the professions.

The planners were interviewed with semi-structured questionnaires that asked about their perceptions of their expertise, autonomy, and accountability to members of the public, as well as their willingness to act politically to further perceived collective interests of planners. The interviews produced a combination of quantitative and qualitative information about planners. Most discussions in the book combine quantitative summaries of responses with qualitative elaboration on prominent themes. The qualitative character of the information leads to a conspicuous reference to "a few," "some," "many," or "most" planners. Although these terms do not satisfy a desire for precise measures, the terms best represent the interview material and suggest at least the magnitude of themes within the responses. The presentation of quotations from interviews enables planners to speak for themselves and provides the reader with the evidence against which the conclusions may be tested.

PART ONE

Problems of Professionalization
in Planning

1

PLANNING AND PROFESSIONS

Planning and professions are both of increasing interest to practitioners, scholars, and the public. "Planning" refers to a variety of activities in which experts employ apparently technical or rational methods for analyzing public problems and recommending actions to respond to them. "Professions" refer to certain groups of practitioners who hold a special, privileged status in comparison with other practitioners and in relation to their clients. Currently planning is carried out by many types of practitioners, including some who explicitly call themselves "planners" and others variously labelled policy analysts, social workers, attorneys, public administrators, engineers, and management scientists.

As the number of "planners" increases, and as the number of goods and services directly or indirectly affected by "planning" broadens, there is increasing concern about whether planning may be considered a profession. Members of the public ask whether "planners" influence public decisions competently and responsibly. Practitioners involved in planning consider whether they might get the privileged status of profession for their work. Specific groups of practitioners, such as "planners," policy analysts, and attorneys, begin to compete for exclusive rights to whatever professional status will attach to planning.[1]

Interest in planning and professions is not purely—or even primarily—intellectual. Efforts to define and discuss "planning" and "professions" are aimed at far more than semantic clarity. Rather, interest in definitions is economic, political, and psychological. People argue about the nature of planning and professions as a way of staking out positions on the allocation of power, status, and wealth.

However, the central conclusion which emerges from the following analysis of planning and professions is that the nature of planning work makes any efforts to imitate traditional professional models self-defeating. Planning is concerned with the understanding

3

and solution of social problems, and any efforts by planning practitioners to acquire traditional professionals' autonomy vis-à-vis clients and other citizens is both inappropriate and certain to lead to ineffectiveness. This conclusion undergirds the main argument of this book and must be emphasized: for planners autonomy is inconsistent with and in conflict with effectiveness. The book is concerned with delineating a new model of profession which is congruent with the work of planning, a model in which planners' effectiveness depends on their using their expertise to collaborate with clients and other citizens in working on social problems.

PLANNING

The practice of planning may be characterized in two ways. Intellectually, it is a process of problem-solving; socially, it is a process of advice-giving. Most commonly, definitions or descriptions of planning refer to it as a particular type of problem-solving.[2] As a method of selecting solutions for problems, planning may be contrasted, for example, with pure guesswork, random choice, and blind stabs into the intellectual dark. Planning is usually also contrasted with decision-making processes which simply favor the choices of powerful political interests. Planning is presented as a strategy for approaching problems with "rationality." This "rationality" is systematized in the adherence to several basic steps in a "planning process." When problem-solving follows this model of planning, then, it is possible for decision-makers to make informed choices.[3]

The role of decision-makers figures prominently in the second view of planning, as advice-giving. Planners' intellectual work takes place and has value only within a political context. No matter how much information planners collect and organize in their analyses, they rarely make final decisions about problems. In the end, decisions—that is, choices of potential solutions for problems—are made by elected officials, their appointees, agency administrators, or councils. The planner only renders advice to these decision-makers.[4] Descriptions of planning which focus on this advice-giving role emphasize that a planner's influence over the final choice by a decision-maker depends heavily on the relationship between the planner and the decision-maker. Characterizations of planners' work as advice-giving usually also incorporate a broader view of "problem-solving" than the discussions which refer to planning solely as problem-solving. In this second view, problem-solving is explicitly a process of attempting to resolve problems which affect social and political interests. In addition, problem-solving is seen as a process which itself takes place in social and political interactions between planners, decision-makers, and other interested parties. Thus problems are identified in a political process, and potential solutions are selected in a political process. Planners are likely to influence the choice of courses of action insofar as they can formulate problems and alternative possible solutions in terms which are congruent with decision-makers' perceptions of the situations in which they are the problem-solvers.[5]

This brief summary of these complementary views of planning indicates why the discussion of planning generates increasing interest. When planning is seen as a process of problem-solving, questions are raised about which problems are important—or legitimate—to try to solve. More specifically, these questions concern whose problems will be worked on and which courses of action will be considered thinkable—feasible and desirable—in the search for possible solutions. These are inescapably political questions, entailing judgments about who will be the clients or, at least, the constituents for planners' work. They implicate planners, with whatever influence they may have, in decisions about the social allocation of valued goods and services.[6] When planning is viewed as a process of advice-giving, related questions are raised about who should be advised. In addition, questions arise concerning who will be permitted to offer advice to whom and whose advice will be listened to. Because no two planners will either view any problem identically or establish an identical working relationship with a client, answers to these questions have unavoidable political implications, even if the implications cannot always be foretold.

Planning in a Political Context

In short, even if planners assert that their work is to provide "rationality" for decision-making, the decision-making is political, and, as a consequence, planners' work is implicitly political. The problems with which planners are concerned impinge on conflicts of perceptions, conflicts of values, and conflicts of interests. Issues about which planners make recommendations are formulated within a social context in which wealth, power, and status are unequally distributed. Parties with different interests have stakes, variously, in having a particular decision or recommendation made or in having no decision made. Even the identification of a situation as a problem for analysis is an action which is likely to evoke support and opposition from interested actors. Planners' control and use of information—in setting an agenda of problems for consideration, in defining a problem, in identifying causes of a problem, and in supporting a recommendation for action—are perceived as political acts, affecting vested interests, and will be responded to in a political manner.

Effective planning in this context requires a recognition of political interests implicated in issues, problems, and potential courses of action. Both individuals and organizations have interests in protecting territory and ways of acting. The bureaucratic organizations in which many planners work themselves derive stability from adherence to organizational rules and regulations, even when these regulations may conflict with apparent mandates to planners to recommend "rational" action. Within bureaucratic organizations individuals and departments are concerned about protecting carefully acquired turf. As a consequence, actual, informal procedures for influencing and making decisions may correspond little to formally delineated procedures. Organizational decision-making may be cautiously incremental, and, in contradistinction to "rational" models of decision-making, selection of courses of action may resemble the matching of already favored "solutions" with problem-formulations which plausibly justify them.

In this context effective planning requires a sensitivity to political and organizational issues. Planners consider problems and recommend courses of action in a context in which many agents with varied interests already respond to a number of incentives. Planners must be able, in turn, to provide these agents with incentives to accept particular formulations of problems, adopt certain recommendations, or implement recommendations in a manner consistent with their intentions. Development of these incentives requires throughout the planning process a sensitivity to the interests and perceptions of different parties, as well as an ability to organize networks of intellectual and political support for specific analyses or recommendations. Further, planning in this context needs flexibility, because actors, their perceptions and interests, and incentives all change as social conditions change.

For practitioners seeking public designation as "planners," these challenges of organizational sensitivity in a political setting come to a focus on the related issues of effectiveness and legitimacy. Which practitioners have the skills which will enable them to offer recommendations which could effectively solve the problems which decision-makers consider important? Which types of training—or, perhaps, even, temperament—are most likely to contribute to this effectiveness? Whom will decision-makers turn to as legitimate advisors in their efforts to identify solutions for their important problems? Whose intellectual skills, biases, ethics, style—or whatever—will give them authority with actors who make decisions about significant social problems? Clearly, the stakes are more than intellectual: for example, what is the most rational approach to problem-solving, or what is the most ethical role for planners to play in decision-making? For claimants to the role of "planners," at stake are their employment and the influence which that may bring. At stake for decision-makers who would make use of planners are their ability to find solutions to important problems, the social and material interests affected by the solutions, and the turns in their careers shaped by others' perceptions of their chosen solutions for problems. At stake for interest groups, community organizations, and other citizens are the distribution of goods and services which they regard as necessary for their well-being.

Competition among practitioners to demonstrate their effectiveness and to gain legitimacy as planners has created confusion about the boundaries between groups of practitioners and a special "identity crisis" among those who have traditionally claimed the label of "planner." Historically, this label has most consistently been claimed by the collection of architects, engineers, and social reformers who have been concerned about the aesthetics, efficiency, and order of the physical development of cities and their suburbs—"city planners."[7] Traditionally, these practitioners have been concerned primarily about land use housing, transportation, sanitation, and other aspects of the physical urban environment. This loose coalition is most closely represented organizationally by the American Planning Association, which has approximately 15,000 members. However, Association membership includes not only planning practitioners, but also elected officials, community activists, and academics who have interests in planning but who may not regard themselves—or be regarded by others—as planners. In addition, several uncounted thousands of others consider themselves planners but do not join the Association.[8] Further, place of employment is misleading as an indicator of who may be considered a planner. For example, employees of "planning departments" may include not only planners, but also administrative staff and legal counsel. Conversely, a "housing department" may do authoritative planning for construction of both public and private housing. Job titles are similarly misleading in identifying planners. Some "planners" may be more appropriately considered budget officers, program analysts, or staff administrators. Some staff members without "planner" in their title may exercise considerable influence in the functions attributed to planning. On top of all this, planning is now being initiated or carried out in substantive fields not of much concern to the traditional "planners": health, education, social services, and energy, for example.

Thus thousands of practitioners, many of whom do not call themselves planners, carry out planning activities in both public and private organizations. Some of these practitioners claim specialized expertise in the use of certain techniques, such as need assessments, economic feasibility studies, budgeting, or cost-benefit analysis. Others focus on their specialized expertise in some functional area, such as land use, housing, health, education, transportation, or recreation. Many who were trained in the mastery of techniques by university planning programs find themselves spending considerable parts of their work day in such non-technical activities as attending meetings and writing memoranda.[9] At the same time, in many organizations relatively technical planning activities are carried out by practitioners not trained in planning programs, such as attorneys, business school graduates, social workers, and policy analysts. The perceived employment threats from these latter practitioners have crystallized the concerns of traditionally oriented "planners" about the meaning of "planning." Efforts to develop working definitions of "planning" are hurried in order to give legitimacy to certain practitioners' claims to "planning" positions.[10] Increasingly, traditionally oriented "planners" have attempted to put forth these definitions as the basis for licensing regulation which would regulate entry into "planning" positions.[11]

Clearly, then, practitioners have high stakes in discussions of planning. In addition, public and private clients and constituents of planners have considerable interest in who does planning. Even if planners may be numerically a small group, their strategic importance appears to be growing and is perceived by others to be increasing. Planners render advice on the allocation of a wide range of public goods and services, for example, housing, schools, roads, recreational facilities, and social services. Planners also offer advice on public decisions affecting the possibility, magnitude, and location of private investment in such areas as housing, medical care, commercial activity, and industrial development. In the private sector planners are asked for recommendations on strategies of development and investment in a number of areas. Although there are no systematic studies of the influence of planners as advice-givers in these situations, there is considerable evidence that planners influence some of these decisions under some circumstances.[12] The economic and political consequences of specific recommendations are often major, affecting the interests of the housing industry, lending institutions, hospitals, middle-income homeowners, racial minorities, the poor, the elderly, and so forth. In a time of economic austerity, when there is restricted opportunity for either private or public investment, decisions and recommendations may arouse still more interest and raise greater conflict. For all these reasons there is growing interest in the nature of planning and planners.

PROFESSIONS

Relationships between effectiveness in problem-solving, legitimacy in advice-giving, and the wealth and power which may attach to this legitimacy are the subject of discussions of professions. As with the discussions of planning, practitioners and citizens who are concerned about the nature of professions feel that economic, political, and psychological stakes are involved, and they mean to assert what they regard as their rightful claims.

The nature and importance of these interests may be illustrated by examining two principal approaches to the study of professions.[13] These approaches may be contrasted in terms of their treatment of four variables. Effectiveness and legitimacy have been discussed in connection with debates about planning, the former representing the desired outcome of the exercise of practitioners' expertise and the latter representing the authority which clients or constituents accord practitioners to exercise their expertise. Autonomy and public accountability refer to two complementary aspects of the relationship between practitioners and their clients or constituents. Autonomy represents the degree of independence which practitioners have in exercising their expertise; public accountability represents the degree to which clients or constituents may question or otherwise constrain practitioners who seek to exercise expertise.

The Attributional Approach

A traditional approach to the study of professions may be called the attributional approach. Writers identify a checklist of attributes which would qualify practitioners for the label of "profession." For example, Greenwood, a social worker, wrote an early article on "Attributes of a Profession" (1957), in which he identified the following determining characteristics: systematic theory, authority, community sanction, ethical codes, and culture. He concluded that social work met this test. Similar positions have been taken in the planning literature, beginning with Howard, who asserted that "Planning is a Profession" (1954) because its practitioners had several crucial attributes, including specialized expertise about urban processes and devotion to serving the public interest.[14] Goode (1960) has reported that most lists of attributes center on two claims: that the practitioners exercise specialized expertise and that they govern their practice by a code of ethics which ensures that this knowledge will be used to serve others.

The attributional approach to the study of professions is a normative approach, concerned with determining who has the right to the title and privileges of "profession." Accordingly, the concept of legitimacy plays a central role in what is posited as a simple relationship between effectiveness and autonomy. In this view, insofar as a group of practitioners can be shown to wield specialized expertise, the practitioners are assumed to be effective in doing whatever they do.[15] Their presentation of professional ethics provides an assurance that this effective expertise will be used for good purposes. Therefore, they are to be accorded the legitimacy of the title "profession" and permitted to practice in the area of their expertise. Permission to practice almost naturally includes the right of autonomy in practice. For insofar as expertise is specialized, only one group of practitioners possesses or understands it, and "professional" ethics by their nature involve self-governance, in which the general public is relieved of any concern about the morality of practice. In this view, then, expertise entails effectiveness; the addition of ethics brings legitimacy; and in the two together inheres autonomy. Because of the emphasis on autonomy, accountability to clients and the public is hardly discussed except by implication in relation to the code of professional ethics.

The simplicity of this model may largely be explained by the concerns of its proponents. They tend to have interests in demonstrating that their own group of practitioners should be regarded as a "profession," and the lists of characteristics tend to support their claims.[16] Central to these discussions is the importance of certain attributes in providing the key of legitimacy to autonomous practice. Thus the implication of the attributional approach for planners concerned about acquiring professional status is that they should define a specialized expertise and establish a code of ethics, and autonomy will follow.

The Political Approach

However, the normative biases of the attributional approach have hindered empirical examination of professions, and these short-comings have contributed to the development of a second, political approach to the study of professions. Writers in this second mode are concerned primarily about the autonomy and accountability of practitioners. Empirically, a number of observers of professions have pointed to inconsistencies among lists of attributes labelled as "professional" and among lists of occupations considered to be "professions." These observers have suggested that, while lists of attributes may serve to justify claims to the "professional" label, they do not help to explain why some claimants are more widely regarded as "professions" than are others. These writers approach the problem of defining professions by examining empirically what attributes or characteristics consistently distinguish occupations which are widely considered "professions" from those which are not. The single distinguishing attribute, they conclude, is the autonomy of the practitioners. They suggest that the degree to which a group of practitioners are accorded the status of a profession is related to their control over the conditions of their practice.[17]

Specifically, "professions" exercise control over entry into and the pattern of work within some defined area of practice. They may control educational or training institutions, licensing or credentialing institutions, the organization of departments in which skills are practiced, and organizations which may wield sanctions against deviants from norms of practice. This control may be enacted into law, as with licensing statutes, or it may reflect organized political power, as with the enforcement of uniform educational requirements. In this way, they may minimize both the likelihood of competing claimants to practice in the demarcated area and the possibility of even intellectual surveillance of practice in that area.[18]

Writers with the political approach observe that the acquisition of the autonomy which attends—really, defines—professional status depends on a political process similar to other political processes. In this process, called "professionalization," practitioners seek to influence relevant decision-makers to grant them autonomy in a claimed area of practice.[19] In this process the alleged attributes of a group of practitioners assume importance as support for a case for autonomy. Whether or not practitioners really have expertise is less important than whether, for example, legislators or citizen groups believe that they have expertise.

When practitioners strive for professional status, three characteristics of their perceived expertise are important in the expectations of decision-makers. First, they expect that the expertise will be specialized. Practically, it will be easier to distinguish one group of practitioners from another when each lays claims to clearly delineated, specialized skills or knowledge which do not overlap. In addition, in American society there is a cultural expectation that expertise, by its nature, is specialized.[20] When the world is perceived as extremely complex, it is believed that knowledge about the world is possible only when the world is broken down—analyzed—into small components and each component is studied in depth. Broad overviews of the world are considered superficial. This cultural expectation is related to a second expected characteristic of practitioners' expertise: the expertise should be useful in solving a problem. Specialization is considered necessary because of a cultural expectation that problems are solvable only when they are defined in narrow, tightly bounded terms. Thus specialization is considered necessary for effectiveness. Third, however, this specialized expertise is expected to be useful in solving problems which are considered important. Issues move into and out of public focus, often without any evident relationship to whether they have been resolved, and expertise will be valued in relation to its correspondence to currently perplexing problems.[21] Thus claims to professional status must be accompanied by arguments that the problems with which the specialized expertise is useful are important and interesting.

With regard to claims that practitioners govern themselves by a code of service-oriented ethics, as with claims to expertise, the perception is politically more important than the reality. Legislators and citizen groups are likely to support granting autonomy and accord legitimacy to practitioners only when they believe that these practitioners are committed to using their expertise in the service of good ends.

The political account of the process of professionalization bears superficial resemblances to the attributional representation of that process. Practitioners present their claims for autonomy to significant decision-makers. These claims are likely to include descriptions of expertise and ethics. The decision-makers consider, among a number of things, the effectiveness of the expertise and the service orientation of the ethics and may then adjudge the practitioners to be legitimate and worthy of autonomy in practice. Yet the thrust of the proponents of the political approach has been to argue that to accept at face value claims and appearances of expertise and ethics is contrary to empirical evidence. When appearances are effective, they do persuade, but they may still not be valid. Further, decisions to grant autonomy to practitioners are often made through a common process of political decision-making that involves considerable bargaining and little scrutiny of intellectual or ethical credentials. In short, the representation of the professionalization process suggested by proponents of the attributional approach is a rationalization of events which endows them with meaning which they may never have had.

In many cases, the relationships among autonomy, legitimacy, and effectiveness may really be just the opposite of those implied by the attributional approach. First, practitioners may organize and succeed in acquiring political and legal support to practice with autonomy. They then acquire legitimacy for their autonomy from the political and legal processes through which they established autonomy. Finally, once they are considered legitimately to have acquired autonomy, they are assumed to be able to practice effectively. The final assumption is explained by the rationalism of the attributional approach, which accurately represents the logic of contemporary American cultural expectations. Expertise and ethics are expected requirements for legitimate exercise of "professional" autonomy. Hence any legitimate exercise of autonomy is likely to be rationalized by assuming that practitioners have the specialized expertise and ethics which would make them effective in the service of the public. Furthermore, practitioners may be accountable to the public only insofar as the political process of acquiring autonomy may open them to scrutiny or exact certain concessions from them. In most political processes, practitioners usually see only representatives of the public. In any case, granting of autonomy tends to seal practitioners off from further accountability to the public or clients in the actual practice of their skills.

Important stakes are involved in the designation of any occupation as a "profession." In addition to prestige, practitioners may gain legitimacy, or authority, to practice in a defined area. Practitioners who gain widespread authority to practice in some sphere effectively acquire autonomy. They may exercise power over entry into practice, as well as the manner of practice. Economically, employment is selectively restricted, and monopolistic control over employment makes it possible for a relatively small group of practitioners to earn relatively large incomes.

The power of "professions" also has consequences for their clients or constituents. Insofar as practitioners restrict the manner of practice to a select few models, individuals, groups, or organizations seeking the assistance of the practitioners have limited choice about the type of service they may have. The fact that choice is limited may itself annoy clients or potential clients. In addition, when a restricted range of services is offered, there is a significant probability of a mismatch between the needs of a client and the activities of a practitioner. In those areas in which planners practice, there is a possibility that communities may not receive appropriate responses to their needs for housing, human services, transportation, economic development, and the like.

This perspective on professions has significantly different implications for planners than does the attributional approach. First, legitimacy and autonomy in practice are likely to come not simply from refinement of expertise and ethics but, rather, from organized political efforts to persuade citizens and legislators to grant planners the privileges of professional status. In addition, engagement in this political activity will require planners to satisfy decision-makers' conditions for granting professional status. In this process of negotiation a specific issue to which planners need to be sensitive is what will constitute plausible demonstrations of their effectiveness. In particular, because of the broad social needs affected by planners' actions, it is questionable whether political decision-makers would agree to grant planners autonomy from their intended clients and constituents. Centrally, the nature of planning is such that effectiveness may be recognized by legitimacy without autonomy. Thus the political approach to professions offers a paradoxical perspective on planning: planners should take political initiatives in order to acquire the autonomy which defines "professions"; however, ensuing political negotiations may lead to "professional" legitimacy without autonomy. Thus, at least for planning, a new status for "profession" may be defined.

The following analysis examines this question in the context of debate about four aspects of professions: autonomy, legitimacy, accountability, and effectiveness.

PLANNING AND PROFESSIONS

Autonomy

Autonomy has evident intrinsic value for practitioners. At the same time, a secular tendency toward bureaucratization of work and current economic austerity increase the value of claims to professional status. The general bureaucratization of work has affected the nature of work to which "professionals" lay claim (Ehrenreich and Ehrenreich, 1977; and Reich, 1972). Conflicts between "professionals" and bureaucratic authority are well documented and increasing (Gilb, 1966; Hall, 1975; May, 1976; and Moore, 1970). At stake is whether certain types of work will be carried out according to norms held by practitioners or whether this work will be conducted consistent with bureaucratic norms for a division of labor and a hierarchical chain of accountability. The conflict concerns whether practicing members of "professions" or organizational managers will decide how work is conducted. Politically, claims to "professional" status serve practitioners in securing a greater measure of discretion in organizations. Consequently, practitioners motivated by pride and faith in their own work norms stand to gain increasing benefits by insisting on "professional" status and the autonomy which accompanies and defines it.

Most planners work in public or private bureaucracies, serving large, collective clients or constituencies. In the public sector, even though planners may work in a department consisting almost entirely of planners, they receive assignments from public officials or high-level organizational administrators. Instructions about how the work may be carried out are usually similarly handed down to the planners. Although individual planners may negotiate discretion in the definition of their work,[22] most planners carry out their work within bounds set by bureaucratic norms. In addition, the flatness of most planning agency hierarchies and civil service restrictions on salaries make it difficult for planners in public bureaucracies to reap rewards of power, status, or income for their work. Planners respond to this situation with feelings that they are forced to do "unprofessional" work.[23] In this situation planners stand to gain greatly by organizing and insisting that they are members of a "profession" which requires autonomy for effective work.

These general tendencies are accentuated in a period of economic austerity like the present. Employment security diminishes, workers become anxious about their earning ability, and competition for jobs intensifies. Because of the security which the autonomy of professional status does offer, conflict over professional designation becomes increasingly bitter. Workers with tenuous claims to jobs present challenges to workers with better or potentially better claims, challenges which might not be made in a period of greater economic security. Thus, as the number of graduates in city planning, policy analysis, management science, public administration, and social work increases more rapidly than the number of positions in planning, city planners are forced into competition with these other practitioners. Aspirations to professional status encourage claims to autonomy, which raise the stakes in the competition to an explicitly political level and discourage reasoned examination of people's needs, tasks which have to be carried out, and any possible division of the planning labor.

Legitimacy

In order to acquire or retain the autonomy of "professionals," practitioners need to obtain the organized political or legal approval of legitimate decision-makers. Traditionally, these efforts have involved the organization of legislative or administrative approval by officials who are regarded as legitimate public representatives, along with some organization of public support through accepted political methods. Functionally, legitimacy may serve as an equivalent to demonstrations of effectiveness. For both practitioners and clients who are anxious about the true effectiveness of services rendered, bestowal of legitimate autonomy provides considerable reassurance.

Two types of developments have made practitioners' efforts to obtain legitimate autonomy more difficult. The bureaucratization of the types of work which would-be "professionals" perform has provoked public questions about control over this work and has made the public accountability of practitioners increasingly important as a condition for the bestowal of legitimacy. Similar questions have been raised as a result of the commoditization of this work (where cost becomes a major characteristic of the work) and by its politicization (where the political power of practitioners becomes prominent).[24] Citizen groups tend to become dissatisfied with traditional means of bestowing legitimacy on practitioners, such as passage of licensing laws and granting of lifetime licenses to practice with few or no further checks on practitioners' performance. Some citizen groups would like to hold practitioners directly accountable to them, not only for a check of initial qualifications to practice, but also for continuing surveillance of relationships with clients. There are slowly growing public pressures to make this type of public accountability a new condition for the granting of legitimacy to practice with any measure of autonomy. Indeed, some citizen groups insist that legitimacy to practice at all should be based on a practitioner's forsaking claims to autonomy and a willingness continually to be accountable to clients and constituents. These issues, along with their implications for planners, are discussed in the following section on public accountability.

A second development involves growing questions about the effectiveness of practitioners in solving important problems. Changes in the relationships between practitioners and clients have stimulated questions about public accountability and, in turn, have encouraged clients to scrutinize services more carefully. In this process, clients have found inadequacies in services rendered. In addition, changes in the types of problems considered important have outdistanced the skills and knowledge of claimants to professional status, with the consequence that many practitioners appear ineffective. Both tendencies have pushed questions about practitioners' effectiveness toward the center of considerations of their legitimacy to practice. These issues, including their implications for planners, are discussed in the section on effectiveness.

Public Accountability

Bureaucratization of the work which claimants to professional status perform has limited the autonomy of practitioners by subordinating them to organizational managers. Bureaucratization has also changed the relationship between the practitioners and their clients. An important ingredient in the relationship between a client and, for example, a self-employed physician or attorney is trust. The client has direct contact with the practitioner, and, although the client may not have access to the esoteric knowledge of the practitioner, the practitioner must act in such a way as to persuade the client that the practitioner is acting in the client's interests. Otherwise, the client may directly fire the practitioner. Although this model reflects an ideal not always realized, it has considerable veracity, and, particularly important, it represents an expectation which many clients bring with them in seeking the services of a "professional."

As the relationship between practitioners and clients becomes bureaucratically organized, clients lose control over practitioners.[25] Public bureaucracies in particular may be singled out as state-managed behemoths which are impermeable to public opinion, insensitive to client needs, and running out of control. Control of the work of bureaucratic employees is made a public issue, and this issue is increasingly articulated in terms of the legitimacy of certain practitioners' claims to professional status. In order to wrest some control over the scope and pattern of these practitioners' work—that is, in order to limit their autonomy—citizen groups contend that the practitioners are not acquiring their apparent autonomy through processes which the citizens regard as legitimate. Citizen groups are insisting that some form of explicit and direct public accountability be considered a condition for the legitimate bestowal of authority to practice. [26]

Proposals for redress of this perceived loss of control take two directions. One is to create some variant of market conditions for the use of the services. The other is to give clients or constituents political participation in processes of decision-making about the delivery of practitioners' services. Each alternative, respectively, reinforces another tendency in the delivery of services which itself detracts from the legitimacy of practitioners' authority.[27]

Economic Controls. Voucher proposals in education (for example, *Educational Vouchers*, 1970) and health maintenance organization proposals in health (for example, National Academy of Sciences, 1973; and Roemer, Kramer, and Frink, 1975) are examples of efforts to re-create or, at least, create quasi-free market conditions in the relationship between practitioners and clients. However, this strategy of creating a more explicitly economic market for practitioners' services reinforces tendencies toward the commoditization of services, a trend set in motion by practitioners.

Historically, the commoditization of services may be seen in the growing proportion of services which are no longer bartered in extended family or community networks but are purchased and recorded as part of the gross national product.[28] Experientially, citizens simply are increasingly aware of the costs of services, which represent a growing economic burden and which are more and more difficult to reconcile with the non-commercial "service ethic." Some people now pay privately for some services which formerly they received publicly, because either the supply or quality of public services is considered inadequate. Social work and education are examples. Citizens witness the delivery of privately provided services in new types of organizations designed primarily to maximize the income of practitioners. Some group practices in medicine are examples. The costs of both publicly and privately offered services grow. Current conditions of economic austerity, combining inflation with recession, intensify concern about the costs of services.

One response to the press of rising costs of services has been for citizens to conclude that, if practitioners are so bluntly going to treat services as commodities, citizens as consumers will go along with this definition by insisting equally directly that they "get their money's worth." Citizen groups have urged the use of cost-effectiveness analyses, competency-based evaluations, and performance contracts, as well as simple limits in costs or expenditures. In these proposals "consumers" will use individual judgment to determine whether a type of service is worth purchasing at all and whether a particular practitioner offers an acceptable service at a reasonable price.[29] The increase in malpractice suits and the extremely large awards offered by juries provide further evidence that "consumers" are prepared to take seriously practitioners' apparent commoditization of services and to hold them accountable for the quality of the commodity.

These developments represent two changes in the relationship between practitioners and clients. They entail an apparent willingness on both parts to redefine their relationship in economic terms. In addition, they involve an insistence by clients on holding practitioners accountable to clients, now defined as purchasers of services. Client responses represent an effort to move decisions about the autonomy of practitioners to arenas where money changes hands. Clients, either individually or through the agencies which allocate their money, would become judges of the legitimacy of practitioners. Judgments about legitimacy would include clients' assessments of the quality and cost of the service. To the degree that clients did not consider particular practitioners legitimate, to that degree the practitioners would lose autonomy because, simply, they would not have clients.

Political Controls. Clients have also responded to their perceived loss of control over bureaucratically organized services by organizing to confront control directly as a political issue. The "citizen participation" movement has been an effort by clients to gain effective participation in decisions about the allocation of resources among goods and services and among particular services, the allocation of services among clients, the hiring of practitioners to provide services, and the dissemination of information about services to clients.[30]

This move has reinforced two other developments which have contributed to the politicization of services. Although aspirants to "professional" autonomy have always used political tactics to gain autonomy, an increase in the number of groups of practitioners striving for this autonomy has made practitioners' use of political tactics more visible. This apparent proliferation of political activity by would-be "professionals" tends to discredit practitioners' claims that they are motivated by public service ethics and that they expect autonomy only as a result of their ethical use of effective expertise. This demoralization of the claims of would-be "professionals" to be above either commerce or politics is reinforced by the economic consequences of practitioners' efforts to restrict domains of practice. Licensing and unionization have the effect of raising the costs of services, again, at a time of economic austerity.

The constricted economic environment in which decisions about practitioners' services are made contributes to another development: the perception that more and more decisions by practitioners about the number, type, and allocation of their services are really political decisions, based on value judgments rather than any specialized expertise. For example, when medical care is scarce and costly, it is difficult for people in need to conclude that the cost and allocation of practitioners' services involves decisions made solely on the basis of specialized expertise. In addition, several groups of practitioners—particularly those involved in "planning" and certain types of social work—are making decisions about matters which have traditionally been considered political, such as allocation of public goods and services.

The politicization of the work of practitioners represents the ultimate demythologizing of the claims of "professionals." As proponents of the attributional approach suggest, "professionals" claim to exercise specialized expertise within the bounds of public service ethics. In order to practice effectively, they require autonomy, and they can be trusted with this autonomy. When clients, perceiving that practitioners' work has become commoditized, insist on holding practitioners accountable for the clients' "money's worth," clients are attempting to change the power relationship between practitioners and themselves. They are insisting that whatever autonomy professionals derive should come from the explicit judgments of informed purchasers of their services. At the same time, this challenge, while casting aspersions on the public service ethical claims of practitioners, leaves claims to specialized expertise essentially intact. Moves to subject practitioners to measures of their effectiveness of competency are based on assumptions that there are practitioners with special expertise and that these practitioners should be rewarded. Further, the ethical claims of practitioners are not really rejected, but only modified. Those practitioners who do satisfy clients as purchasers of services will be considered to be, in fact, conforming to the tenets of a public service ethic. The judge of conformity to the ethics may be changed, but the ethics and propriety of the ethics are not seriously challenged. Rather, in the operations of the market "true" "professionals" will be separated from pretenders.

The politicization of the work of practitioners takes the challenge much further. One moderate political challenge to practitioners resembles the economic challenge. In this case, clients do not question the right of certain expert and ethical practitioners to autonomy but do reserve for themselves the right to participate directly in decisions about which practitioners they will be.[31] In a more radical challenge, some clients are contending that whatever practitioners do should be considered political and should be subjected to whatever procedures clients consider legitimate for decision-making. These clients are both calling for some form of explicit and direct public accountability of practitioners and insisting on setting their own criteria for judging the practitioners.

Implications for Planning. These developments have serious implications for people in planning. Because most planners work in public bureaucracies, they are subject to citizens' general concerns about control. If planners are interested in professional status, it will be difficult for them to ignore citizens' growing calls for more direct public accountability of practitioners. The calls for economic accountability are probably less significant for planners. The relatively small number of planners who work as private consultants have always worked with clients in commercial relationships in which both parties have been clear about the importance of clients' satisfaction to planners' further work with them. In the public sector the proportion of the public budget which is spent for planning is relatively small. The "taxpayers' revolt" more often takes aim against operating agencies than against the planners who may recommend decisions affecting those agencies. Economic concerns about planning may be most often expressed by representatives of industries significantly affected or regulated by planning. Representatives of the housing industry or medical institutions, for example, may contend that the costs of their operations are raised by the paperwork requirements of the planning process and by the planning decisions themselves. In a number of cases, as with medical institutions, this charge may simply be a way of diverting the attention of citizens who are concerned about the economic accountability of practitioners employed in these institutions. It should be noted that these concerns are not really questions about the cost-effectiveness of expenditures on planning per se, but, rather, questions about the cost-effectiveness of planning decisions to institutions required to change their operations. In the short run, because most planners either do not have or have not used power to affect the activities of major institutions, these types of challenges are not likely to be overbearing. They could increase as planners acquire either the statutory or organized political power to affect the institutions.

In the short run, citizen calls for political accountability are most likely to affect planning. Symbolically, "planning" often stands for what many citizens do not like about government, particularly bureaucratically organized government. "Planning" represents public intrusions into private life. Practically, "planning" does involve decisions about the allocation of socially valued goods and services. When planning was introduced as part of Progressive reform in the early twentieth century, a primary claim of the early planners was that they would attempt to do what local governments had been doing all along, but would inject "rationality" into decision-making. Thus the ties of "planning" to public, political decision-making processes are intrinsic and historically explicit.

Insofar as planners want some measure of autonomy in their work, they may be drawn in two directions. In their conflicts with organizational managers, who would increasingly bureaucratize planning, planners would need to insist that the application of their specialized expertise to the service of the public interest requires that they have greater discretion in defining and executing their work. At the same time, this possible resolution to this conflict is unlikely to resolve the conflict with citizens concerned about public accountability. Few citizens make distinctions between claimants of "professional" status, such as planners, and the managers who supervise them; both are "bureaucrats" who restrict public access to decision-making.

Citizen concern about participation in decision-making was one force which contributed to the institutionalization of "citizen participation" in planning. It is written into planning statutes and informally institutionalized in planning processes. Growing citizen concern about the political accountability of practitioners like planners is likely to lead to increased citizen insistence on some form of participation in planning decisions. Planners could, at least in the short run, minimize the influence of citizens by structuring their participation in such a way as to co-opt leading critics and by restricting discussion of planning issues to technical, esoteric language (Arnstein, 1965; and Steckler & Herzog, 1979). However, although planners have used both tactics, neither is consistent with planners' ethical claims to serving the public interest. Practically, both tactics have shortcomings. Community groups are increasingly sensitive to ornamental forms of participation which take their time and give them the smallest tokens of power. Citizens confronted with esoteric language may not be able to understand technical issues involved, but they do recognize that their political influence is at stake. Increasingly, as in health planning councils, citizens are insisting that technical issues be clarified before they commit themselves to a decision (Checkoway, 1981).

In the context of growing demands for direct public political accountability of planners, planners' desires for increased autonomy may be unlikely to be realized. More importantly, this autonomy may be in direct conflict with planners' effectiveness, as the next section suggests.

Effectiveness

The seriousness of problems on which practitioners work generates concern that practitioners can be effective in handling the problems. Anxiety about the seriousness of problems encourages both practitioners and their clients to believe practitioners' claims of effectiveness.

However, evidence of significant mistakes by practitioners is accumulating. In medicine, for example, the record of iatrogenic health problems (caused by physicians in the process of treatment) increases (Illich, 1976). The number of practitioner errors may have increased. In addition, the scrutiny of practitioners has increased. Citizens have responded to a perceived loss of control over some practitioners by attempting to hold practitioners accountable for either their cost-effectiveness or their political responsiveness.

There is still another explanation for the continuing discoveries of and complaints about mistakes. Practitioners are being expected to solve more and more difficult and complex problems. In education, for example, some of the criticism of teachers appears to come from their failure in their imputed responsibility to assure graduates of secure, well-paying employment (Baum, 1978). The creation of intricate medical technologies encourages the expectation that physicians will be able to prolong and improve the quality of almost any life. Retrospectively, the poverty warriors of the 1960's are accused of having been seduced by simplistic or inchoate social scientific knowledge into believing, as both they and most citizens wanted, that they could solve all problems of poverty.[32]

Controversy about the assessment of the social programs of the

1960's is most instructive for considering the prospects for planners. The harshest criticism is that practitioners were not effective because they had inadequate expertise, their ethical claims were misplaced, and their claims to autonomy were illegitimate. Here two observations are necessary. The first is that problems of the magnitude and complexity of the War on Poverty had never before been attacked. The second is that most problems which planners are presented with today are similarly complex and difficult.[33] Poverty, energy, housing, income distribution, education, environmental quality, health, transportation—the list of problems which "planners" are being asked to solve is virtually endless, and each problem is unmanageably complex. There are unsettling gaps in substantive knowledge—for example, how to increase the tax base of older cities while simultaneously not displacing or depriving disadvantaged residents, how to increase the supply of energy while simultaneously not doing irremediable damage to the environment or people's health, or how to increase the productivity of industry while simultaneously not disrupting the lives of workers.

Yet this list is misleading. There is, indeed, little knowledge about how to solve these problems. However, there is also limited agreement that these problems are important. Perhaps crucially, there is limited agreement that these formulations of problems are correct—either because the dilemmas posed have little empirical validation (that is, the conflicts are problems of perception, not of social dynamics) or because some of the values implied by the statements of the problems are unimportant or illegitimate. In short, it is not easy even to define the problems which "planning" is supposed to solve. Community groups disagree about both the empirical characteristics of social conditions and about the values which should be used to assess these conditions. Thus formulation of consensually acceptable problem-definitions is itself a problem for planners.

It is difficult to separate the content of planning problems as social problems from the social context of planning problems. In examining the reasons why plans often have not been implemented, contemporary planners have rediscovered an axiom which the planners who worked with the Progressive reformers understood:

implementation of a plan requires intellectual and political support from significant social groups.[34] For a proposed course of action to be implemented as a possible solution for a problem, several social agreements are necessary. There must be agreement that the course of action is consistent with important values; there must be agreement that the course of action is feasible; there must be agreement that the course of action is a plausible possibility as a solution for the problem under consideration; there must be agreement that there is a problem requiring a solution; and there must be some general agreement about the nature of the problem.[35] "Planning," then, inextricably includes organizing. It includes organizing of agreement about solutions and problems, as well as agreement about the allocation of resources to certain problems. These organizing problems, if they may be distinguished from the other, intellectual, problems, are no less complex and difficult than the intellectual problems.[36]

That planning does involve organizing should have been evident from the initial examination of why "planning" is a subject of growing public interest. The problem-solving and advice-giving of planning are intimately tied to decisions about the allocation of valued goods and services. In the public sector "planning" is a central component of government.

Four decades ago Mannheim (1940) made a particularly strong argument about the unique responsibilities of planning as a part of government. Decisions about the allocation of goods and services, he suggested, were secondary to the pressing primary obligation of planning. Writing in a period of anarchic relations among nations and disintegration and demoralization of national institutions, Mannheim contended that planning should be, first of all, an effort to re-establish the possibility of governance among and within nations. Traditional procedures for making decisions were no longer well accepted while social relationships had become increasingly complex, change was growing more rapid, and technical tools began to pose the threat of widespread destruction. Planning, Mannheim urged, should become a means of mediating potentially destructive conflicts and establishing new widely legitimate rules for social decision-making. Planning, he contended, had the reponsibility to be concerned with organizing. What planners had to organize was nothing less than new decision-making procedures which could gain public legitimacy for social decisions.

The crisis which Mannheim described has not passed. Current conditions of economic austerity increase the significance of each decision in which government allocates diminishing goods and services to fewer people. Attacks on bureaucratically inaccessible decision-making processes grow. Nor have experts gained much legitimacy as surrogates for politically open decision-makers. Practitioners claiming authority on the basis of their expertise increasingly have been charged to demonstrate their public accountability. Citizens' protests about the justice of specific planning decisions express doubts about the legitimacy of basic procedures for making decisions. Instead of creating a solution to the problem of governance, "planning" has become a public symbol of the problem.

It is in this context that questions of planners' effectiveness are to be assessed. Initially most planners saw themselves as introducing some rationality into processes of public and private decision-making. With time they have found specific recommendations challenged. Increasingly they have found public resistance centering on the choice of rules and criteria for any decision-making. Any practitioners who want to work as "planners" will have to confront and demonstrate their effectiveness in dealing with problems of governance.

The implications are profound. In order to satisfy new public expectations for "planners," practitioners will not be able to meet traditional public expectations for "professionals." Effectiveness in working on problems of governance requires violating conventional expectations about "professional" expertise in two ways. First, in contrast with many commonly recognized "professions," the expertise required in "planning" is demonstrably not technical. Rather, it involves social design and negotiation. It entails organizing intellectual and political agreement among complexly constituted and continually changing groups. Unlike many types of technical expertise, it is not free of the context in which it is practiced.[37] Thus, as a consequence of working on a problem which citizens regard as important, "planners" will have difficulty making the clear, specific public representations of their expertise conventionally expected of "professions."

This difficulty is related to a second way in which the expertise required for "planning" will violate traditional expectations of "professions." For reasons discussed earlier, "professions" have been expected to exercise an expertise which is specialized— narrow but deep, well-defined, and readily applicable to easily bounded problems. These assumptions make it possible to distinguish the members and domains of different "professions," as well as to justify the granting of autonomy within defined lines. In contrast, the problems of governance are elusively difficult to bound. The appropriate expertise is difficult to define, in part because changing situations require changing expertise. Finally, the problems of societal governance are, by definition, anything but narrow. The extent of these problems constitutes their importance. In order to be effective with these important problems, "planners" will be compelled to develop a general expertise, making use of but primarily overseeing the application of more specialized expertise.[38]

Just as "planning" confronts problems and offers types of expertise which deviate from the traditional "professional" model, the meaning of "effectiveness" itself is changed. The problem which "planning" is expected to deal with is a loss of legitimacy for social decision-making institutions. The solution to this problem is the creation of legitimacy for some such institutions. In contrast with traditional "professionals," this type of solution is not represented by any single decision, which might be regarded as the end of a problem. Instead, legitimacy resides in a continuous process of making decisions, in which citizens generally consider the rules underlying the decisions reasonable and fair.[39]

Moreover, a crucial component of this legitimate process is to be a specific type of public accountability for "planners." "Planning" decisions have suffered an attrition of legitimacy because citizens have felt excluded from deliberations, and citizens have indicated that they will accord legitimacy to the process of "planning" only insofar as they are involved in some direct way in the process. Citizens will not grant prior legitimacy to "planners" to practice on the basis of perceived credentials. Instead, citizens will continually grant legitimacy to "planners" on the basis of their ongoing actions. The specific forms of citizen participation will be less important than their effect in assuring citizens that "planners" are accountable to them. In short, the outcome of planners' expertise, their effectiveness, must be the creation of a process of social decision-making in which decisions are considered legitimate because the decision-makers are accountable to the public. This is in evident contrast with traditional expectations of and possibilities open to "professionals."

Finally—and most significantly of all—these new expectations of "planners" radically change their possibility of acquiring autonomy as a "profession." Public accountability lies along a continuum with autonomy. When citizens will accord "planners" legitimacy to the degree that they make themselves accountable to the public, to that degree planners must practice without autonomy. The traditional "professional" model is turned on its head. Effectiveness with problems which citizens regard as important will give practitioners legitimacy as practitioners. However, inherent in the requirements of effectiveness is continuing engagement in a process of public accountability which limits the autonomy of practitioners. In the case of "planning"—and, by implication, for many other types of social practice—autonomy is in conflict with effectiveness. It may be possible for planners to secure some measure of autonomy in practice, but the consequences would be the isolation from public accountability which would limit their legitimacy and, in the end, hinder their effectiveness at any but relatively trivial tasks.

CONCLUSION

Two conclusions may be drawn from this analysis. The first is that planners, if they are committed to effective planning, will need to sacrifice any aspirations to the type of autonomy which "professions" have traditionally enjoyed. It is unlikely that planners will gain much autonomy under any conditions; the challenge to them is whether they will develop their practice in such a way as to be effective in dealing with important problems. Second, however, if planners, indeed, do succeed in devising effective solutions to the crucial problem of legitimacy in governance, they will, nevertheless, be accorded the prestige which currently is granted "professions."

Their role suggests that the changing nature of problems which citizens consider important may lead to a redefinition of "professions." While prestige will continue to be awarded, autonomy will be limited.

NOTES

1. Stylistically, "planning," "planners," "professions," and "professionals" will be put in quotation marks on two occasions. "Planning" and "planners" will be put in quotation marks when they refer to the self-label of a specific group of practitioners, the city planners who have traditionally claimed these labels. Any of the four words will be put in quotation marks when they refer to the practitioner or public conceptions of "planning" and "professions" mentioned in the first paragraph. Otherwise, it will be assumed that planning activities and professional status have been sufficiently well defined in the text as to have independent meanings which may be discussed apart from public conceptions. Because quotations marks are distracting, and because they may inadvertently cast aspersions on the planning competence or professional status of particular practitioners, quotation marks will be avoided whenever possible.

2. Traditionally, city planners have developed less or more comprehensive plans for urban development. These plans have set forth goals for future actions. This type of planning has been characterized as "goal-oriented" and has been contrasted with the "problem-oriented" planning described here. Faludi (1973) formulates the distinction as one between a "blueprint mode" and a "process mode" of planning. The distinction is useful in pointing to differences in orientation between the intentions of earlier planners with relatively undeveloped cities before them and contemporary planners who cope with contingencies which arise in complexly developed cities. A move toward a more "problem-oriented" view of planning has also been encouraged by an appreciation of the social complexity of the settings in which planning may be done and the intellectual difficulty of establishing clear expressions of ideal states for these dynamic settings. This change in the intellectual description of planning appears to bring verbal accounts more into line with the social and psychological dynamics of planning: individuals and organizations are usually likely to consider planning more in response to an experienced problem than in pursuit of an unreached goal. The pursuit of any but the simplest goals entails the solution of some problem or problems.

3. For a succinct description of this model, see Banfield (1955). For a discussion of ways in which strict requirements for intellectual "rationality" can be adapted to the social and psychological rationalities of the settings in which planning is done, see Etzioni (1968). For a good description of how the steps of the problem-solving process may be carried out, see Puget Sound Governmental Conference (1974).

4. City planners have always recognized this relationship but have long denied or disregarded it. When their plans were readily implemented by early social reformers, the fine points of the advice-giving relationship were unimportant, because advice given was most often accepted. Continuing discussion of the proper relationship of planners to agencies of local government—for example, whether planning decisions should be made by the city executive, an independent planning commission, or the city council—has recognized the advice-giving role of planners. One thoughtful weighing of alternative relationships is Kent (1964). Yet a pervasive hostility by planners toward "politics" has expressed planners' concern that "nonrational" considerations of political interest influenced choices of action but also, centrally, planners' resentment that their recommendations were often disregarded. The most consistent response to this frustration has been to deride the perceived petty-mindedness of political actors, rather than to examine the advice-giving relationship and to consider ways of acquiring influence in this relationship. One prominent planner who had no trouble with this latter alternative was Robert Moses, whose power is described by Caro (1975).

5. For well-analyzed case material presenting planners in advice-giving roles, see Benveniste (1977) and Meltsner (1976). For conceptualizations of the problems which planners may encounter in communicating their "rational" concerns to "political" decision-makers, see Argyris (1971) and Churchman and Schainblatt (1965).

6. For two cogent presentations of the view that planning entails a chain of political decisions from the initial selection of a problem for consideration, see Forester (1978) and Seeley (1967).

7. For a review of the history of the United States city planning movement, see Birch (1980) and Scott (1969). For representative expressions of the issues comprising this group's crisis of identity, see Catanese (1970) and Levin (1977, ch. 1).

8. Perceptions of the American Planning Association are discussed in Chapter Six.

9. See Bergman, et al. (1976) for one study describing the immersion of "planning" graduates in non-technical activities.

10. Indicative of this concern is a conference on "The Role of Policy Analysis in the Education of Planners," sponsored by the Department of Urban Studies and Planning at the Massachusetts Institute of Technology in October, 1979. On one level, the conference agenda involved exploring the respective contents of "policy analysis" and "planning" and considering the degree to which "planning" students currently learned "policy analysis" and the degree to which they might benefit from more training in "policy analysis." On another level, the conference agenda involved the concerns of educators of "planners" that educators of "policy analysts"— meaning, in this instance, business management—might be attracting students away from "planning" programs and placing graduates in positions which "planning" graduates traditionally could have counted on. One not-so-hidden agenda item was for "planning" programs to demon-

strate that they already teach business management ("policy analysis") skills to their students, in order to reassure both potential applicants and potential employers of graduates.

11. Practitioners in New Jersey lobbied for approximately two decades before seeing the enactment in the late 1960's of the first State licensing procedures for "planners." Continuing controversy about the appropriateness of the definition enacted into law is discussed in Chapter Six.

12. Perhaps the most optimistic, even at times euphoric, description of the likely influence of planners is Galbraith (1971). Galbraith contends that the combination of the complexity of decision-making situations and the magnitude of the stakes involved compel decision-makers to follow the advice of such technical experts as planners. He tends to downplay the importance of political considerations in decision-making. One set of case studies designed to identify the influence of planners in a variety of decisions is Bolan and Nuttall (1975). Two accounts which provide both description and analysis of ways in which planners may influence decision-making are Benveniste (1977) and Meltsner (1976).

13. The following brief discussion of the literature on the professions is by no means intended to be exhaustive. Rather, it is meant to highlight some contrasts in focus within the study of professions. For more extensive reviews and analyses of this literature the reader is referred to Freidson (1971), Larson (1977), and Vollmer and Mills (1966).

14. For a review of discussions of the professional status of planning, see Beauregard (1976).

15. It might be more accurate to say that the assumption is most likely to be made when practitioners describe their own colleagues. However, the most common adherents to the attributional approach are claimants for members of their own occupation.

16. Conversely, others may have interests in demonstrating that certain other practitioners should not be regarded as "professions," and their lists tend to deny the professional label to those practitioners. Many disputes among health care practitioners take this form. For examples, see Feldstein (1977). Finally, to be sure, there are disinterested writers in the attributional mode who simply want to understand occupations.

17. For an articulate review of the literature on professions and a clear argument for the political approach, see Freidson (1971).

18. For an analysis which focuses on professions as monopoly control over cognitive specializations, see Larson (1977).

19. Vollmer and Mills (1966) were the first to give serious attention to a process of professionalization. Their analysis is weakened by pervasive ambiguities about the defining characteristics of a "profession" as a standard against which to measure the progress of various occupations. However, they provide considerable case material which illustrates the efforts made by practitioners in seeking the autonomy about which writers with the political approach are concerned.

20. This cultural expectation has been linked to the requirements of a capitalist industrial political economy by Habermas (1970). The implica-

tions of this expectation for the claims of would-be professionals are discussed by Ehrenreich and Ehrenreich (1977). I have discussed the origins of this expectation in industrialization and its specific consequences in planning in "Toward a Post-Industrial Planning Theory" (1977). The reader is referred to these sources for a detailed discussion of influences on this expectation and its consequences for professionals.

21. Schon (1971) has discussed the fluctuation of concerns into and out of "good currency." It is beyond the scope of this work to venture into the sociology of knowledge sufficiently to discuss the conditions under which particular conditions become regarded as social problems. Blumer (1971) offered an early argument that the definition of social problems is not related to the inherent characteristics of situations defined as problematic, and he outlined a social process through which a situation may become considered a problem. Writers on the left have suggested that national public and corporate policy focuses tend to be influenced by corporate considerations of what is necessary to maximize stable economic growth and to maintain the social control necessary for this growth. For examples of this position, see Gordon (1977).

22. See Benveniste (1977) and Meltsner (1976) for case examples.

23. Needleman and Needleman (1974) provide evidence of this. Additional evidence is provided in later chapters of this book.

24. The next section describes commoditization and politicization in detail, with particular attention to their effects on public demands for accountability. They are mentioned here to indicate reasons why the terms of legitimacy for "professionals" are changing.

25. In some ways, also, as suggested in the discussion of conflicts between would-be professionals and manager, practitioners lose control over clients.

26. For extensive discussion of these issues, see May (1976), Moore (1970), and Wilensky (1964).

27. For stylistic simplicity this discussion refers to "practitioners" and their "services." As in other sections, "practitioners" is a generic term used to refer to workers who claim or aspire to professional status. The content and product of their work are subsumed in the label "services," even though only a portion may regard themselves as "service workers," some may produce tangible goods, and others, such as planners, may manipulate information and produce reports. The use of the term "service" seems apposite both because most current aspirants to professional status do consider themselves service workers and because all codes of professional ethics state or imply service to the public.

28. This one-sentence reference to a historical tendency does not begin to reflect the complexities and unevenness in this development. For example, Polanyi (1957) describes the transformation of social feudal relationships into commercial market relationships. Bell (1973), Gans (1962), and Sarason et al. (1977) offer representative descriptions of the contraction of the size and resources of extended family or community

networks and their partial replacement by commercial providers of services. Bell (1973), Fuchs (1968), Illich (1975), and Wilensky and Lebeaux (1965) provide different perspectives on the increasing organization and growing economic importance of commercial providers of services. The reader interested in a deeper exploration of historical tendencies should begin by consulting these works. In the discussion here, more important than a thorough understanding of the historical tendencies is a recognition of ways in which citizens experience them in the present through their growing discovery of themselves as consumers of service commodities.

29. A pure market arrangement would discriminate against the poor, who have little or no income to spend. Because schooling is a universal requirement, voucher proposals provide for universal distribution of vouchers, sometimes with extra large vouchers to the poor to pay for their extra needs and to enable them to compete with others who could supplement vouchers with their private incomes. In health care Medical Assistance and Medicare represent vouchers for two populations (the poor and the elderly) who are least likely to be able to afford as much medical care as they may need.

30. For representative discussion of citizen participation efforts, see Arnstein (1965), Burke (1979), and Perlman (1975).

31. Fein (1970) is helpful in distinguishing this moderate political position from the more radical position described below. He notes that community groups opposing teachers in Ocean Hill-Brownsville, for example, included both positions.

32. Although the tone of Moynihan's (1970) criticism of the War on Poverty is carping, unsympathetic, and charged with the enlightenment which comes with retrospection, he is right that poverty warriors and their constituents often colluded in believing that they understood social dynamics better than they really did. However, they made these leaps of faith because of their conviction that the problems of poverty were sufficiently crucial as to warrant risks. Further, any assessment that the War on Poverty was only a failure is simplistic, also a misunderstanding of social dynamics. An evaluation of the War on Poverty is beyond the scope of this discussion. More balanced accounts, which include analyses of the conflicts of interest raised by these programs, are provided by Marris and Rein (1973) and Ryan (1976).

33. Actually, most problems presented to other practitioners, such as attorneys, physicians, engineers, and social workers, are also complex and difficult. As will be argued with respect to planners, unless a problem is trivial, any practitioner's perception that it is relatively narrow and easily bounded is simplistic.

34. This support, as the discussion of the poverty programs suggests, is necessary but not sufficient. Consensus without effective knowledge will not lead to successful implementation of a plan.

35. Cohen, March, and Olsen (1972) suggest that such a formulation of

necessary agreements is excessively rationalistic. In particular, they would raise questions about the need for agreement about the nature of a problem. They characterize a solution as "an answer actively looking for a question" and contend that "you often do not know what the question is in organizational problem solving until you know the answer" (p. 3). Wildavsky (1979) has made the latter point at length in describing public decision-making in the realm of planning. It is useful to acknowledge that retrospective reconstructions of social action often impute more rationality to the actors than ever was the case. Nevertheless, it is reasonable to say that these agreements, if not explicitly reached, are implicitly settled upon. At the least, participants in decision-making have the legitimate opportunity to interrupt a process of decision-making by insisting that agreement has not been reached on one or more of these issues. These arenas of agreement represent potential veto points for participants. The ability of a party to enforce the veto depends upon that actor's political resources. Finally, it may be possible to compromise with Cohen, March, and Olsen and Wildavsky by suggesting that, at the least, action requires agreement among affected, politically active parties on two conditions: that there is some problem requiring action and that a particular course of action is a plausible response to the problem.

36. For cogent discussion of planning as organizing, see Forester (1978, 1982a, and 1982b).

37. Here the appearances of both "pure" and "applied" science misrepresent the realities of their practice. Although they may be represented publicly as the precise application of universalistic procedures, actually, the work entails numerous personal judgments and is modified to meet the demands of the specific context of practice. For example, Mitroff (1974) provides a revealing study of space scientists, in pointing to the subjectivities which intervene between the application of ostensibly context-free methods and the actual practice of science. Freidson (1971) provides numerous examples of the way in which physicians' clinical judgment guides their application of biological knowledge and medical techniques in working with patients.

38. There is a time-honored debate in city planning over whether planners should be generalists or specialists. Usually this debate is expressed in terms of whether planners should be experts primarily in some substantive field, such as housing or health, or in some aspect of the process of planning, such as need assessment or budgeting, which may be applied to all or most substantive fields. The former are considered the specialists and the latter the generalists on the premises that significant planning "problems" should be defined by subject area and that subject areas are discretely distinguishable. This debate is summarized by Faludi (1978). Faludi discusses the issues in different language, in terms of the relative importance of "substantive" and "procedural" knowledge in an earlier book (1973). The thrust of the argument developed here is that members of the public are increasingly coming to the conclusion that problems of legitimate process are more important than—take precedence

over—problems in substantive areas. Specialized expertise in substantive areas is, clearly, useful in recommending solutions for substantive problems. However, it is contended here that planners who have only this specialized substantive expertise are likely to have diminishing influence without support from others with general, processural expertise.

39. There is in planning also an old debate concerning whether planning should be concerned primarily with producing specific outcomes or with ensuring a reasonable ongoing process of deliberating about social problems. This debate is related to the specialist-generalist debate in the following way. If specialists are people who work on problems in substantive areas, then the "solutions" to these problems are specific products in housing, health, or some other field. In contrast, if generalists are people who work on problems in the process of planning, then the "solutions" to these problems are reasonable types and amounts of progress in a process of planning. This debate also is summarized by Faludi (1973 and 1978). The argument developed here is that citizens presently regard problems of process as more crucial than problems of specific outcomes. This is not to argue that such specific problems as poverty, malnutrition, and poor housing are not worthy of immediate attention. Rather, it is contended that solutions to these problems are not likely to receive widespread support unless some planners work on re-designing the process through which problems are identified, recommendations are developed, and implementation is attempted.

REFERENCES

Argyris, Chris. "Management Information Systems: The Challenge to Rationality and Emotionality," *Management Science, 17,* 6 (February, 1971), pp. B-275 - B-292.

Arnstein, Sherry R. "A Ladder of Citizen Participation," *Journal of the American Institute of Planners, 35,* 4 (July, 1969), pp. 216-224.

Banfield, Edward C. "Notes on Conceptual Scheme," in Martin Meyerson and Edward C. Banfield, *Politics, Planning, and the Public Interest.* New York: Free Press of Glencoe, 1955, pp. 303-330.

Baum, Howell S. "Toward a Post-Industrial Planning Theory," *Policy Sciences, 8* (1977), pp. 401-421.

Baum, Howell S. "Legitimation Crisis in Education," *Journal of Educational Thought, 12,* 3 (December, 1978), pp. 159-175.

Beauregard, Robert A. "Professional Closure and Environmental Change: The Case of Urban Planners." Mimeographed, Department of Urban Planning and Policy Development, Rutgers, New Brunswick, 1976.

Bell, Daniel. *The Coming of Post-Industrial Society.* New York: Basic Books, 1973.

Benveniste, Guy. *The Politics of Expertise.* Second edition. San Francisco: Boyd and Fraser, 1977.

Bergman, Edward M. et al. *The Practitioner Viewpoint: An Exploration of Social Policy Planning Practice and Education, Part II: The Findings.*

Chapel Hill: Department of City and Regional Planning, University of North Carolina, 1976.

Birch, Eugenie Ladner. "Advancing the Art and Science of Planning," *Journal of the American Planning Association, 46,* 1 (January, 1980), pp. 22-49.

Blumer, Herbert. "Social Problems as Collective Behavior," *Social Problems, 18,* 3 (Winter, 1971), pp. 298-306.

Bolan, Richard S., and Ronald L. Nuttall. *Urban Planning and Politics.* Lexington: D.C. Heath, 1975.

Burke, Edmund M. *A Participatory Approach to Urban Planning.* New York: Human Sciences Press, 1979.

Caro, Robert A. *The Power Broker.* New York: Vintage, 1975.

Catanese, Anthony J: "Where is the Planning Profession Heading?" *Journal of the Town Planning Institute, 55,* 1 (January, 1970), pp. 5-8.

Checkoway, Barry, ed. *Citizens and Health Care.* New York, Perganon, 1981.

Churchman, C. West, and A. H. Schainblatt. "The Researcher and the Manager: A Dialectic of Implementation," *Management Science, 11,* 4 (February, 1965), pp. B-69 - B-87.

Cohen, Michael D., James G. March, and Johan P. Olsen. "A Garbage Can Model of Organizational Choice," *Administrative Science Quarterly, 17* (1972), pp. 1-25.

Educational Vouchers. Cambridge: Center for the Study of Public Policy, 1970.

Ehrenreich, Barbara, and John Ehrenreich. "The Professional-Managerial Class," *Radical America, 11,* 2 (March-April, 1977), pp. 7-32.

Etzioni, Amitai. *The Active Society.* New York: The Free Press, 1968.

Faludi, Andreas. *Planning Theory.* New York: Pergamon Press, 1973.

Faludi, Andreas. *Essays on Planning Theory and Education.* New York: Pergamon Press, 1978.

Fein, Leonard J. "Community Schools and Social Theory: The Limits of Universalism," in *Community Control of Schools,* ed. Henry M. Levin. New York: Simon and Schuster, 1970, pp. 76-99.

Feldstein, Paul J. *Health Associations and the Demand for Legislation.* Cambridge: Ballinger Publishing Company, 1977.

Forester, John. "Planning in the Face of Power," Journal of the American Planning Association, *48,* 1 (Winter, 1982), pp. 67-80. (a)

Forester, John F. "Critical Reason and Political Power in Project Review Activity: Serving Freedom in Planning and Public Administration," *Policy and Politics, 10,* 1 (1982), pp. 65-83. (b)

Forester, John F. *The Planning Analyst's Questioning: Toward A Communicative Theory of Design.* Working Papers in Planning, Number 9, Department of City and Regional Planning, Cornell University, Ithaca, 1978.

Freidson, Eliot. *Profession of Medicine.* New York: Dodd, Mead, and Company, 1973.

Fuchs, New York: The Free Press, 1962.

Gilb, Corinne J. *Hidden Hierarchies: The Professions and Government.* New York: Harper and Row, 1966.

Goode, William. "Encroachment, Charlatanism, and the Emerging Profession: Psychology, Medicine, and Sociology," *American Sociological Review,* 25 (1960), pp. 902–914.

Gordon, David M., ed. *Problems in Political Economy: An Urban Perspective.* Second edition. Lexington: D.C. Heath, 1977.

Greenwood, Ernest. "Attributes of a Profession." *Social Work,* 2 (1957), pp. 44–55.

Habermas, Jürgen. *Toward a Rational Society.* Boston: Beacon Press, 1971.

Hall, Richard H. *Occupations and the Social Structure.* Second edition. Englewood Cliffs: Prentice-Hall, 1975.

Howard, John T. "Planning is a Profession," *Journal of the American Institute of Planners,* 20 (1954), pp. 58–59.

Illich, Ivan. *Medical Nemesis.* New York: Pantheon, 1976.

Kent, T.J., Jr. *The Urban General Plan.* San Francisco: Chandler Publishing Company, 1964.

Larson, Magali Sarfatti. *The Rise of Professionalism.* Berkeley: University of California Press, 1977.

Levin, Melvin R. *Community and Regional Planning.* Third edition. New York: Praeger, 1977.

Mannheim, Karl. *Man and Society in an Age of Reconstruction.* New York: Harcourt, Brace and World, 1940.

Marris, Peter, and Martin Rein. *Dilemmas of Social Reform.* Second edition. Chicago: Aldine, 1973.

May, Judith V. *Professionals and Clients: A Constitutional Struggle.* Sage Professional Papers in Administrative and Policy Studies, 3, series number 03-046, Beverly Hills: Sage Publications, 1976.

Meltsner, Arnold J. *Policy Analysts in the Bureaucracy.* Berkeley: University of California Press, 1976.

Mitroff, Ian I. *The Subjective Side of Science.* New York: Elsevier, 1974.

Moore, Wilbert E. *The Profession: Roles and Rules.* New York: Basic Books, 1970.

Moynihan, Daniel Patrick. *Maximum Feasible Misunderstanding.* New York: The Free Press, 1970.

National Academy of Sciences, Institute of Medicine. *Health Maintenance Organizations; Toward a Fair Market Test.* Washington: National Academy of Sciences, 1973.

Needleman, Martin, and Carolyn Emerson Needleman. *Guerrillas in the Bureaucracy.* New York: John Wiley, 1974.

Perlman, Robert. *Consumers and Social Services.* New York: John Wiley, 1975.

Polanyi, Karl. *The Great Transformation.* Boston: Beacon Press, 1957.

Puget Sound Governmental Conference. *A Comprehensive Human Resources Planning Guide.* Seattle: Puget Sound Governmental Conference, 1974.

Reich, Michael. "The Evolution of the United States Labor Force," in *The Capitalist System*, ed. Richard Edwards, Michael Reich, and Thomas Weisskopf. Englewood Cliffs: Prentice-Hall, 1972, pp. 174–183.

Roemer, Ruth, Charles Kramer, and Jeanne E. Frink. *Planning Urban Health Services*. New York: Springer, 1975.

Ryan, William. *Blaming the Victim*. New York: Vintage, 1976.

Sarason, Seymour B. et al. *Human Services and Resource Networks*. San Francisco: Jossey-Bass, 1977.

Schon, Donald A. *Beyond the Stable State*. New York: W.W. Norton and Company, 1971.

Scott, Mel. *American City Planning Since 1890*. Berkeley: University of California Press, 1969.

Seeley, John R. "Social Science: Some Probative Problems," in *The Americanization of the Unconscious*. New York: International Science Press, 1967, pp. 149–165.

Steckler, Allan B., and William T. Herzog. "How to Keep Your Mandated Citizen Board Out of Your Hair and Off Your Back: A Guide for Executive Directors," *American Journal of Public Health, 69*, 8 (August, 1979), pp. 809–812.

Vollmer, Harold M., and Donald L. Mills, eds. *Professionalization*. Englewood Cliffs: Prentice-Hall, 1966.

Wildavsky, Aaron. *Speaking Truth to Power*. New York: Little, Brown, and Company, 1979.

Wilensky, Harold L. "The Professionalization of Everyone?" *American Journal of Sociology, 70* (September, 1964), pp. 137–150.

Wilensky, Harold L., and Charles N. Lebeaux. *Industrial Society and Social Welfare*. New York: The Free Press, 1965.

PART TWO

What Planners Say

2

PLANNERS' EXPERTISE

What do planners believe they know, what skills do they think they exercise, and what problems do they regard as their domain? This chapter examines planners' perceptions of their expertise.

Questions explored the personal meaning of this expertise by asking planners how successive career choices led them to work in planning as a way of exercising specific skills on particular problems. Planners were asked why they originally chose to go into planning, what goals they set for themselves once in planning, and what strengths they believe they contribute to their day-to-day work.

These matters are closely related. Studies of vocational choice indicate that people tend to make choices about occupations on the basis of their perceptions of the match between their personal traits and the characteristics of a type of work (Holland, 1962, 1966, 1968, and 1973). Thus the choice of planning, like any other occupational choice, would seem to be a process in which individuals look for a type of work which would match their personality, their interests, and their skills.

Consequently, one would expect to find close relationships among the types of concerns which planners express in describing their attractions to planning, their goals in planning, and their strengths. Moreover, it would appear that the expertise which planners develop reflects not only conscious calculations about the types of skills which may be effective in solving significant problems, but also nonrational, subconscious "decisions" to do what is most compatible with traits developed relatively early in life.

ATTRACTIONS TO PLANNING:
EARLY IMAGES OF PLANNING

Planners were asked two questions concerning their entry into planning. They were asked when they made a decision to enter planning. In addition, they were asked what attractions planning held for them at the time of the decision. As with any questions which call upon people's memories, it is difficult to be certain that what people relate accurately reflects their state of mind at some previous time. In addition, people have a tendency to rationalize subsequent events by citing actions or motives in the past which would justify what followed. Nevertheless, the consistency and the candor of the responses suggest that they do accurately represent the concerns which led people into planning. Thus, while the responses may neglect or overlook some motives, including some which were unconscious, they do not seem in any systematic way to distort the process of choosing planning.

The psychological importance of the decision to become a planner is illustrated by stories related by three planners recalling early memories. One planner described an event in his youth which he felt represented a personal decision-making process leading him into planning:

> My mother thought city planning was a good idea. She had influence over my decision. I'll tell you a story which is important to me. When I was twelve sitting on the beach in North Carolina, I was drawing in the sand. My mother said, "I see you are drawing a city." Soon another boy came along and asked what I was doing. I told him I was drawing a city. He asked if he could help. I told him to draw the airport. Soon a number of kids had come along, and I gave each of them an assignment. Someone was drawing a shopping center, someone was drawing housing, and so on. I was supervising all of them. We were a team planning a city.

Someone else, who entered planning through architecture, remembered,

> When I was in high school, I started dreaming about a piece of land I would have, including details of the land which I would have . . . hills, a stream, a house there. It just happened. But when I graduated, I decided to go to architecture school.

One other planner recalled his reaction to the Second World War as a motivation to become a planner:

> The war had an effect on me. I wanted to do something large scale and creative. There were apparently powerful feelings in me that had not been released before: anger at things that were wrong and

evil—a destructive feeling, but I wanted to be socially creative. War is a big thing, and it is socially destructive. I had to do some powerful things of a creative nature to help other people. Also, I think a pioneering urge was in it.[1]

Others describe the decision to go into planning in fortuitous terms. For example, they had an enjoyable experience in a summer job in planning, or they were excited by a university course in planning. Some who were already practicing architecture or engineering reported favorable reactions to planning projects in which their normal work involved them. Yet there are questions why these people were excited by planning courses or planning jobs. Responses to the question about the attractions which planning held for these people help to understand motivations to enter planning.

In examining what planners say about their attractions to planning it is useful to look at other occupations which they may have considered in addition to planning. Three-fourths (76 percent) said that they had at some time in their lives considered some type of work other than planning. With few exceptions, almost every other occupation considered was a professional or white-collar occupation. Law, engineering, architecture, human services, and science were most frequently mentioned. These interests are reasonable in the context of the socioeconomic status of the planners' parents. Forty-eight percent of their fathers held white-collar positions; 34 percent held managerial positions or were proprietors; and 16 percent were in blue-collar positions.[2] Thus interest in the professions can be understood as normal status aspirations for a group with this background.

When asked why they did not pursue one of their interests other than planning, the respondents most frequently stated that personal values precluded another choice (53 percent of stated reasons); second, they mentioned limitations in personal ability (26 percent); less frequently they mentioned limited opportunities (10 percent) or objections to the type of life style associated with an occupation (8 percent). It would be difficult to know how often a value conflict was alleged as a cover for limitations in ability. What is perhaps most significant about statements about other occupations considered is that they draw a profile of general interest in white-collar and, in particular, professional work. In this context responses to the question about attractions to planning shed some light on the initial motivations of planners.

Planners' statements about what attracted them to planning may help to understand planners' expertise in two ways. First, they give an idea of the type of activity which future practitioners consider planning to be. Second, insofar as planners' initial attractions to planning persist, the statements provide an indication of the types of motives which planners will seek to satisfy through their work. Implicitly, "planning" may tend to become what planners imagine it to be.

Planners' responses about the attractions of planning were analyzed for the themes mentioned, and four themes dominate. The most common attraction, referred to by 38 percent of the sample, was the possibility of doing large-scale design or comprehensive guidance of development. Architects and engineers, in particular, contrasted the narrow focus of projects in these occupations with the broader scope and opportunities of planning. The following statement typifies this interest:

> Architecture was involved with only one or two buildings; that was too small for me . . . I was more interested in a broad perspective of planning, as opposed to individual buildings.

Some architects tied the interest in large-scale design to an explicit concern in dealing with large-scale problems. For example, one private consultant noted,

> Most of us younger architects felt that the practice, as limited to single building types, was not an adequate response to urban problems. We saw [the opportunity to work on] broader problems as an attraction.

The possibility that planning could provide a handle with which to deal with extensive social problems was emphasized by another practitioner, from a social science background:

> I had a lot of broad interests, and planning seemed to be the most possible of doing as many of all of these as possible. The fact that it is a very broad area of activity seems to be an area for constructive government, for dealing with policies and programs of government that affect services.

The last statement points to a second type of attraction, mentioned by 34 percent of the sample.[3] Many people saw planning as a source of leverage for social change. It seemed to address pressing urban problems:

> Planning was attractive to me because it seemed to be dealing with substantive issues of the day that were important to me: the whole urban crisis.

> I wanted to be part of the solution rather than the problem. I wanted to deal with the problems of the cities. I saw it as a noble profession, as contrasted with being in business, selling Pepsi Cola, et cetera.

A number of newer planners mentioned the influence of social problems and social change values of the 1960s on their choice of planning:

> Having been in school in 1968 with all the riots and all the problems, I was into the problems of the city, society, economics, into the race problems. But I did not feel like a social worker [who would] teach people the right way to live. I thought this would let me do some of the things which I liked about sociology but in a more rational way, versus doing just social work.

> Social change—it was a place where you could have an impact. Intellectually, it was challenging. I was trained as a generalist, and I would do a lot of things, and I could contribute to change. I was reading *Future Shock*. Planning was everything!

A third type of attraction, often mentioned in combination with one of the first two, was cited by 34 percent of the sample: this was the possibility that planning could bring influence and power. The statements above include self-assurances that planning would "work": it would enable the planner to accomplish the goals of large-scale design or social change. One planner noted succinctly,

> I've always wanted to see things accomplished over a relatively short period of time. Planning seemed to provide that kind of opportunity.

Another mentioned that he "would like to have influence over things that occur."

Finally, 36 percent recalled a number of pragmatic considerations for entering planning. While mentioning one of the other attractions, they often added that planning had appeared to offer good economic opportunities, respectable professional status, or a general basis for moving into a number of other fields. One planner now working for a county agency reminisced:

Hard to remember [what attracted me to planning]. On a personal level, I had a friend who was a planner. We thought we would set up business together. In an intellectual sense, the notion of a multidisciplinary way of examining issues affecting develop ment of a city [interested me]. . . . I could become interested in functional entities. I just kind of drifted into things. It was not a structured planned decision. Maybe this is not all so uncommon.

The types of attractions which planners mentioned tend to be related to their undergraduate background, as the literature on vocational choice would suggest (Holland, 1973). This association may be considered additional evidence that personal traits influence motives for going into planning.[4] (Types of attractions to planning are not significantly associated with planners' ages, types of graduate training, places of employment, or organizational roles.) As Table 2-1 shows, architecture and engineering undergraduates were attracted to planning primarily by opportunities for large-scale, comprehensive design. Social science undergraduates were most likely to enter planning in order to effect social change. They

TABLE 2-1.   ATTRACTIONS TO PLANNING, BY UNDER-
GRADUATE MAJOR

	Attractions				
Major	Large Scale	Social	Power	Pragmatic Considerations	Total
Architecture	7	3	1	3	14
Engineering	6	1	5	2	14
Social Science	6	13	11	13	43
All	19	17	17	18	71

$X^2 = 13.05$
$P < .05$
$V = .303$

(V is a measure of association for r x c tables introduced by Cramer. It is defined in the following way:

$$V^2 = \frac{X^2}{N \ \mathrm{Min} \ (r - 1, \ c - 1)}$$

where Min (r - 1, c - 1) refers to either r - 1 or c - 1, whichever is smaller. The value of V varies from 0 to 1 for any r × c table.)

were also most likely to be explicitly concerned about planning as a source of social power.

These statements describe an occupation of practitioners concerned with exercising influence over large-scale change in the physical or social evironment. These are the most frequently cited themes, and they do seem to reflect the most common conscious motives for entering planning. Still, there seem to be other, perhaps subconscious images of planning which attracted a number of practitioners, and several additional quotations help to understand the affect which surrounds the choice of planning for many.

One theme which may be quickly taken for granted because of the historical association of city planning with architecture is that of building. This theme deserves emphasis. Planners see themselves as builders of society. One county planner referred to this motive quite simply in a passing comment: "I always tell people that . . . if I were not in city planning, I would be a carpenter." Yet the type of building involved is far more complex than work with hammer and nails. One planner, when asked about other occupations he had considered, mentioned "theatrical technology: like working behind the scenes at the theater."

This image reappeared in another planner's comments about professional ethics: "A planner is a stage designer." When considered for a moment, this image is powerful: the planner sets the stage on which social life is carried out. The planner works behind the scenes of everyday action to bring about success.

This image is pretentious. Although mentioned explicitly by only these two planners, the feeling of personal importance associated with such an image recurs. Some people mentioned their perception that planning could be a source of social power for solving urban problems. Others referred to a greater, more personal type of power which planning could bring them. One planner mentioned that, in choosing planning, he "would like to have influence over things that occur" and noted that his career choice was influenced by his parents, "especially by my father, who thought he was saving the world from disease [as a research scientist]." Another planner spoke more grandiosely of a theme which seemed to run under the surface of a number of responses. He had been attracted to planning because it held out "a sense of history, a sense of doing something that seemed very important." This theme was reiterated by another planner, who referred to "the fact that you could really make a monumental and historical change . . . egotism. As an aside, there is a street named after me, and a stream."

These responses add an affective component to the considerations which attracted planners to their work. Not only did they aim to influence broad environmental change, but many viewed themselves as master-builders who could affect the course of history. An important question in the examination of subsequent material is how this initial image of planning has affected planners' identification of their expertise and their effectiveness.

PERSONAL GOALS IN PLANNING PRACTICE

After being asked what attracted them initially to planning, the planners were asked what they now attempt most to accomplish in their practice. Most of the responses contained highly phrased, general objectives for society: planning better communities, creating environments which meet people's needs, promoting social justice, and improving the rationality of decision-making. Statements about goals in practice may have two types of meaning. Biographically, they indicate how individual practitioners have translated their initial attractions to planning into what they regard as plausible practical goals. At the same time, these statements represent only espousals of desirable goals, and it is important to look, as subsequent discussion will, at planners' aims in day-to-day work. Socially, statements about goals in practice indicate how practitioners choose to define the domain and purposes of "planning."

The themes in most of the statements can be grouped into one of three categories. The largest group, offered by one-third (32 percent) of the sample, concern goals in the physical environment, such as making changes in the physical environment to meet human needs, helping to balance growth and development, and contributing to physically well-designed communities. The tone of these goals is expressed in the following quotations. One county planner, evoking the image of planner-as-builder, described his concerns about the ends of his planning generally:

> Making an environment, the things I touch, more useful to the people involved, whether they know it or not . . . enhancing the quality of life.

An administrator reflected on what he tries to do through the activities of his department:

> Improving a community's living environment . . . seeing people receive improvements of services, physical improvements that they envision should be part of the community . . . whatever they saw as the needs of their community.

An architect-planner, giving special emphasis to a concern with the ways in which people use the physical environment, said that he was interested in

> solving human problems. It is the same thing as when I work as an architect. I want to be responsive to a wide range of human needs. . . . There are psychological and aesthetic needs that I feel are important to try to satisfy. I think my design background, my planning background have made me aware of a wide range of human needs, and I try to meet them. What I try to do is to be more satisfied with practicing as an architect, but expanding my definition of what it is to be an architect.

Almost one-third (28 percent) of the sample mentioned various social goals, including increasing social justice, improving social equity, and in a number of ways meeting human needs. For example, one planner with many years of experience commented that

> In terms of distributing benefits, I try to distribute benefits to people who are disadvantaged. I try to put the costs where people can pay for it. That is difficult because the government process is financed by a regressive process.

A planner in an urbanizing county offered the following overview of his goals in contributing to the shaping of this urbanization process:

> The dangers that the county will approach will be like the problems of the cities. Others may be worse because the county does not have the infrastructure that the city does. I see myself as working for the county, helping the county to become aware of some of the problems which are on the doorsteps and to develop some institutions which would help it to do that. I see this as being planning a series of employment programs. That is one of my goals.

A transportation planner in a state agency described his goals this way:

> I guess [my goals are] increasing or improving the living situation

for as many people as possible through my particular field. I obviously do not have money to give to the poor. . . . Creating a better environment for as many people as I can, while simultaneously I consider freedom of mobility of the individual a high priority.

A third group of planners, representing 16 percent of the sample, said that they aim to get results, regardless of the specific content. The following statements are representative of this view. One planner of several decades' experience, reflecting concern that many plans are filed without any follow-up action, said that he worked for

implementation of plans. [I am] not satisfied to come up with documents that go on a shelf. Attached to every planning document should be a section that shows where it can be done, how it can be financed, when it can be implemented.

A planner-developer, who first suggested that he did not have any specific goals, emphasized results as a necessity for his making a living:

I am not out to change the world. I was never out to change the world. . . . I have no great humanitarian goals. Money is more important.

Another planner emphasized the accomplishment of results as important for a sense of competence and satisfaction with work:

End results, unfortunately, are the only measure of your accomplishments, and everyone would try to achieve that. In architecture the success is quite short term. But in planning, you may never do that. There is a rate of achievements in planning, rather than a successful project.

By and large, the statements about goals express the same pretensions which drew these people into planning initially. Here planners generally present themselves as working to accomplish broad-scale changes in the environment. In demarcating a domain, they variously lay claims to problems in both the physical and social environments. Only those with goals in the social environment touch on problems which might be construed as the problems of governance outlined in the first chapter, but none of these planners moves from mention of substantive problems to an explicit discussion of procedural problems.

The third group of planners, those emphasizing the accomplishment of results, may be an exception to the interest in broad changes with their apparent pragmatism. Yet their statements about the importance of results highlight uncertainties which bother many planners: whether plans will be accepted and in any measure implemented, and how to evaluate personal effectiveness in such a way as to gain a sense of accomplishment and competence. Planners in the last group have chosen to concentrate on concrete results *per se* and to be less exacting about the nature of projects. Other planners eventually come to different terms with these uncertainties, as later discussion will show.

As was the case with initial attractions to planning, the type of goals which planners emphasize is associated with their undergraduate backgrounds. This finding would suggest that personal traits influence the goals which planners espouse when they become practitioners (Holland, 1973). (Differences in emphasis are not significantly associated with differences in planners' age, type of graduate training, place of employment, or organizational role.) As Table 2-2 shows, architecture undergraduates are concerned primarily with accomplishments in the physical environment. Social science undergraduates are the most concerned about accomplishing social goals. A substantial number of social scientists are concerned also about goals in the physical environment; this concern would seem to be a product of their employment in physical planning agencies. Engineers, though they work on the

TABLE 2-2. PERSONAL PLANNING GOALS AND UNDER-GRADUATE MAJOR

	Personal Planning Goals			
Major	*Social*	*Physical*	*Results*	*Total*
Architecture	3	6	3	12
Engineering	1	1	4	6
Social Science	10	9	1	20
All	14	16	8	38

$X^2 = 11.44$
$P < .03$
$V = .388$

physical environment, are most of all concerned about getting results, regardless of their specific content.

Still, there is an affective component to many responses which these categories do not convey. A number of planners, for instance, confess having difficulty identifying any personal goals in planning. For example, one planner suggested that the general status of planning is so low that individual planners may never be able to set and reach personal goals until their work acquires broader social legitimacy:

> My immediate concerns are with [the agency's] staff. I have a tremendous concern—maybe it grows out of personal insecurity— with having the section and department legitimized. Often we are the laughing stock. [We must] strive constantly for the credibility of our section and our section's work.

Another planner shared some of these concerns and said that he need a position in which he would have power before it would make sense to set personal goals:

> Personally, I want to have my own shop. I want to be a director. . . I want the profession to have more respect within the local government. I think the profession is viewed as an outsided meddling in the business of government.

A private consultant who had worked in planning for several decades expressed a sense of resignation to not having much control over what he got from his work:

> I don't have any ambitions any more along these lines. I am now so busy with production.

A strongly stated but broadly representative view was provided by one city planner asked to indicate what he tried to accomplish as a planner:

> Nothing. The way I see it, I'm here at my desk. I'll do whatever they ask, just as long as it's not zoning. One thing which we used to do, which no one liked to do, was land-using the city. Now it is done by a computer.

The example which this planner singles out is zoning; other planners identify other tasks which they do not want to be assigned. What this planner's statement represents is a broad sense of discouragement, a readiness by planners to do what they regard as creative work but a belief that they will not be asked and should not expect anything. A number of planners share this feeling even while they express the desire to serve far-reaching ends through planning.

These statements create a picture of contrasts. On the one hand, approximately two-thirds of the planners identify some goals toward which they say that they strive in practice. Most of these goals might be characterized as concerned with the improvement of society, even if most of them are rather vaguely stated. However, many planners, including some who espouse these goals, say that they feel that they have little power and that, consequently, goals for practice do not mean much. Even among those who identify goals for their practice very few express confidence that they make much progress toward their broad goals in narrow daily work. Put differently, many planners simultaneously lay claim to a wide domain and express doubts about whether they can control the domain. These hints at a sense of powerlessness should be kept in mind in examining responses in the next section to a question about planners' strengths in practice, as well as in considering subsequent statements about planners' autonomy.

HOW PLANNERS EXPECT TO ACCOMPLISH THEIR GOALS

In these statements planners portray themselves as a group of practitioners concerned with enacting broad changes in the environment. They espouse a number of highly stated goals for their actions, but many also admit to a sense of impotence about their ability to accomplish their goals. In this light it is important to ask what expertise planners believe they apply in practice which might enable them to reach their goals. It is possible, for example, that planners' goals, and the domain they demarcate, are reasonable in the positions which they occupy but that they have chosen inappropriate skills to lead them to those goals. One question asked planners what they regard as their strengths in practice.

The tone of the responses is set by one successful administrator who impulsively retorted, "I didn't know that I had any [strengths]!" A number of planners responded to the question with a long pause. Others declared succinctly, "I don't know." Following any such preface, most planners moved ahead to provide some answer to the question.

Some descriptions of personal strengths were simply general observations about being able to draw on rich personal experience. Other planners offered their views that they had so far succeeded by being jacks-of-all-trades. A typical statement was this:

> One of the greatest strengths that planners have . . . is an attempt to put together eclectic processes that work toward good solutions. . . . someone that is a generalist who tries to put it together.

Finally, a number of planners offered responses which referred to some skills which they believed that they had mastered and which distinguish them as practitioners. The types of expertise which planners did mention as their strengths may be placed in two categories: intellectual skills and interpersonal/organizational/political skills. Approximately two-thirds (68 percent) of the sample described their strengths in terms which emphasized intellectual skills. One-third (30 percent) portrayed their strengths in terms which included skills in interpersonal or political processes, sometimes combined with intellectual skill.[5]

Intellectual Expertise

Of the planners emphasizing intellectual stengths, a few made brief general reference to such areas of expertise as "design" or a "sensitivity to waterfront," with the implication that the skills involved are well understood and require little elaboration. Somewhat more extensive statements summarized themes common in textbook descriptions of planning. For example, planning is a process of problem-solving:

> [strength] in analyzing design and . . . in formulating ideas . . . the ability to evaluate alternatives: ability to identify different threads or facets of a problem, to identify all of the various forces that are at work on a particular conflict, and to come up with a scheme which resolves these conflicts.

A number of planners referred to expertise in analyzing information as a means of developing proposals which meet people's needs:

> I think I am good [at] analysis and evaluation of the results. I am also good at developing procedures and schemes that serve the immediate needs.

I think the thing probably is in synthesis. I am not a data freak. I enjoy getting together all the information because it is necessary. But the challenge is to say, what does it all mean? Which I would call the synthesis phase. That is what I can contribute the most.

Another planner articulated several planners' concerns with the future implications of actions:

[In discussing my strengths, I would emphasize] the ability to remove myself from the day and look at the future to get a decent reading on what is happening... in order to have an air of predictability which you can be relatively sure about.

These statements are typical of the responses of the two-thirds of the planners who emphasized intellectual strengths as their primary expertise. The comments both describe the planners as practitioners and present an image of the process of planning. These planners depict themselves as intellectual problem-solvers. They collect information, organize it to formulate alternative solutions for problems, evaluate the alternatives in light of their likely future consequences, and make recommendations to follow.

It is important to note the affect attached to this problem-solving: it brings the planners enjoyment. A number of planners specifically mentioned the opportunity to engage in problem-solving when asked earlier about what attracted them to planning. A county planner described his attraction to planning with an emphasis on "the appeal of the problem-solving, and monkey-puzzle appeal was pretty consistent. I still enjoy solving problems, doing things." A local planner mentioned a common attraction, the possibility of inter-disciplinary collaboration in problem-solving: "like working in a dynamic intellectual environment. . . . You could have an intersection among different specializations—entirely different perspectives—in problem-solving. I enjoy problem-solving." Thus planners describing their expertise as intellectual both offer an assessment of their strengths and refer to a type of activity which brings them considerable pleasure.

Nevertheless, planners' statements about intellectual strengths are pervaded by vagueness. Planners mentioned few specific skills. Rather, in attempting to identify their strengths, they referred to and adumbrated a general way of thinking about problems.[6] Most of the planners interviewed employ this way of thinking regularly. Yet their descriptions of it bear a noteworthy affect. As initial quotations indicated, many planners expressed disappointment with their inability to provide a clearer articulation of what this way of thinking involves and what intellectual or other assets they could contribute to it. Is there possibly something about the work of planning that is, if not vague, at least difficult to find language to describe? This question is explored in Chapter Seven.

In summary, it may be recalled that these planners said earlier that they seek to accomplish goals related to re-ordering society and the physical environment. Now they say that in practice they wield intellectual skills in order to achieve these goals. If these statements are taken at face value, they would imply that planners believe that there is something about the force of their ideas that should make social and physical changes come about. At the same time, planners' vagueness in describing their intellectual expertise suggests that they are not certain what about their ideas might bring about environmental changes. In addition, expressions of pleasure with problem-solving suggest that a number of planners may engage in intellectual activity primarily because it brings them intrinsic enjoyment and secondarily because they believe that it may contribute to social or physical change. Finally, these comments need to be examined in the context of allusions to a sense of powerlessness in work. It is possible that a sense of powerlessness contributes to vagueness in describing expertise.[7] Or the hints at powerlessness may express these planners' real assessment of their expertise: in practice their ideas alone may not give them influence to enact the ends which they seek.

Interpersonal Expertise

In contrast, the planners who characterized themselves as having interpersonal or political strengths, either alone or in combination with intellectual strengths, present a different picture of their expertise and a different image of the planning process. A number of them see themselves as being able to provide a bridge between the world of ideas and organizational practice. A veteran planner described this skill as "my ability to deal with complex matters, to integrate them and to help other people understand them, so that they can make intelligent choices, without sacrificing too much of the detail." Administrators are most frequently expected to work with others, and they tended to be particularly inclined to identify interpersonal expertise as their strength. One administrator expressed the viewpoint of many administrators when he called attention to his skills "as a manager, synergist, where I can bring together different disciplines, where I can orchestrate things, and out of it comes something physical. That is what I do best." Another administrator, with two decades of experience, emphasized, as did many planners, what he considered the power of a general ability to "get along with people":

> My personal greatest strength is an ability to work with people. I am not a great administrator, and I am not a fantastic organizer. But I have been able to break through barriers and get people to talk with each other. We have to resolve differences which will occur unless we do communicate. Coordination, communication is so vital in these things.

With regard to facilitating communication, a regional planner talked about the importance of distinguishing conflicts in interest from differences in language:

> [My greatest strengths as a planner are] probably in the area of coordination and synthesis and understanding what different people mean—finding some language which both can understand and agree on. In an organization like this, it is like a United Nations. You have all sorts of disciplines inside. On the council you have all sorts of disciplines on the outside. Some of them do not use the same words. Some of them use the same words to mean different things. A lot of the air needs clearing: what is being said, what is meant.

One county planner provided an exceptionally articulate description of what is involved in working with others in organized decision-making processes:

> I am practical. [It is] the combination of personality and training as a strategist. If there is anybody who can figure out a way to make something happen in a system as complex as this, it is me. . . . I seem to have a higher tolerance, patience. Basically being a secure person. . . . It takes coming into the situation and looking at it, understanding that there are constraints. . . . It's like, in a situation as complicated as this, the person who defines the problem is ahead of the game. If somebody has defined the problem, what they have got is one perspective on it. You work to bring about some consensus. A combination of being able to tolerate a high degree of ambiguity and yet constantly seeking to make order out of it.

These statements about interpersonal expertise depict a different planning process than that suggested by planners emphasizing intellectual expertise. Here planning is described as a political process in which planners contribute to social and physical changes by clarifying issues, communicating with interested actors, and facilitating agreements among parties with possible differences in interests. Implicitly these planners are saying that ideas in themselves have little force to accomplish broad planning goals without the organization of coalitions in support of the ideas.

In addition, significantly, these planners, in describing their expertise, are addressing some of the problems of governance outlined in the first chapter. Without ever referring directly to "governance," they contend that solving a problem depends on finding a common language for interested parties to communicate their concerns, breaking through barriers of mistrust, negotiating some consensus about the definition of the problem at issue, helping actors to accept ambiguity and uncertainty, "and yet constantly seeking to make order out of it." Only after this social process has been worked out is it possible to move toward an apparent solution for a substantive problem. Thus implicitly they are saying that governance at some level is a problem which they as planners work on. Whether they are more effective or effective in different ways than planners emphasizing intellectual expertise is a question which will be explored in the next three chapters.

Planners making statements about interpersonal expertise resemble the planners talking about intellectual expertise in sharing some vagueness about specific skills used in practice and in sharing also some personal dissatisfaction about being unable to be more specific. However, the comments contrast sharply in form with the statements about intellectual expertise. These comments tend to be longer and more articulate discussions of the planners' strengths than statements about intellectual strengths. This noticeable difference suggests that, at the least, planners claiming interpersonal strengths felt more comfortable in the interview situation and, more than that, probably feel confident that they comprehend and work well in planning situations, even if their personal contribution may seem vague. This greater fluency, coupled with an almost complete absence of comments about powerlessness, raises the question whether this group of planners may be employing skills in some way well matched with requirements of the organizational environments in which they do planning. This question is examined in the next three chapters.

This is how planners portray their expertise. From these statements two themes emerge. The first concerns planners' perceptions of the relationship between their goals and their expertise. Most planners espouse goals of broad change in the physical or social environments. The majority of planners tacitly describe the process of planning for these changes as a rational intellectual process. They present their expertise as the creative organization of information in order to solve problems. They rarely refer, in contrast, to the political interests of parties involved or relationships among these parties, and they do not regard themselves as social or political actors of any type. A minority of planners differently describe the planning process as an inter-personal and political process, and they are conscious of acting politically. They represent their expertise as the creative organiza-tion of people who have information in order to formulate and solve problems. This group appears to be more optimistic about its influence over decisions.

A second theme concerns planners' difficulties in describing their expertise with specificity and their feelings about these difficulties. A significant number of planners are not certain whether they have strengths—or, at least, whether they have strengths which might distinguish them from other practitioners. On top of this, even though almost every planner identifies some intellectual ability as a strength, few planners can describe clearly just what skills are involved. Finally, even though most planners are involved in interpersonal processes in organizations, few mention having any strength in this area, and few who claim interpersonal skills are very clear about what they are.

Planning Strengths and Personality Orientations

The statements quoted here suggest that planners emphasizing intellectual strengths may differ significantly from planners empha-sizing interpersonal strengths. Subsequent analysis will indicate that there are consistent patterns of behavior associated with the alternative emphases regarding expertise. Accordingly, it would be helpful to understand the sources of the personal emphasis.

Some hypotheses may be quickly eliminated because of lack of statistical support. For example, none of the personal characteristics of age, sex, or class origin (indicated by father's occupation) is associated with emphasis of strength.[8] In addition, these emphases do not appear to reflect the content of formal education, insofar as there is no statistical association between emphasized strength and either undergraduate major or type of graduate program.[9] Further, hypotheses that these emphases may reflect socialization or self-selection into planning practice are not supported. There is no statistical association between strength emphasized and either years of experience in planning or the planner's rank in the employing organization.

An explanatory hypothesis is suggested by the literature on vocational choice, referred to earlier. As noted, that literature provides evidence that an individual's choice of an occupation is a reflection of that individual's perception of the occupation and an expression of the individual's personality orientation (Holland, 1973). These findings would suggest that, particularly in the context of the diverse character of planning activities, differences in emphasis regarding personal strength might similarly reflect differences in personality orientations. This hypothesis was tested in the analysis of information collected in the study.

The literature on vocational choice indicates that choice of under-graduate major and thoughts about alternative occupations of interest may both reflect distinctive personality orientations (Holland, 1973; and Holland, personal communication). Accordingly, each planner's undergraduate major and list of alternative occupations considered was coded and analyzed within a framework provided by Holland in his studies of vocational choice (Holland, 1968 and 1973). These two separate codes were then combined through a procedure suggested by Holland into a single summary code of personality orientation for each planner. From these individual summary codes a profile could be developed for the sample as a whole. The full procedure followed is described in the notes for this chapter.[10]

The analysis of personality types for the sample of planners as a whole, shown in Table 2-3, reveals a profile of types with the pattern IS/A. This suggests that the primary disposition of planners as a group is Investigative, which is associated with intellectuality and rationality. Clinically, Holland (1978b) suggests, people high on this dimension are concerned with science, mathematics, and theory. They are inclined to think problems through, rather than to act them out. They tend to deprecate social, political, and business activities (Holland, 1978b, pp. 10-11). Considerably less dominant are two other dispositions holding an equal secondary position: Social and Artistic. The Social disposition is associated with intuition in problem-solving and an intellectual and ethical sense of social responsibility. Clinically, people with the disposition have social interests, are inclined toward teaching or therapeutic roles, and have interpersonal and role-playing competence (Holland, 1978b, p. 11). The Artistic disposition may be associated with originality. Clinically, people with the disposition tend to be introverted and may resemble "the stereotype of the artist in some ways—may be immature, anxious, sensitive and feminine" (Holland, 1978b, p. 12). The meaning of such a profile may be suggested by its similarity to the modal profiles for people who are physicians (ISA) and those who are economists (IAS) (Holland, 1978a).

TABLE 2-3. PROFILE OF PERSONALITY TYPES OF
URBAN PLANNERS FOR STUDY SAMPLE OF 50

Type	Score[a]	% of max. score[b]	Rank
Realistic	28	18.7	5
Investigative	108	72.0	1
Artistic	66	44.0	2
Social	66	44.0	2
Enterprising	42	28.0	4
Conventional	3	2.0	6

[a] Summary scores from codes for undergraduate fields of study and other occupations considered.
[b] Maximum: 150 (= a primary type score of 3 for each of the 50 members of the sample).

For purposes of comparison the undergraduate backgrounds of 2,000 members surveyed by the American Institute of Planners (AIP, 1974) were coded, and a similar profile was prepared.[11] Interestingly, as Table 2-4 shows, this profile is less differentiated but different. This profile is IAR, in which the Investigative type is still primary but the Artistic type is secondary and a Realistic type is tertiary. The Realistic type is associated with practicality and conventionality. Clinically, people like this type are "hardheaded," more skilled mechanically than interpersonally, and repelled by problems requiring a sensitivity to others' feelings or their own (Holland, 1978b, p. 10). This pattern is the same as the profile for physical scientists. The difference between the profiles of the study sample and that of the national AIP membership study suggests that there may be distinct subtypes of planners, characterized by different personality orientations, within the occupation of planning. This possibility brings the discussion back to the hypothesis of an association between differences in strength emphasized and differences in personality orientations.

TABLE 2-4.   PROFILE OF PERSONALITY TYPES OF
URBAN PLANNERS FOR AIP SAMPLE OF 2,000

Type	Score[a]	% of max. score[b]	Rank
Realistic	94	38.2	3
Investigative	135	54.9	1
Artistic	102	41.5	2
Social	81	32.9	4
Enterprising	28	11.4	5
Conventional	4	1.6	6

[a] Summary scores from codes for undergraduate fields of study.
[b] Maximum: 246 (= a primary type score of 3 for all of the 82% of the survey sample for whom undergraduate fields have specified significant representation.

The codes for the planners in the study sample were re-examined with the purpose of attempting to distinguish subgroups. Because the two samples analyzed differed in the presence of either a Social or a Realistic orientation to the exclusion of the other, this difference was pursued as a possible difference between subgroups. A re-examination of the codes for planners in the study sample revealed two groups of planners distinguished along these lines: those who have a Realistic disposition without or more dominant than a Social disposition, and those who have a Social disposition without or more dominant than a Realistic disposition. For the study sample, 88 percent of the planners fall

TABLE 2-5.   SUBGROUPS OF PLANNERS FOR
STUDY SAMPLE OF 50

Type	R-dominant Subgroup (N = 16)			S-dominant Subgroup (N = 28)		
	Score[a]	% max. score[b]	Rank	Score[a]	% max. score[c]	Rank
Realistic	23	47.9	2	2	2.4	5
Investigative	42	87.5	1	53	63.1	2
Artistic	22	45.8	3	32	38.1	3
Social	1	2.1	5	62	73.8	1
Enterprising	9	18.8	4	23	27.4	4
Conventional	0	0.0	6	1	1.2	6

[a] Summary scores from codes for undergraduate fields of study and other
  occupations considered.
[b] Maximum: 48 (= a primary type score of 3 for each of the 16 members of
  the subsample.
[c] Maximum: 84 (= a primary type score of 3 for each of the 28 members of
  the subsample).

TABLE 2-6.   SUBGROUPS OF PLANNERS FOR
AIP SAMPLE OF 2,000

Type	R-dominant Subgroup (N = 53% of 2,000)			S-dominant Subgroup (N = 29% of 2,000)		
	Score[a]	% max. score[b]	Rank	Score[a]	% max. score[c]	Rank
Realistic	94	59.1	2	0	0.0	6
Investigative	132	83.0	1	52	59.8	2
Artistic	75	47.2	3	27	31.6	3
Social	10	6.3	4	71	81.6	1
Enterprising	8	5.0	5	20	23.0	4
Conventional	0	0.0	6	4	4.6	5

[a] Summary scores from codes for undergraduate fields of study.
[b] Maximum: 165 (= a primary type score of 3 for all of the 53% of the
  survey sample for whom undergraduate fields have specified significant
  content).
[c] Maximum: 87 (= a primary type score of 3 for all of the 29% of the survey
  sample for whom undergraduate fields have specified significant
  content).

into one of these two subgroups. Table 2-5 shows the profiles for these two subgroups in the sample. It shows that there are two distinct subgroups: IRA and SIA. A similar analysis was performed for the AIP sample. As Table 2-6 shows, the same two subgroups appear, and the pattern of the six dispositions was almost identical.

The next three chapters will examine patterns of practice which are associated with—and which appear to be consequences of— the respective emphases on different strengths and expertise. For now, on the basis of the discussion of personality orientations associated with Realistic and Social dimensions, some speculation about planners' use of their expertise is possible. Insofar as planners are concerned about problem-solving, it may be hypothesized that planners emphasizing different strengths may be likely to define "the problem" differently and to identify different types of information as germane to "the problem." For example, planners emphasizing interpersonal expertise and having Social personality dimensions[12] would seem more likely to include perceptions of actors' feelings, organizational dynamics, and political interests in a definition of a problem and to gather information about these matters in analyzing the problem and formulating recommendations. In contrast, planners emphasizing intellectual expertise and having Realistic personality dimensions would seem more likely to restrict the definition of a problem and recommendations to technical, economic, and quantifiable considerations. This possible difference suggests a hypothesis regarding planners' perceptions of the advice-giving role of planners. Planners emphasizing interpersonal expertise and having Social personality dimensions would seem more likely to recognize the social relationships involved in advice-giving and to collect and to organize information in a way which would respond to concerns of decision-makers. In contrast, planners emphasizing intellectual expertise and having Realistic personality dimensions would seem more likely to construe advice-giving simply as the written transmittal of "objective" information to their organizational supervisors. These planners would seem likely to overlook or ignore decision-makers' interests and social relationships.

Although the findings about associations between planners' emphasized expertise and their personality orientations are only suggestive, the potential implications are major. For example, it is possible that problems in practice are associated with particular emphases in strengths. Earlier discussion suggested that planners emphasizing intellectual expertise may be less likely than planners emphasizing interpersonal expertise to recognize and confront the social complexities of planning problems in general and the problems of governance in particular. Here it is suggested that emphasis of expertise—with any consequences for planners' effectiveness—may reflect personality orientation. Personality orientations take their basic shape early in life and may be unaffected by institutions of higher education (Holland, 1973).

Thus there appears to be one subgroup of planners who are primarily Investigative, secondarily Realistic, and tertiarily Artistic. The orientation of this subgroup (IRA) is the same as those of surgeons (Holland, 1978a). A second subgroup are primarily Social, secondarily Investigative, and tertiarily Artistic. The orientation of this subgroup (SIA) is the same as those of social scientists and social workers. In the study sample the IRA group comprise 32 percent of the planners, and the SIA group comprise 56 percent.

The discovery of these two subgroups of planners, distinguished by their personality orientations, raises the question of whether these personality orientations may be associated with the differences in planners' emphases on their strengths, or expertise. A statistical examination of relationships between personality orientation and emphasis on intellectual or interpersonal strength, in Table 2-7, does show a relatively significant association ($p < 10$). While these findings are not conclusive, the associations are suggestive. They indicate that an emphasis on intellectual expertise is particularly likely to come from planners with a Realistic personality dimension, whereas an emphasis on interpersonal expertise is especially likely to come from planners with a Social personality dimension. These associations suggest that planners' differences in the expertise which they emphasize may reflect differences in underlying personality orientations. Specifically, the data suggest that planners who are relatively more comfortable with others' and their own feelings are more likely to develop, exercise, and refer to interpersonal, organizational, and political strengths as practitioners. In contrast, planners who are relatively less comfortable with feelings are more likely to develop, exercise, and refer to intellectual strengths as practitioners.

TABLE 2-7.   TYPE OF EXPERTISE EMPHASIZED
AND PERSONALITY ORIENTATION

	Dominant Personality Orientation		
Expertise Emphasized	*Social*	*Realistic*	*Total*
Interpersonal	12	3	15
Intellectual	16	12	28
All	28	15	43

$X^2 = 3.33$
$P < .10$
$V = .278$

NOTES

1. This last comment recalls Erik Erikson's eerie suggestion that Adolf Hitler's frustrations as a would-be city planner may have led him to unleash the vast destruction of the Second World War:

> As a youth, Hitler had wanted desperately to be a city planner; he walked around for days (and as if in a daze) rebuilding his hometown of Linz. To rebuild, of course, he had to imagine all the large buildings destroyed, but no doubt he tried to be "constructive" on a vast, if almost delusional, scale. It was when he finally sent his plans for a new opera house in Linz to a prize committee which paid no attention to them that he finally broke with society and disappeared, to reappear only as an avenger. But in his very last days, after having destroyed much of Europe and having finally been cornered in his bunker, he carefully planned his self-liquidation, but not without putting the last touches on his plans for the opera house in Linz, which he had almost come to build. To such an eerie extent does a late-adolescent commitment persist even in a person of excessive destructive needs (1968, p. 192).

2. One respondent's father was a farmer. Other characteristics of the sample, as well as the strategy for selecting the sample, are discussed in the Appendix.

3. Because planners might mention several attractions to planning, the groups mentioning each type of attraction are not mutually exclusive, and the percentages add to more than 100 percent.

4. The role of personal traits in influencing planners' perceptions of "planning" is discussed in the final section of this chapter.

5. Responses had the following distribution of emphases: 42 percent mentioned intellectual skills alone; another 26 percent mentioned intellectual skills but gave secondary importance to distinctly interpersonal skills; 8 percent mentioned interpersonal skills first, with secondary emphasis on intellectual skills; finally, 22 percent mentioned exclusively interpersonal or political skills. One person did not provide a response to the question.

In this study the responses are analyzed in two categories, on the basis of primary emphasis: intellectual or interpersonal. Other studies asking similar questions of planners (Howe and Kaufman, 1979; and Vasu, 1979) have analyzed the responses in three categories: essentially, the intellectual, the interpersonal or political, and an intermediate category containing mixed responses. There are two reasons why this analysis uses two categories. First, this dichotomy helps to understand the meaning of positions at the opposite ends of a continuum. Second, empirically, when the responses are divided into three categories—intellectual, mixed intellectual-and-interpersonal, and interpersonal—the results do not provide additional explanation of planners' statements beyond that provided by two categories. Although there certainly are planners who combine intellectual and interpersonal skills, efforts in this study to distinguish an intermediate group on the basis of responses to the question on personal strengths are not successful. They do not identify a distinctly different group, and they reduce apparent differences between the intellectual and interpersonal groups.

For purposes of comparison, it is possible to examine the distribution of three categories of planners in this and the two other studies:

— This study: intellectual: 42%; intellectual/interpersonal: 34%; interpersonal: 22%;
— Howe and Kaufman (1979): "technical": 27%; hybrid": 51%; "political": 18%;
— Vasu (1979): "technical": 48%; "moderate": 32%; "advocate": 20%.

Differences in questions asked and methods of analysis limit conclusions which may be drawn from this comparison.

6. Their description of the work of planning is similar in many respects to that offered by a sample of graduates of social policy planning and public policy programs (Bergman, Hemmens, Lieberman, and Moroney, 1976, p. 39). Describing their reasoning skills, those respondents reported spending 45 percent of their time using some form of "common sense" and another 30 percent of their time using "logical or systematic thought." Thus either the work of many planners involves general skills, or there is a common generality to descriptions of planning work. These possibilities are examined in subsequent chapters.

7. The converse is also possible. Difficulties in identifying clearly what planners do may make it difficult for them to identify ways in which they do have influence. This possibility is explored in the final section of the book.

8. Although the sample has a proportion of women similar to that among planning practitioners nationally, because this proportion is small, in a sample of this size it is not possible to make a good statistical test of the relationship between sex and other variables.

9. Respondents who had attended graduate programs in planning were asked to characterize the orientation of their programs. Although no prior labels were suggested as part of the question, most of the labels offered

by the 37 planners with graduate degrees in planning fell into four categories: physical planning (14), "general planning" (8), economic planning (5), and social planning (4). Because the same program was sometimes characterized differently by two or more alumni, it seems clear that the responses represent planners' personal experiences of the "message" of their programs, rather than a summary of a program's policy statement or catalogue description. Subsequent comments about differences between these policy statements and the orientation of personal coursework support this interpretation. Thus it was possible to look for associations between strengths which planners emphasized and both the type of graduate degree which they received (for example, planning, social work, or public administration) and, if they had a planning degree, the orientation of their particular program. No significant associations were found.

10. John Holland offered suggestions for procedures which might be followed with the data available (personal communication). Normally, his Vocational Preference Inventory (1978b) or Self-Directed Search (1972 and 1977) would be administered to a group of subjects to get an indication of their vocational preferences and personality orientation. In the case of this study of planners, subjects had been asked several questions which called for the types of information elicited by these two instruments. Holland suggested that responses to the questions about undergraduate major and other occupations considered might provide indicators of the personality orientations of the planners in the sample.

For this purpose Holland's (1978a) classification of modal personality dispositions for various occupations was employed. In this classification system Holland has assigned to various occupations codes which reflect the scores for members of these occupations when tested with either of his instruments or some variation of the instruments. In a small number of cases scores reflect hypotheses about the likely characteristics of workers in an occupation based on an analysis of the characteristics of the work. Holland has suggested that undergraduate majors (such as history or architecture) may be considered to have equivalent meaning to the occupations (such as historian or architect) which graduates of such programs may hold. Undergraduate majors were coded accordingly. In Holland's system occupations and the personality characteristics of workers may be coded with any combination of six letters, corresponding to six empirically discovered discrete traits. For simplicity an occupation or an individual is given a three-letter code, representing a primary, a secondary, and a tertiary orientation.

The six types of orientation, discussed in more detail in the text, are (1) Realistic (practical-minded, mechanical, and masculine); (2) Investigative (scientific, problem-solving, and intellectual); (3) Social (sociable, feminine, concerned with feelings, and concerned with social reponsibility); (4) Conventional (conforming, unoriginal, status-oriented, and concerned with self-control); (5) Enterprising (dominant, adventurous, risk-taking, and needing achievement); and (6) Artistic (aesthetic, original, unconventional, and introverted). These brief descriptions, while indicative of individual characteristics, clearly, do not adequately represent either the conceptual or clinical complexity of traits involved.

Within this framework, each individual's field of undergraduate study was translated into an occupation directly linked to the field and assigned a three-letter code from Holland's (1978b) classification. In most cases field of study was readily translatable into an occupation. For example, an undergraduate architecture major could be translated into the occupation of an architect and then assigned the code AIR (primary orientation Artistic, secondary orientation Investigative, and tertiary orientation Realistic). A history undergraduate could be translated into the occupation of a historian and assigned the code SEI (primary orientation Social, secondary orientation Enterprising, and tertiary orientation Investigative). When an individual had studied more than one field, the code for the separate fields were combined into a summary three-letter code. A similar procedure was followed in coding responses to the question about what occupations other than planning the individual had considered. Finally, for each planner the codes for field of undergraduate study and for other occupations considered were combined into a single summary code, which could subsequently be used to develop a profile of the sample as a whole. In all cases, summary codes and sample profiles were developed by taking weighted sums of individual codes, multiplying the primary characteristic by 3, multiplying the secondary characteristic by 2, counting the tertiary characteristic once, and selecting the three highest ranking resultant characteristics.

11. The same procedures were followed as with the study sample, with the exception that percentages of respondents with similar backgrounds, rather than individual planners, were used as the unit of analysis.

12. It should be recalled that not all planners emphasizing interpersonal strengths have Social personality dimensions. Rather, those with Social personality dimensions are especially likely to develop interpersonal abilities and strengths.

REFERENCES

American Institute of Planners. "AIP Membership Has Not Changed Much Since 1965: Average About the Same but Salaries and Education Higher," *AIP Newsletter* (1974), pp. 1-3.

Bergman, Edward M., George C. Hemmens, Susan A. Lieberman, and Robert M. Moroney. *The Practitioner Viewpoint: An Exploration of Social Policy Planning Practice and Education, Part 2: The Findings.* Chapel Hill: Department of City and Regional Planning, University of North Carolina, 1976.

Erikson, Erik H. *Identity: Youth and Crisis.* New York: W. W. Norton and Company, 1968.

Holland, John L. "Some Explorations of a Theory of Vocational Choice: 1.

One-and two-year longitudinal studies," *Psychological Monographs*, 76 (26, Whole No. 545) (1962).

Holland, John L. *The Psychology of Vocational Choice: A Theory of Personality Types and Model Environments*. Waltham: Blaisdell, 1966.

Holland, John L. "Explorations of a Theory of Vocational Choice: VI. A Longitudinal Study Using a Sample of Typical College Students," *Journal of Applied Psychology*, 52 (1968), pp. 1-37.

Holland, John L. *Making Vocational Choices: A Theory of Careers*. Englewood Cliffs: Prentice-Hall, 1973.

Holland, John L. *The Occupations Finder*. Revised edition. Palo Alto: Consulting Psychologists Press, 1978. (a)

Holland, John L. *Manual for the Vocational Preference Inventory*. Revised edition. Palo Alto: Consulting Psychologists Press, 1978. (b)

Howe, Elizabeth, and Jerome Kaufman, "The Ethics of Contemporary American Planners," *Journal of the American Planning Association*, 45, 3 (July, 1979), pp. 243-255.

Vasu, Michael Lee. *Politics and Planning*. Chapel Hill: University of North Carolina Press, 1979.

3

PLANNERS' AUTONOMY

PLANNERS' AUTONOMY IN PRACTICE

Planners present themselves as problem-solvers who are working for broad changes in the physical and social environments. Most planners offer an intellectual expertise for solving these problems. These claims are pretentious. How much influence do planners actually exert in practice?

The contextual discussion of the first chapter offers two reasons why planners' influence may be limited. First, members of the public increasingly expect that "planners" will solve not only specific substantive problems but also general problems of social governance. Accordingly, planners would acquire influence to the degree that they are effective in solving governance problems. However, planners' descriptions of their expertise suggest that planners' aims and much of their proffered expertise may not be matched to these problems. Hence planners' presentation of expertise itself makes influence problematic. Second, planners would like to acquire autonomy because it would bring them both the influence and prestige of a "profession." However, the requirements of effectiveness with governance problems suggest that autonomy is unlikely, although limited influence is possible.

A central question, then, is this: Are the goals and expertise of planners appropriately matched to the environments in which they work? This chapter examines planners' descriptions of their working conditions. These descriptions are scrutinized for comments about difficulties in working or constraints on planners' autonomy. In particular, statements of planners are analyzed for an explanation for the following common sentiment:

> I guess there are moments of depression, which I think everyone in the field has. ... What are you really doing? What is the long-range impact? If I didn't show up for six months, what difference would it make? The government would run without my department. It would run without my department. It would run without my section. It would run without me.

73

The Variability of Single Optimal Solutions to Problems

Often the realities of work are different from the image which attracted people into it, as well as the goals which they set for themselves in practice. The first hint that this may be the case in planning comes in response to a question which asked planners how often in their experience they discovered a uniquely correct solution to the problem on which they were working. The question evoked lengthy responses, in which planners appeared to see themselves asked to describe—and justify—the quality of their work. This type of reaction is not surprising, because the question touches on concerns central to the traditional ideology of planning. The classical rational model of planning suggests that, given sufficient time and information, a planner can identify a single optimal solution to a problem. Apparently, planners felt pressed to measure themselves against this standard and called to rationalize any deviations from the standard.

Responses to the question split in two directions. Forty-four percent stated that they "frequently" or "always" found a single solution, whereas 32 percent stated that they "rarely" or "never" saw a single solution, while the remainder said that single solutions appeared "sometimes."

A large number of the comments that followed supported the traditional position that a sufficiently skilled and informed planner could, indeed, identify an optimal solution for a problem. Several planners contended that this solution would appear "if you do your work well enough" or if you have time to work on it." Confidently, a veteran planner expressed this point of view: "Well, with a professional background you usually try to come up with alternative solutions, and as a rule there usually is one which sort of naturally is higher than the rest of them." One planner noted his surprise that, contrary to his initial expectations, he normally did find optimal solutions:

> Before I started working in planning, [because of] a lot of the literature which I read, I more or less was of the opinion that —this was sort of a philosophy or theory of mine—that the best you can do is gather the data and develop alternatives, and there will be two or more alternatives which will be fairly close, and there will be a lot of values involved, and it boils down to a value judgment. The actual decision will be a value judgment which may not need the

work of the planner to have the value judgment made. But in the
different projects which I have undertaken...the end result in my
mind [is] that one option stands out as being clearly superior to the
others. In terms of what I read, that is not the way a planning
process should work. Maybe that is because I make the technical
process.

Several planners observed that a combined intellectual and
political process of considering alternatives helps to winnow down
the choices to a single solution. For example, one noted,

> It depends on what stage of the process you are talking about. I tend
> to focus in on the project level thing. The environmental statement
> requires that you consider all alternatives and also that you consider
> not doing anything at all; in other words, you are required to start
> out without biases. Now the process is very much an open one. It is
> difficult to give you a flat out answer to the question. After public
> hearings are held, it is only at that stage that you select the final
> alternative. We are forced into a situation of having to consider
> alternatives without biases at the outset and at the end evaluating
> projects in terms of cost, city input, economic, social, and physical
> impacts, and then recommending alternatives. At that stage we do
> know what the best alternative is.

At the same time, it is helpful to consider the observation of an
education planner that people tend to develop emotional attach-
ments to and rationalizations for whatever recommendation they
end up making:

> Ultimately we have to make a recommendation. After you work
> with it long enough, you become convinced that it is the solution.
> But getting to that point, I am aware that it is heavily dependent on
> your assumptions, how you interpret the data. I have been in
> education planning long enough to see this. That is enough to
> convince you.

In contrast with these views, there are several ways in which a
second group of planners describe constraints which the world sets
on their ability to reach a single optimal solution. Some limitations
appear to be intrinsic to planning. First, a number of planners
contended that the social world is simply too complex for unique
solutions to problems. Some planners just asserted that problems
permit multiple solutions:

> There is usually more than one solution. Saying there is usually one
> right way means there is only one thing you are trying to do, and if
> there is only one thing you are trying to do, you are doing it wrong.

A local administrator pointed to the human component of problems and argued that unique solutions are rare "because. . . . problems are dealing with people." This human world, a veteran planner noted, is extremely complex:

> The type of project I work on is so complex that it is really a decision tree. Normally we are not even smart enough to see where the project is going to lead us. The way you pose the problem influences the outcome. It is not an optimization process, but really a suboptimization process.

Further, noted a consultant, social processes complicate the problem-solving process:

> The nature of this work is that there is no clearly defined right and wrong decision because it is measured against factors which are constantly changing. The technical aspect is a little bit easier, but it still operates within social and organizational aspects. There is a great variety of compromise and tradeoff which is necessary.

Interestingly, a relatively new planner reported the opposite effect of experience on his view of planning from that described by another planner above:

> When I first got out of planning school, I would have said [that I found a single unique solution] frequently or always. The longer I work, the lower my rating is. The older and wiser you get, the grayer things get. If you had asked me several years ago, I would have said frequently. If you ask me several years from now, I may say rarely.

In this complex world, one architect-planner suggested, reaching a recommendation is less a matter of science and more an art of making a judgment:

> On most planning projects we consider many alternatives. Issues become the application of which criteria, whose criteria are to be met. There are many things which are not measurable. It becomes an intuitive, instinctive process to some extent.

Finally, there is a paradoxical, if not perverse, quality to problem-solving in such a complex world, as one veteran planner asserted: "The more problems we try to solve, the more problems we create."

In the views of these planners, then, the social world and social problems are complex, there are neither single correct problem definitions nor single correct solutions, and making recommendations from alternatives requires exercising judgment. In contrast with two groups to be examined next, these planners are relatively sanguine about carrying out their work in this manner. In their portrayal of the complexity and fluidity of the environment of planning they give the impression that they may appreciate the problems of governance described earlier. The description of the uneven emergence of problem-formulations and solutions recalls the descriptions of the planning process offered by planners emphasizing interpersonal expertise. And yet there is little overlap between these two groups: most of the planners who report never or rarely discovering single unique solutions claimed strengths with intellectual skills.[1] This lack of overlap suggests that these are two groups who appreciate different types of complexity in planning. Those reporting infrequently finding single unique solutions seem to be describing the intellectual complexity of planning problems, without much reference to the social context in which problems are defined and perhaps solved. The group emphasizing interpersonal strengths appears to be concerned with the complexity of this social context. They have direct contact with the individuals and groups whose actions cumulatively contribute to the intellectual complexity encountered by the first group. Although neither group uses the language of "governance," the group emphasizing interpersonal expertise appears more attuned to governance problems. At the same time, it is significant that in one of these two ways more than half the sample (54 percent) testify to the uncertain complexity of the planning environment.[2]

Responding to the question about finding single optimal solutions, a third group of planners point to legal constraints on their recommendations, and they are not happy about these constraints. For them statutory requirements and regulations limit the alternatives which they may consider and may force them to make recommendations which do not fully satisfy them. A county planner with many years' experience commented,

A lot of stuff which I do has to do with framing work to meet requirements. This is different from [recommending what is] appropriate. It is what is dictated. I can meet all requirements and still feel I am not doing a good thing. I guess what I really do is try to optimize the two. I take the organizational values and constraints and then try to get my own values. I try to get 70 or 80 percent. I think that is par for the course. Unless I could re-write regulations or guidelines. Then we could get 100 percent. We have managed to do this. That is one of the most satisfying things: changing the rules of the game, so that the game can be most satisfying.

In other words, this planner frequently sees single optimal solutions to problems, but for reasons he does not like.

One other group of planners refer to ways in which political processes of decision-making distract attention and preferences away from reasonable or optimal solutions. These statements express a common hostility of many planners toward "politics," although these planners disagree about whether "politics" lead toward or away from finding a unique solution:

> I know planning is supposed to [examine many alternatives]. I was taught in school that there are not supposed to be any strict answers. That is true technically. But if you add in the political factor, a single answer emerges. Things are not as complicated as they appear to be. [I can] distinguish what I think is the solution, but it is not what is the most feasible solution [politically].

A planner who had worked as advisor to a county executive concurred that there may be differences between planners' preferences and ultimate political choices. However, he contended that it would be undemocratic to permit planners to make decisions:

> This does not mean that [the alternatives not chosen] are less adequate. They are only less satisfactory, but we cannot do it politically. And I think this is an important thing for planners to realize. I do not think planners should ever back a public official into a position where he has only one choice. Sometimes planners decide to play God and say this is It. They have got to come up with options for a man who has got to make decisions.

These are four different sets of responses to a question concerning the degree to which planners find single optimal solutions to problems. The first group express considerable confidence that they can discover and recommend optimal solutions. The second group believe that intellectual mastery over problems is limited by the complexity of planning, with the consequence that planners infrequently discover obviously optimal solutions. The last two groups are concerned that legal requirements or political processes so limit planners' discretion in recommending reasonable alternatives as to make the question about discovering optimal solutions moot. Recommending optimal solutions to problems is regarded as the core of planning work. These last two groups, comprising approximately one third of the sample,[3] are complaining that "regulations" and "politics" prevent them from doing good planning and from having the influence which good planners should have.

Analysis of the pattern of responses suggests some explanation for planners' perceptions of the frequency with which optimal solutions appear.[4] Planners' responses are not associated with such personal characteristics as age, sex, or class origin. Nor are they associated with either field of undergraduate education or type of graduate training. With regard to work experience in planning, the responses are not associated with years in planning, but they are significantly associated with planners' roles in the organizations where they work, as Table 3-1 shows.

TABLE 3-1. IDENTIFICATION OF UNIQUE SOLUTION, BY PLACE OF EMPLOYMENT AND ORGANIZATIONAL ROLE

Employment, Role	*Unique Solution*			
	Never/ Rarely	*Sometimes*	*Frequently/ Always*	*Total*
Public agency: administration[1]	4	6	5	15
Public agency: staff	2	4	11	17
Private firm	10	0	6	16
All	16	10	22	48

X^2 = 15.11
$P <$ .01
$V =$ .397

[a]"Administration" includes all ranks from section chief up.

Planners in lower-level staff positions in public agencies are most confident of their ability to find a unique solution when working on a problem. Their assuredness contrasts with what may be either greater conservatism or greater flexibility on the part of agency administrators, who report less frequently finding unique solutions. These differences may reflect differences in responsibilities of or constraints on planners in these two roles. Staff members have the luxury of working out optimal solutions for problems, whereas administrators bear the responsibility of presenting recommendations which are acceptable to a politically heterogeneous public. This contrast seems to be a source of conflict between staff and administrators, wherein staff members have difficulty understanding why their "correct" solutions are not automatically adopted by their supervisors. This conflict is illustrated in later discussion in this chapter. Private consultants have the greatest expectation of finding a range of possible solutions to problems. They generally explain that, whatever their personal conclusions as planners, their final proposal has to reflect the client's wishes tempered by planning regulations.

The responses to this question identify concerns of many planners that their reasoned recommendations are consistently constrained by statutory requirements, regulations, and political considerations. In particular, planners who report feeling constrained most often are found in lower-level staff positions in public agencies. Thus a number of planners do indicate that, whatever their planning goals, they confront significant hindrances in their work. These obstacles limit what is likely to be implemented. In addition, they prevent planners from recommending specific alternatives which they consider optimal solutions for problems on which they are working.

Defining "Good" Planning Projects: Results and Goal Displacement

If a significant proportion of planners feel that their work is constrained by the legal and political contexts in which they work, it would be important to know how planners set standards for their work. In order to explore this consideration, planners were asked to describe a planning project in which they had participated which they regarded as particularly good.

Notably, one-fifth (20 percent) of the planners found such a question difficult to answer at all. One veteran planner stated succinctly, "I don't know how to answer that." Some others, like a staff member of a county housing department, offered a blanket negative assessment of their projects: "There are not many that I would consider particularly good." A number of planners noted that it was difficult to settle on criteria for "good" planning: "'Good,'" one regional planner commented, "is a tough question."

The specific difficulties which planners find in identifying "good" projects begin to point to some characteristics of planning work which practitioners find troublesome. For example, a planner for an urban county, after describing an adroit job of carrying an imaginative solution to a recreation problem through a complex political process, concluded, "No harm done, only cost a lot of money, may be some benefits some day." The reference to "some day" highlights an uncertainty which many planners experience in assessing their work. For example, another planner, when asked if there were "good" projects which he could describe, replied, "Not that I have worked on. . . . I have not had enough opportunity to see something straight through." For many planners the time that may elapse between the initiation of the writing of a plan on paper and any subsequent action to implement the plan makes it difficult to see the outcomes of planning efforts. This hiatus is a problem because planners want to see their ideas used and implemented. When planners cannot see such tangible results clearly, they have difficulty feeling that their work has been completed. There seems to be something inherent in the planning process which may make it difficult to identify "good" projects.

Almost all planners eventually could single out a project which they regarded as "good," and two-thirds (68 percent) identified a project in which their work had results. A social planner spoke for this group as a whole when he said, "I got satisfaction out of it that it is actually happening." A planner in zoning enjoyed the short amount of time required for his proposals to be implemented:

> Generally it is rewarding in current planning. You see projects happen. It is an intrinsic reward, not an extrinsic reward.

Another planner emphasized the bricks-and-mortar element of results:

> I could see the visual things which were coming out. I am not administration oriented. I am physical development oriented.

For some planners, acceptable results may include the successful organization of political support for a proposal:

> The plan, once developed, is supported by the community. If they support it, it will go through every level of approval.

A number of planners hold a still more modest view of results which are necessary for a project to be "good." For them it is sufficient that their ideas be used at some point by other actors in the planning process. For example, one regional planner observed, "The analysis was done, and they used it." Another planner could accept this use of her ideas even when they were never implemented:

> At least something came out of it. The ideas have been used, even though the plan has never been adopted.

Nevertheless, simply seeing results is insufficient for a number of planners. This feeling is conveyed by an experienced planner who answered the request to describe a "good" project with a question of his own:

> "Good" from a technical standpoint, or "good" because you got through with it?

Consistently, a second characteristic common to a large proportion of projects described as "good" is the perceived high intellectual quality of the work process. Almost two-thirds (60 percent)[5] of the sample referred to the intellectual challenge, the opportunity for personal creativity, or the possibility of executing a "model" planning process in the preparation of a plan in a "good" project. Whereas planners emphasizing intellectual expertise and planners emphasizing interpersonal expertise were equally likely to mention the achievement of results in describing a "good" project, planners emphasizing intellectual strengths were somewhat more likely (through not significantly so statistically) to emphasize the intellectual quality of the planning process.

The importance of employing rigorous planning methods, almost regardless of results, is indicated by one planner working with a state cabinet agency:

> The project came too late to have an impact, but the methodology was good.

Another planner emphasized method, elaborating,

There was a methodology to doing it. It was a series of sequential things. It was a framework for planning. This was funded to a level where we could do it the way it should be done.

Other accounts read like excerpts from textbook descriptions of a rational planning process:

[The project] provided an opportunity to step back and take a comprehensive look at problems in the city and get an overview.

The important thing was, I could make use of all the techniques of planning, from a systems point-of-view.

One consultant recalled many specific details of the project:

It involved urban design. . .working with maps. . .surveying. . .directing the surveyors' work. . .seeing the accomplishments of the office. . . .For example, we were working on presentation methods using two projectors. Design, in terms of physical design, physical forms. . .traffic patterns, building blocks. We didn't build a model, but [another consulting firm] had a model of the area, and I provided some input.

Several comments reveal the pleasure which planners may derive from carrying out a precise intellectual problem-solving process:

Everything we proved with statistics. We had it all backed up. There was no emotion about it, it was strictly thought out, and it worked beautifully. We had the community behind us. We had politicians behind us. That is why the job was most gratifying. [Note: although "there was no emotion" interjected into the process, it "worked beautifully" and "was most gratifying."]

[It was] truly a selection of alternatives process. . . .a real storybook process.

A third characteristic of "good" projects, mentioned by approximately one-fourth (28 percent) of the planners, concerned the social or political process of planning. Here planners recalled that decision-making had been based on extensive participation or that a final recommendation succeeded in reconciling many opposing interests. Several planners discussed the importance of citizen participation in the "good" project or in planning generally:

In policies, the development of large citizen task forces was extremely helpful. [It] provided the opportunity to try to recognize different viewpoints which exist and try to represent them.

[There is] the need to involve citizen groups, to set up a process that produces not only an end project but also makes people happy with it, that creates a constituency for the end product. [There are two reasons] for participation: one, for people to spend enough time to understand what is going on and make their interests known, and, two, to give outside people opportunities to coach and give information to the inside people.

Another planner's description of the strategy which he developed to move a plan ahead matches in its sense of beauty some of the descriptions of "storybook" intellectual processes described above:

It took us ten months to turn around the process to where the council could select a [landfill] site. We set up a citizen group. It took us ten months to re-open the decision-making process within the government to select a site which was acceptable to the general public. We definitely had a strategy which was acceptable to the general public. We definitely had a strategy and an approach that we were trying to implement. Our strategy was not to present to the council [only] one site, to divorce a technical decision from a political decision, for our department to consider the technical aspects—and allowing the political decision-makers to make a value judgment in relation to the non-quantifiable, the political value judgment.

Although it is difficult to generalize about the characteristics of the planners who prefer projects with participatory decision-making, one quotation from a local district planner reveals the personal pleasure which these planners do derive from the interaction of widespread participation:

I know I am going to go out and work with people. I like that kind of feedback, rather than working in a house of paper all the time.

Finally, a small fourth group (16 percent) noted that their "good" projects helped to meet community needs. Planners' concerns here are represented by the following two comments, one from a relatively young planner and one from a relatively older planner:

[The project resulted in] something tangible that people wanted. The community wanted services, and something tangible resulted from our efforts.

I was able to take planning techniques and apply them to the racial issues. . . . I considered a planning project good if somehow benefits were distributed to low income or disadvantaged groups.

Planners offering these observations tended to be the planners emphasizing interpersonal strengths, but the number involved is too small to draw any firm generalization.

Both the form and the content of the statements about "good" projects present contrasts with earlier statements about attractions to planning, goals, and strengths. Formally, the length of the quotations here accurately mirrors the greater volubility of planners when discussing specific projects than when discussing their personal goals or expertise. This difference suggests several interpretations. One possibility is that planners speak more about those things for which they have ready language and less about those things for which they lack language. The university training of planners covers the technical aspects of planning projects at great lengths and almost completely overlooks the role of the planner as a social actor. There is little in the formal education of planners to teach them to express a consciousness of self. Further, although planning education is undergoing change, planners have traditionally been taught to manage information and make recommendations in a manner free of personal judgment and emotion. As a result of this socialization, planners would be likely to talk more about the products of their work than about themselves as workers.

It is possible also that planners simply feel more comfortable discussing planning projects as objects rather than themselves as subjects. The literature on vocational choice suggests that people who undergo the socialization of formal training for planning may do so with the conscious understanding that they will be encouraged to act in ways consistent with their feelings. Thus planners may develop limited language for describing themselves because they have limited comfort examining themselves. The descriptions of "good" projects provide some, albeit inconclusive, evidence for this interpretation. Even though these descriptions contain liberal first-person references, most of these statements refer directly to the objects of planners' actions, rather than to the planners' intentions, strategy, or motives. The image of the planner as theatrical technician attributes great importance to the planner's role but focuses attention on the action of others, on the stage. These two interpretations of the form of the comments are not mutually exclusive, nor is either one conclusive. They suggest directions for further study.

The content of the descriptions of "good" projects contrasts with earlier statements in a way which raises questions about planners' influence as practitioners. It is noteworthy that almost none of the planners identified a project as "good" because it contributed to the high-level goals which they identified for their work. Although most selected as a "good" project some instance in which their work had results, most of the examples focused purely on the implementation, partial use, or endorsement of some of their ideas, without attention to the content of the ideas or the role of the ideas in any coherent system of goals.

This point can be highlighted by drawing a contrast between the pattern of responses to this question and an ideal model of the planning process. Most models of the planning process begin with an identification of clients' or constituents' needs. This identification of needs is the beginning of a rigorous intellectual process of collecting and organizing information to discover reasonable interventions. The intellectual analysis may be accompanied or succeeded by a social process in which clients, constituents, or significant decision-makers contribute their ideas, seek to influence recommendations, and offer political support for certain alternatives. If the intellectual and social processes are well organized, a proposal will be implemented, and the results should help to meet the needs initially identified. Although it may be argued that this is a rationalistic ideal for the planning process,[6] it is the model espoused by most of these planners in their discussion of goals and strengths in practice. However, the descriptions of "good" projects favor a planning process with priorities—if not necessarily stages— which are the inverse of this model. First in importance is implementation of something. Second is high-quality intellectual work. Third is social participation in planning. Last is the meeting of client or constituent needs.[7]

Although it is not customary for practitioners always to enunciate the theoretical principles underlying their actions, the almost complete absence of references to earlier espoused goals or needs in the project descriptions stands out. One possible interpretation of this paucity of references to goals is that planners may be acting without concern for the long-range consequences of their work. This possibility would be a matter of concern to those who view planning as intrinsically involved with assessment of the consequences of alternatives. A more specific interpretation is that planners may act on projects without serious consideration of social goals which are implicated in the projects and which the projects could serve. This possibility, which is explored further toward the end of this chapter, poses questions about the ethical direction of planning activities. It also raises practical problems for planners seeking legitimation as "professionals."

An alternative interpretation of the scarcity of references to goals is that most planners may take goals for granted and not feel a need to mention them. This interpretation is difficult to accept in the context of a careful scrutiny of the descriptions of "good" projects. Overwhelmingly, these descriptions, rather than referring to the projects' outcomes, focus on facets of the process of carrying out the projects. Planners mention intellectual rigor, good methodology, careful use of statistics, creativity, rational consideration of alternatives, learning, comprehensiveness, use of many techniques, working with people, recognizing different viewpoints, involving citizen groups, and so forth. These emphases suggest, instead, that many planners may simply be more concerned about the structure of the work process than about the value of the outcome. If this is so, how do planners become distracted from earlier concerns about goals to concerns about process? Scattered complaints about constraints on achieving espoused goals suggest that frustration may lead to goal displacement. Planners may focus on aspects of the work process as something over which they believe they have some control and from the execution of which they may derive some satisfaction. This possibility is examined more carefully in a later section of this chapter.

Planners' Difficulties Assessing Their Work

Many planners imply that they could do better work if they were not constrained or overruled by legal regulations or the political process. A significant number of planners describe "good" projects less in terms of goals for planning outcomes than in terms of the quality of the planning work process. Potentially conflicting expectations could make it confusing for planners to evaluate their work. It is possible to get a better picture of planners' efforts to make sense of problem-solving in organizational settings by considering their responses to a question about how often they have difficulty assessing their work.

TABLE 3-2. IDENTIFICATION OF UNIQUE SOLUTION
AND DIFFICULTY ASSESSING WORK

Difficulty assessing work	*Unique Solution*			
	Never/ Rarely	Sometimes	Frequently/ Always	Total
Never/Rarely	5	5	9	19
Sometimes	8	·4	10	22
Frequently/Always	3	1	3	7
Total	16	10	22	48

In Table 3-2 the responses to this question are presented in conjunction with responses to the question about the frequency of single unique solutions for problems. This table identifies two relatively large groups, each of which poses a question for further consideration. One group can be found among the 38 percent who report that they "rarely" or "never" have difficulty assessing their work. Half of these planners (18 percent) also state that they "frequently" or "always" find unique solutions for problems. Thus for this group, representing almost one-fifth of the sample, the work of problem-solving is reportedly a relatively straightforward task.[8] Yet, if planning problems and the environment of planning are so complex, how can these planners find problem-solving such a simple matter?

A second, larger group, comprising 26 percent of the sample, report both that they "frequently" or "always" discover a unique solution to problems and that they at least "sometimes" have difficulty assessing their work. (Comments following the question suggest that "sometimes" actually occurs rather frequently when problems in assessing work are involved. Respondents appear to have understated the frequency of difficulties.) These responses seem paradoxical and also raise a question: if planners readily perceive optimal solutions for problems, why should they have difficulty assessing their work?

Narrative comments provide answers to the questions posed by these two groups. There is a tendency for one approach to assessing work to be taken by the first group and another approach to be taken by the second group. Nevertheless, each approach is taken by many planners, and the comments should be taken as broadly indicative of the ways in which planners try to make sense of problem-solving in a complex environment.

The first group of planners indicate that problem-solving is a relatively simple matter, even though there are many indications that problems and the environment for planning are complex. This group simplifies the definition of problem-solving in such a way as to make their work simpler and easier to assess. An indication of how they do this is offered in a county planner's characterization of typical projects:

> Technically, you know what you did. [But you] don't know the significance ever.

This planner makes a distinction between "technical" components of problem-solving and the "significant" social context of problem-solving. The former can be evaluated by internal standards; the latter is difficult to evaluate. This distinction is formulated a little differently by another planner, who said that, with regard to the "quality" of her work, she "rarely" had problems assessing it but that, with regard to the "form of presentation" of that same work to others, she "sometimes" had difficulties. Both planners indicate that there is something about the way in which their work may or may not be used which makes assessment of it difficult. Hence a number of planners resort to a separation well characterized by a planner with many years' experience:

> In terms of whether or not the work I do is *right,* I don't have all that many qualms about. Whether or not it is *useful* is where I am on softer grounds where assessment is concerned. [For example, I don't know whether my last major project] is related to improving life in the city.

For these planners two aspects of the use of their work appear to be problematic: first, whether decision-makers will adopt their proposals and, second, if their proposals are implemented, whether citizens will make use of and benefit from the products. At the same time, the planners would like to be able to assess their work and to derive a sense of competence from it. Consequently, they deliberately exclude the problematic aspects from a definition of their responsibility and restrict their view of problem-solving to performing "right"—or high "quality" or "technically" correct—analysis of problems and recommendation of solutions. When "planning" is simplified to mean the satisfaction of these internal standards, then problem-solving can become a relatively straight-forward activity.

The second group of planners appear to differ from the first primarily in their inability to convince themselves to redefine their responsibilities in technical terms. Although they often feel, as do the first group, that they do competent technical work, they seem to have difficulty gaining a sense of accomplishment from that alone. Their explanations of their difficulties in assessing their work center on their inability to see satisfying results from their efforts. Perhaps they are more candid than the first group. Certainly, they express concerns which are unsettling to many planners.

Some of these planners may attempt to rely on an internal, technical standard for their work but find the effort unconvincing. A long-time city planner expressed a common disquietude:

> Because it is usually through my own value system [that I judge my work, I am] not quite sure whether what I try to do, other people consider valuable.

Hence many planners, as the descriptions of "good" projects suggested, look to the results of their efforts in order to assess their work. However, they have understandable difficulties assessing their work when they cannot discern results. The most common problems were summarized by an administrator who said that assessing work is difficult

> for a very specific reason: the plan hasn't been built yet.... We all need to go back to our communities. [There is always a] grayness about where you began and someone else finished off. [It is difficult to] evaluate yourself as a role player within a context of many role players.

Thus, first, because the planning process is usually lengthy, planners—especially those in agencies without implementation responsibility—are likely to have to wait a long time before seeing any results. In addition, because the relationships among actors in the planning process are intricate, it is usually difficult to identify particular results with the efforts of a single planner. Finally, because many planners do much of their work in offices isolated from community members, planners often have added difficulty seeing the effects of their efforts or assessing their value to community members.

This second group of planners are prepared to assess their work by its "form of presentation," its "significance," and its "usefulness," but their analyses of problems in evaluation indicate that they find the organizational process of planning confusing. A number of comments point to intellectual difficulties in grasping the complexities of the planning process. For example, some planners report that they start out with broad goals in mind but are unable to identify the results of their work with those goals. An administrator who claimed interpersonal and organizational skills observed,

> I think that at the beginning of any project or process you establish your goals which you want to achieve, and you work from your goals down to your plan to carry out your goals.... By the time of implementation, it appears to be a kind of compromise. When you implement the plan, you wonder if it corresponds to the original goals. I think that happens almost on a daily basis.

A city planner who said that he had rare difficulty assessing his work emphasized, nevertheless,

> the very complex nature of the work itself. The rules and regulations of the legislation are very complex, and so sometimes the technical complexity makes it difficult to assess. The other part is in terms of human behavior. Human behavior itself is very complex. Social scientists are just beginning to understand what makes people tick.

This uncertainty may not only make assessment of work difficult; it may also be painful and almost overwhelming, as this comment by a county planner shows:

> So much of what we do is subjective, seat of the pants, intuitive— and, so many times, not politically feasible....You think, maybe I don't have technical training, maybe I should go home, maybe I don't know anything. Another thing: community development is a lengthy process....When you're assessing your job, you need some day-to-day encouragement. It is difficult to assess a twenty-year package. How do you know if you're right or wrong? Checkpoints help. Another thing is, you're dealing with such a complex idea, the city. I don't think I can ever understand that. Maybe we can never understand that. I don't know.

Other planners in this group reveal the confusion of the organizational process of planning in references to difficulties in controlling their roles in the process. Perhaps they share some of the intellectual difficulties just expressed, but what they emphasize is problems in influencing actors and events in the planning process. For example, a consultant characterized planning projects as unpredictable:

> Projects often end up going for a great period of time, from start to when they open the doors. . . . A lot of the people I worked with will be gone by then. So there is a great separation between my early efforts and what the product looks like. It is easy to lose sight of the other things which you do along the line before you get to the final product. Or you could go through the entire thing, and the project is aborted.

A county planner pointed to difficulties related to

> the stage of the thing when you pick it up. Either that it is not clearly defined. It leaves you with a lost feeling before you get into it. When it is all done, nothing becomes of it. Those kinds of circumstances.

It may be difficult to assess one's work because resource constraints force the planner to do quick work without reflection:

> Part of the problem is that you do not have time. The job has to be done. You have to come up with quick solutions. You do not have time to sit back and reflect on how you might do it five different ways. . . . I could say that it would frequently be the case that you do not have the time to think about the best way of doing it. I am not convinced that winging it is the best way to go. The biggest problem with the job is that you really do not have the time to do the breadth and analysis which you know you should do. You continually have to suboptimize. You have to use people who do not have the skills to get the job done. Or you do not have the time to do the research. The people and time constraints are significant.

The experience of not having control over the planning process feels confusing, as a planner with frequent assessment difficulties revealed:

> Very often I have a nagging feeling that I would have liked to have done it slightly differently. . . . There are always those things which you wish you had said. You don't necessarily see it right away. You simply don't know. Yet the last thing which happens when they put

the final coat of paint on the building, that is what you plan for.
Eventually when it gets built, you have the question, did we do it
right? It is more of the self-doubt than assessing your work.

This lack of control over the planning process is also disturbingly
frustrating, as a similar planner noted:

> I personally have a relatively high feeling of frustration. The long
> period of time required to accomplish these things to wait out some
> of these processes. I would far prefer to have a shorter span. It is
> this thing: am I really accomplishing anything? Am I really
> accomplishing anything, or am I churning a lot of water? I often feel
> frustrated. I find, looking back at my experience, a good 85 per cent
> of my work has come about. You cannot take argument with that,
> but it takes so long. Maybe I do not have enough perseverance. I
> doubt if I'll ever get any credit for this, but I guess that is the
> planner's lot. An architect gets his name attached to a building, but a
> planner never gets his name attached to a city, unless he makes a
> mistake.

One other feeling runs through planners' comments, irrespective
of how much difficulty they report in assessing their work:
isolation. A state planner cannot assess her work "because I am
response-oriented. And if I don't get a positive response, I don't
know. Often in planning you don't get a positive response." This
comment is echoed by a regional planner: "I don't get any
response. Or I get a negative response." One planner copes with
this situation in a Walter Mitty-like fashion. He believes he has the
competence to know how the agency's projects should be done,
"but I never tell anyone. I am a dreamer, but at the same time I am
realistic." Several planners attribute their feelings of isolation to the
turbulence of the planning environment, in which there are few
fixed standards to measure work, but this analysis is not necessarily
reassuring. For one planner this understanding only tempers the
feeling of isolation with a cynical tone:

> There is really no fixed standard to evaluate [your work] by, and the
> kinds of feedback you get are not necessarily ones which I consider
> valid. Half the time I don't think they know what they are talking
> about. Or... you think they don't want to rock the boat.... If you
> are working for [a large commission], it is impossible to achieve a
> consensus about what you are supposed to be achieving. I think this
> is one of the most difficult things about working with a regional
> planning agency in a controversial arena. So it is rare that you get a
> project that it is not difficult to get everyone to agree on. Just choose

whom you want to make enemies out of. You just try not to take it personally.

Another planner concludes that the environment is so turbulent and that he is so isolated, that he is dispensable, worthless:

> It gets difficult sometimes when you are into too much. You tend to lose a sense of priorities. You need to pull away and look at the scheme of things. It is hard to know how quickly a project will grow, how much attention I should pay to that right now. I guess there are moments of depression, which I think everyone in the field has. . . . What are you really doing? What is the long-range impact? If I didn't show up for six months, what difference would it make? The government would run without my department. It would run without my section. It would run without me.

The question about assessing work leads planners to look at the effects of their efforts. Most planners report that they have difficulty seeing results from their work. They say that they neither control nor influence planning outcomes in consistent significant ways. This is a puzzling situation, insofar as "planners" usually are employed because their expertise is considered an integral part of organizational decision-making. The planners interviewed explain the apparent paradox by observing that they work in isolation— from colleagues and constituents.[9] And it is clear that this isolation is not accompanied by any of the autonomy which "professionals" would desire. What is not clear is whether this isolation is a necessary component of planners' roles, whether, nevertheless, many planners carry out their roles in isolation, or whether this isolation is only a subjective cognitive experience of planners who are more connected to other workers than they think.

Cognitively, many planners refer to two types of isolation. First, there is an isolation of the work which they do in their roles from the work which others do in their roles. Typically, planners report that they perform competent intellectual work and submit it to the appropriate recipient. Then something which most have difficulty comprehending or describing—something "crazy—happens to their work. It may be lost and never received by anyone. Or it may be received but never read. Or it may be read but never responded to. Or it may be responded to, but nothing happens as a result. Or, eventually, something may happen, but so much time has elapsed since their work, that it is difficult to know whether the occurrences are related to their work. Or something may happen, but it bears so little resemblance to what their work referred to, that it is difficult to know whether it reflects their work.

Planners refer to a second type of isolation, which helps to compensate for the "craziness" of this situation: this is an isolation of their professional identity from what they do in their roles. They describe splitting themselves—one part inwardly adhering to particular standards for "good" work, the other part carrying out various actions in the organizational process of planning in which they seem to have little influence and of which they can make little sense. In order to make sense of their work and to maintain some sense of competence, many planners engage in this psychic contraction and retreat.

Planners describe two ways in which they cannot control the organizational planning process. Many cannot comprehend it intellectually. In addition, many indicate that they do not have the skills to influence it interpersonally or politically. Clearly, the two types of control are related, and each type of difficulty contributes to the other. The immediate result is what planners portray as a loss of control over their work once it becomes part of the organizational process of planning. Beyond this, this lack of control over the way in which their work is used might explain the emphasis simply on *some* use of their work when identifying "good" projects. Further, this felt lack of control over use of their work could explain the focus on their own intellectual or creative contribution to the work while it is directly in their hands.

In the comments on difficulties in assessing work, planners claiming intellectual strengths were slightly more likely than planners claiming interpersonal or political strengths to report difficulty evaluating their efforts. This difference suggests that planners who regard themselves as political actors comprehend the organizational process of planning better and can act in it with more predictability and influence than planners who regard themselves as rational intellectual analysts. The difference suggests, similarly, that an emphasis on intellectual expertise may for some planners be an act of personal splitting which leads to the social isolation which many report experiencing.

Recommended Changes: Power for Planners, and No Politics

More information about how planners make sense of their role and how they perceive constraints on their influence can be provided by responses to a question about what changes in the environment of planning would make it easier for them to accomplish the goals for which they strive. Planners' recommendations require them to make assumptions about the dynamic structure of the planning process and about crucial points of leverage in this process.

One-tenth (10 percent) of the planners in the sample named specific superiors in the organization where they worked as culprits and said that their replacement would cause major transformations and make proper planning possible. Comments include complaints about "the secretary" of a cabinet department and the expressed desire for "a new deputy director" of a housing department. There are calls for "bold action." What would be needed, a typical response indicated, is

> change at the top. We need much more of an activist director. We have had a director who is very concerned about his own job, because he will not take risks. Mostly he takes a reactive planning stance, rather than a proactive stance.... It is distressing within the Department of Planning [because] the Department of Planning is seen as obstructionist.

Effective planning would be possible if only someone would

> fire two, three people at the top of the department, this division, and the heads of administration in other [related departments]. Get somebody with a little desire to work closely with but not quite so shilly-shallying about dealing with people with potentially hostile political constraints.

One-fifth (20 percent) argued that there should be fewer bureaucratic restrictions on technical planning and that the planning process should somehow be depoliticized. With one exception these were all planners employed in public agencies. Many of their comments, rather than specific recommendations for changes, were reiterations of complaints that the analyses and recommendations of planners were given little weight and passed over in public decision-making processes. For example, one agency administrator began his observations with a brief Madison-

ian defense of the process of interest-group politics but turned
quickly to criticism of the usual outcomes of this process:

> I think the political process is a healthy one. It gives a whole lot of
> people an opportunity to participate. But, at the same time, it results
> in decisions that are counter to good planning or management
> decisions. So planning people are faced with having to deal with
> straw man issues, to accommodate problems that are perceived
> problems, not real problems. And the political issues are based on
> the pacification of interest groups simply because these groups are
> vocal. I don't think local officials take heat well. They will work
> compromises that serve the interests of existing citizens but in the
> long run will be shown to be short-sighted. A specific answer is that
> you ought to build road A from X to Y even though people who live
> there don't want it. There is little way to balance [the interests of a
> few hundred neighborhood residents] against those of the many
> affected. . . . When you get down to specific facilities projects, that is
> when it is the responsibility of local officials to represent both sides
> of the issue, not only those who are most vocal.

A planner in a regional agency pointed to similar problems when
governmental units act as competing interest groups:

> I feel hampered sometimes in the activities and the positions which
> we can push as they relate to local jurisdictions as components of
> our council. Or if they are sensitive to things we might do which are
> critical of them. . . . Here it is easier to criticize the state than local
> jurisdictions, because, even though this is a state agency, our clients
> are the local jurisdictions.

Several planners complained that public decision-making is either
formally or informally structured to minimize the influence of
planners. A planner who had worked in public agencies at several
levels of government pointed to the selection of membership for
citizen boards and advisory councils as a primary means through
which politicians collaborate with "private sector interests" to stifle
the influence of public agency planning staffs in decision-making.

Others in this group offered a range of recommendations for
changes which would minimize the political component of the
planning process and would increase the influence of planners. At
one end, one planner focused on changing the statutory authority
of the planning department:

> I think a lot of the frustration has to do with the function of our
> agency. If our agency had the responsibility to say yes or

no....We're virtually powerless to do anything about it....We comment on others' plans....We have the authority just to be heard, and a lot of time we are not doing even that. Nobody wants us to tell them what to do.

This planner represents ·the view that, in some unspecified way, the planning department should be given new statutory authority to enforce conformity by other agencies with its plans. Other planners acknowledged the role of informal influence and talked of ways in which planners could have more power within existing governmental decision-making processes. An administrator in a local agency simply called for a new, direct connection between the agency and the most powerful actor in decision-making: "We need easier and more frequent access to the County Executive's office, because that is where the power exists." More concretely and specifically, another planner described his goals for changing the planning process in his county:

> One thing would be...we're trying to work now...to change the planning process and the planners—changing the level of responsibility which planners take within the local government. We're trying to stick it to them [the planners]! Out here the Council are the planners. I'd like to see them not see themselves as the planners. What I see ultimately as helping us to do a better job is changing the roles and responsibilities and organizational structure of the county.

A third group, comprising two-fifths (42 percent) of the sample, argued in more general ways that planners should have more power, should receive more support for their efforts, and should have a larger budget for their work. In this group a number of planners, most of them private consultants, complained that the ways in which government intervened in planning, primarily through the issuance of regulations, both seriously constrained planners from influencing outcomes and damaged the quality of outcomes. An architect-planner with many years of experience represented most in this group when he advocated a "reduction in rules and regulations and review processes, most of which are meaningless and which discourage creativity." Sympathetic with the purpose of the regulations but disturbed by their effects, another consultant called for "more flexibility in the system," whereby there "would be tradeoffs" on such things as housing densities, the location of roads, and road widths. In order to do this, there should be "somebody to look at projects on a project-

by-project basis, not fall back on a manual." Others saw more
caprice and less good intention in governmental actions. A private
consultant, representing the views of both consultants and some
public agency administrators complained:

> We need a changed attitude or approach in government to allow
> things to be done in different, newer, better ways. One of the
> greatest obstacles to the kind of things I would like to do is
> government agencies. Government itself is set up as an obstacle to
> private enterprise.

In addition to stifling creativity, a state health planner suggested,
regulations and review processes generate side-games which focus
on controlling aspects of the review process, rather than planning a
sensible outcome:

> Administrators in hospitals have to deal with nurses, doctors, health
> planning agencies. You can cut out the worst abuse, but you also
> stifle any innovation and creativity, because there is such a narrow
> path through the regulations. What I see from where I am is a
> system where I watch so many people who are relatively powerless.
> But so much of the theatrics are attempts to gain control. But it is
> much ado about nothing. Partly it is because the problems are so
> complex. People catch one little corner of it. But they have only one
> tiny side. It is like a stalemate. They have such a little share of the
> power that they can't do anything with it.

Other planners, in both the public and private sectors, contended
that planning would remain peripheral to decision-making in the
absence of greater public financial investment in planning activities
and new programs. They believe that planning that is to be more
than simple compliance with regulations, that is to search for
creative solutions for major problems, would require larger
budgets than planners and operating agencies now have available.
An administrator argued that money is the sole constraint on good
planning:

> I think the only constraints right now are money, funding at two
> ends: funding for the actual improvement of capital projects or
> related services, and we would probably need additional staff. Right
> now there is no constraint on the philosophy of a county. They kind
> of challenge us to do more than we can physically do. But there are
> no political roadblocks to serving the community.

Another planner, a veteran of several decades' experience, agreed
about the importance of a larger budget for planning but

suggested that it is important to understand the ways in which legislative bodies see—or don't see—the need for planning. A long-time proponent of environmental programs, he expressed some disappointment with the limited support he had received from local councils, but he attempted to put the need for greater support into perspective:

> This gets into problems of dollars, taxes, money, income, zoning, regulation...and I honestly do not have any nice neat answers to any of this. Money is limited. The principal element needed is understanding on the parts of those controlling these things. I can understand the problems of the councilmen. This is not easy, because the people themselves do not understand.

Planning programs would receive more money, he suggested, when planners succeeded in convincing citizens and their representatives of the value of planners' work.

For some planners all these concerns about increasing the power of planners reduce to the challenge of increasing public sympathy for planning. An administrator argued that planners must excite the public imagination about planning's potential:

> There has to be political change, education, have to be voters willing to pay money for these things, have to be city managers and elected officials who can see the long picture....I guess it is trying to educate people and politicians to see a better world.

An architect-planner emphasized the importance of the type of creative work which planners contribute:

> The key is public awareness that environment is important, that a different kind of environment does make a difference....We just completed the final phase in the redevelopment of a school complex. We created an environment that has people thrilled.

Other planners would echo this statement with arguments about the importance of public awareness of the social environment and the potential of social programs. What they share is a belief that they have the ability to improve the quality of people's lives, if only people would give them support to move ahead.

There are two contrasting views about the short-term likelihood of changing public perceptions of planning. The more optimistic view, probably a minority view, is expressed by a planner who takes an active political role:

One of the biggest priorities is more responsibility for business to work with neighborhood organizations and, I guess, more of a trust between government and people, especially large government. There has to be more trust on the part of government that people can do things for themselves. And the only way to do this is to build power for the people but also to bring in business, in partnership with people power.

What is probably the majority view is expressed by an architect-planner, who identified two obstacles to planners' status and influence. Citizens appear to fear the potential of planning as a threat to their liberties, and, at the same time, planners have not provided clear evidence that they are equal to the challenge of important problems:

> The biggest obstacle is the general status of architecture and planning in this country. As a profession, architects and planners are not highly thought of. We really have not met the challenge, either by education or practice, of coming up with solutions to problems of urban and rural development in this country. We are not a planned economy. There is a basic conflict between the market and planning. So many decisions are made by private enterprise and government, and it is not a coordinated process. It is like the deck is stacked against coming up with solutions.

Collectively, the various recommendations for changes have a remarkable quality. Most represent an insensitivity to the organizational environment of planning. Some comments convey a lack of appreciation for bureaucracy as a complex organization of people. The suggestions that the replacement of single individuals in authority would significantly change the planning environment imply that relations in organizations can be reduced to the interactions of individual personalities. At another extreme, the recommendations that the planning process be depoliticized treat the organizational process as if it were an abstraction: it is something which can somehow be either "politicized" or "depoliticized" while remaining substantially intact. Moreover, the desire that the planning process could be depoliticized stands in evident conflict with the recommendation most frequently offered by planners, calling for power for planners and support for planning. This recommendation, embodying complaints that planners have too little influence over decisions, suggests that power exercised by planners would be somehow apolitical. In addition, the recommendation implies that the acquisition of power by planners would not itself require political action. In reality, the empowerment of planners would be by its very nature a political process. Yet few of the planners calling for more power begin to specify organizational strategies which could bring them power. Most of these planners do not even refer in sufficiently tangible ways to the organizational settings in which they presently work as to be able to think about strategies for power.

Planners who claim to have interpersonal or organizational strengths do not differ significantly from planners claiming intellectual strengths in relation to the types of recommendations for changes which they offer or in terms of the relative abstractness of their recommendations. These findings suggest that, insofar as planners claiming organizational expertise may feel influential in the planning process, many may be focusing on interpersonal relations in the organization, rather than on the overall direction of work. In this respect they apparently resemble other planners in lacking an overview of the process as a whole.

When talking about changes which they would make, many planners variously describe the sensation of working on an assembly line where the workers on both sides of them are invisible. Many are not certain where their work comes from. They know who gave them their immediate assignment, but they do not always know what larger problem and picture their assignment fits into. Once they have carried out their assigned work, they submit their product, usually a written document, to another person, generally the same one who gave them the assignment. In this process they may have some influence over how their assignment is presented to them or, at least, how they execute their assignment, but what becomes of their work product is for many planners more or less a mystery. In reality the report or recommendations traverse organizational lines of communication, buffeted by political pressures along the way. But planners evidently do not have a picture of these organizational lines in their minds. Consequently, when they speak of changes, they refer to what they do see directly—namely, individuals who give assignments—or they refer abstractly to a process whose character they only dimly imagine.

These responses add to early comments about constraints on

planners' autonomy. The primary recommendation for change expresses the feeling that planners have less power than they should have. At the same time, these comments suggest at least one additional reason why planners may have limited power. In response to earlier questions planners cited external constraints in law, politics, and organizational "craziness." In response to this question they revealed a weak understanding of the organizational environment of planning. This lack of understanding appears to be one internally imposed constraint on planners' autonomy.

REDEFINING THE WORK OF PLANNING

Criteria for Effectiveness in Day-to-Day Work: From Public Wants to Personal Needs

A majority of planners start out with broadly stated goals. Yet many express a sense of powerlessness in meeting these goals. On close inspection, it appears that many planners lack a clear understanding of the organizational environment in which they work or an understanding of the ways in which organizational strategies might give them influence. Is it possible, then, that, in the face of this frustration and perplexity, planners redefine their expectations so as to find some satisfaction in their work? To explore this possibility, the planners were asked what they looked for as indicators of their effectiveness in their work.

Two-fifths (42 percent) said that they regarded implementation or use of their work as the primary criterion of their effectiveness. Either some part of their recommendation may be put into practice, or, more modestly, some part of their analytic work may be used by others. How much or which part of their work is accepted tends to be less important than some acceptance. At one end of a continuum, one planner argued for the importance of concrete results:

> One thing I look for, rather than the adopted plan—I don't consider that a measure of effectiveness at all. I look for facilities, actual physical development taking place according to principles that I have been involved in establishing.

An administrator indicated that he kept a mental scorecard of the times his point-of-view influenced final outcomes. He wanted to know,

Do I get my own way? That doesn't mean that I cannot compromise at points, because I have, but I look at the percentage, of how often it goes where I thought it should go.

Others said that they wanted to have their work read and to feel confident that it had some influence on decisions. A planner in housing wanted to know "who might read my report . . . whether it is cited or copied or referred to by other people . . . if it's used to swing or sway a decision that would be made by the public sector." Somewhat more modestly, a staff planner in a state agency wanted to have his ideas accepted by his administrator and eventually influence policy in the department. He emphasized

primarily, acceptance by the Secretary of his department. Secondarily, as actual accomplishments, in terms of achieving legislation or achieving budget funds which I initiated or helped to plan. But primarily I see my role as being a technical advisor to the head of the organization in planning-related ideas, and his acceptance of these ideas is the best evaluation I can have that I am having an impact.

A second group of two-fifths (44 percent), including a few from the first group,[10] said that they look for supportive feedback from their immediate client or from the constituency for or with whom they are planning. Although they find it most desirable to be commended for doing work which actually improved others' lives, they indicated that they also value clients' comments that they liked working with the planner or respected the planner's intentions. A planner in an urban county emphasized good working relationships in the community:

[I value] being taken seriously by my director, working directly with the staff of almost every county department. The response I get from the community when I am with them tells me that they believe what I am doing.

More modestly, a planner who had worked with county government for several decades said that he would be pleased when his point-of-view were merely understood by important community actors:

[You look at] simply the degree to which those with whom you're working at least recognize the need to take a longer-range point-of-view. In the case of the recreation program in the county, for example, the degree to which the County Council, the County Executive at least indicate that they know what you're talking about.

For some planners community members' judgment may be valued because it provides a balance to what is considered the unfair lack of appreciation accorded work by agency administrators. Another public agency staff planner angrily said that he looked for support from constituent groups in order to get a deserved sense of competence. He concentrated on

> what I get by way of feedback from community groups and developers. For example, I am frustrated with this department. I am seriously thinking of getting out of this damned place. [I have a good reputation with people in other agencies,] but I don't have so much luck with some of my superiors.

For private consultants client satisfaction has a special, economic importance. A long-time consultant emphasized the necessity of getting a combination of results and client satisfaction:

> [I look for] the results, one hundred per cent results. Relations with the client? Very definitely. It is quite difficult to keep up with the client. Every penny you spent, it is his money. I would like to see my client come back to me.

Another consultant similarly pointed to the absolute value of the client's satisfaction:

> The satisfaction of the client [is the only indicator of effectiveness]. I don't judge my work. It is the client who judges my work. It is up to the client to judge if you have done his work. His satisfaction is your satisfaction. You can have any criteria—it depends on whom you get. As long as the client is satisfied, I am satisfied.

A final group, which included one-third (32 percent) of the planners, emphasized the importance of approval or compliments from agency colleagues as a sign of their effectiveness. The following comments are typical of this focus:

> [I look for] responses from other people, verbal responses, how people react. When I do workshops, I give out feedback sheets. I've even started doing that with our staff, after our management meetings. I have not perfected that yet, but yesterday I had good results.

> [What is primary for me is] whether my work meets criticism, praise, compliments.

Some planners value praise from their colleagues because of its scarcity. Rare compliments provide some measure of personal value, as a local planner observed:

[I look for] no editing [of what I write]. . . . There is not that much backslapping and congratulations. When I have done something decent, I get some congratulatory remarks from colleagues. I do not need that all the time, but now and then it is nice. Often here you feel you are being taken for granted.

These statements about indicators of effectiveness contrast markedly with earlier broad statements about what planners seek to accomplish in practice. More significantly, the ways in which planners redefine their aims reflect their organizational environment, even while they make little mention of the organization. For example, whereas two-thirds of the planners describe themselves as practitioners with intellectual strengths, two-thirds identify interpersonal responses from clients or colleagues as their primary criterion for effectiveness, and most of the rest identify some form of implementation requiring interpersonal effectiveness. Planning takes place in organizational settings, and planners come to evaluate themselves in terms of their ability to enact the outcomes expected of them in their roles or their ability to obtain the rewards accessible to them in their roles. The influence of the organization is similarly evident in planners' movement from the initial goals of accomplishing broad social or physical change to the striving for almost any kind of acceptance of their work and, crucially, personal approval and compliments from others with whom they work.

The influence of organizational structures on this transformation of goals is evident in an association between particular choices of criteria for effectiveness and the roles of the planners most frequently mentioning those criteria, as Table 3-3 shows.[11] For example, private consultants are concerned first about implementation of results and clients' approval, which translate into economic survival. Public agency administrators, working under many expectations similar to those of private consultants, consider themselves effective when they are able to contribute to implementation and when they receive praise from such clients as elected officials and community leaders. Only rarely does a planner insist that what is implemented be part of his or her overall planning goals. Rather, as the last quotation about client satisfaction suggests, they are willing to work for results which meet the immediate objectives set by their client or constituency.

Finally, lower-level staff in public agencies are quite different. Very few are concerned about implementation of any type, or any use of their work. Fewer than a fourth are interested in a response from constituents. Rather, two-thirds look for comments from others in their agency to tell them whether they should consider themselves effective.

TABLE 3-3. INDICATOR OF EFFECTIVENESS, BY PLACE OF EMPLOYMENT AND ORGANIZATIONAL ROLE

Employment, Role	Indicator of Effectiveness			
	Implementa- tion, Use of Work	Client, Consti- tuent Praise	Colleague Praise	Total
Public agency: administration[a]	10	8	4	22
Public agency: Staff	2	4	11	17
Private firm	9	9	1	19
All	21	21	16	58

X^2 = 17.98
$P < .01$
V = .394

[a] "Administration" includes all ranks from section chief up.

The responses of lower-level public agency staff are also accompanied by a special affect: cynicism about their agencies' work and pessimism about having any influence over agency decisions. Directly and indirectly, a majority of these staff members suggest that they know how to do high quality work but that they are either ignored or asked to do mediocre but politically acceptable work. A number of planners express a sense of futility or internal defiance toward administrators, whose motives appear arbitrary. These feelings come across in side comments like the following:

> [I am concerned about] my satisfaction, period. . . . Sometimes I am doing bits of work, and I am able to say it is a good piece of work, whether they like it or not.

Others complain about being ignored or sent mixed messages by their superiors:

> [I check to see,] did I get things in on time? Do I think I did the job adequately, given what little direction I was given?

> As far as superiors, you kind of look for indications that they are giving your views some consideration. . . . whether they are willing to set up meetings to hassle down something. Here things are too funneled as far as decisions go. Everything goes up, and nothing comes down. There isn't the authority which goes with the responsibility.

The very low importance which staff planners attach to implementation—or even the use of their work by someone—is remarkable. Their consistent expressions of cynicism or pessimism suggest that their extreme emphasis on interpersonal relations with agency colleagues represents in part a response to the feelings of powerlessness expressed by a number of planners. Although the feeling and responses of lower-level staff planners lie at the end of a continuum for planners in the sample, their orientation epitomizes a problem experienced by many planners. They tend to limit their influence and any resultant satisfaction by conceptualizing the setting for their work in such a way that they do not "see" the organizational process within which planning decisions are made. At the same time, desiring some satisfaction in work, they turn their attention to those rewards which are accessible to them within the organizational process. Thus, although many planners apparently do not "see" or understand the organizational process, they are very much affected by it in redefining their work.

Diversion from Broad Goals for Planning Action to the Details of the Planning Process

There is a constrast between the expansive initial statements of planners about their goals and the subsequent confined statements about what they concentrate on in their work. Earlier, planners reported that they were attracted to planning by the possibility of gaining power to make large-scale changes in society. They viewed themselves as master-builders. They referred to controlling the development of the physical environment and taking steps to form a more equitable society. They presented themselves as grand problem-solvers. Their intelligence would make this possible.

In later descriptions of their actual work, these pretensions have receded. While a number of planners suggest that they do find the optimal solutions to solve major problems, they report that laws and political actors hinder them from presenting the solutions. When they describe "good" projects, they recall projects in which their ideas were somehow used but quickly move from possible outcomes to the intellectual quality of the work process. It is enough to have the opportunity to follow a logical problem-solving process, whether or not the suggested solution is used. They describe difficulties assessing their work or understanding why it may or may not be used. Their recommendations for changes in the situation are vague. When asked what they really accept as indicators of their effectiveness from day to day, many do look for the possibility of satisfying clients with results. However, many also settle simply for compliments or general praise from other planners in the agency as the ultimate sign of their effectiveness. It is a long distance from aspiring to build a more equitable society to settling for some comment to the effect of, "I see you are working on something, I haven't had a chance to look at it, but it seems like you are doing a good job."

Three possible explanations for this redefinition of the work of planning have been mentioned already. First, it has been suggested that the formal education of planners does not teach them to interpret specific issues which they are asked to analyze in terms of a broader theoretical framework. Perhaps discussion of social, ecological, or physical design ideals is so abstract that the ideals are not translated into specific projects which could embody them or specific actions which could contribute to their enactment. Perhaps the discussion of these ideals is so separated from training in the use of planning methods that the theoretical framework and the skills become mentally compartmentalized and strategically unrelated. Or perhaps the presentation of ideals is minimal, training in the use of methods is emphasized, and the curriculum conveys the message that planning is the execution of methods without relation to goals. The traditional emphasis of planning on a value-free practice would reinforce the last of these possible messages.[12]

The literature on vocational choice suggests that people may choose to enter an educational program in planning with one of these messages because the emphasis of the program is seen as consistent with already existing personality orientations. That is, the formal education of planners may not teach students to interpret specific issues in terms of broad ideals in part because students may prefer to look at projects in isolation from a theoretical context. This hypothesis requires testing, but it suggests some of the possible complexity of the influence of planning education on planners' perceptions of their work, a theme returned to in the final chapter. Insofar as planning education does affect planners' definitions of their work, whether or not personality plays a significant role, there appears to be an emphasis on working on discrete projects serially, in isolation from other projects or a context of ideals. If this were the case, then it would not be surprising that many planners devote most of their energy to ensuring that they can follow a model logical process of problem-solving, with much less thought to the outcome of their efforts.

A second possible, complementary explanation has also been suggested earlier. To whatever degree planners hold serious goals for their work, the conditions of this work may either distract or discourage planners from concentrating on their original goals. Planners depend for their livelihoods on satisfaction of clients. (In the case of planners in public agencies, elected officials are the immediate clients.) Few planners have the opportunity to select a client on the basis of affinity to the client's goals. Moreover, few clients, whatever their goals, are engaged in sustained efforts toward the fulfillment of comprehensive plans in the service of their goals. At the same time, few planners have the opportunity to work for a long period of time for some client with such sustained efforts toward attractive goals.

Third, there is another possible, more specific way in which the conditions of planning work may affect planners' redefinitions of their work. Responses to questions about the frequency with which planners found single optimal solutions and about the criteria used to judge effectiveness in work tended to be associated with planners' organizational role. Private consultants tended to emphasize striving for clients' satisfaction with a project and noted that they infrequently find any single correct solution in this process. Public agency administrators tended to feel that single optimal solutions appear somewhat more often but, nevertheless, emphasized that they work for the satisfaction of their client with a project. Lower-level staff members differed from both other groups in both respects: they tended to feel confident that single correct solutions become evident relatively frequently, and they rejected client satisfaction and implementation in favor of colleague compliments as their primary criterion for effectiveness.

Preceding discussion has pointed to ways in which these different roles may condition planners' expectations. Private consultants must satisfy their clients and must be sufficiently imaginative or flexible to find the ways which will please their clients. These are the conditions for financial success. Administrators in public planning agencies confront similar requirements. Elected officials expect their assistance in planning and implementing projects which will satisfy voters. Most top-level planning administrators serve at the pleasure of specific elected officials and must attend to their clients' satisfaction.

The statements of lower-level staff members may be interpreted in several ways. First, the nature of their positions is that they may be insulated from many day-to-day political pressures, with the consequence that they have the encouragement—or, at least, the opportunity—to think through solutions to problems in the absence of political constraints. They might then be particularly likely to feel that they do discover optimal solutions to problems. Some directors may encourage this free thinking with recognition that it will create intellectual tension in the department. Still, the denigration of use of their work expressed by lower-level planners and the emphasis on colleague compliments requires explanation. On the one hand, their lower-level positions may quite simply remove them from the opportunity to influence recommendations directly, and they may choose not to count on this influence as a way of shielding themselves from any possible disappointment. Similarly, their emphasis on praise and compliments from others on the staff suggests a reasonable approach to looking for emotional rewards in a situation where instrumental influence on decisions may be tenuous.

However, a second line of interpretation is possible. To begin with, there is a noticeable strain of resentment expressed in statements about often finding optimal solutions but not caring about their implementation. The education of planners leads them to expect to provide well-considered solutions to problems and to influence decisions by virtue of their intelligence. Accordingly, disappointment of this expectation may lead some planners in lower-level positions to exaggerate the correctness of their solutions and to understate the importance which they attach to the use of their work.

Some additional information about possible sources of resentment may be provided by the age distribution of planners in different organizational roles, as shown in Table 3-4. Although there are no statistically significant associations between planners' ages and their organizational positions, some tendencies may be noticed. Among planners in public agencies, those age 35 and younger are likely to be in lower-level staff positions, whereas those over 35 are likely to be in administrative positions. These patterns suggest a normal path of upward mobility associated with seniority in an agency. Hence some resentment of lower-level staff planners might be interpreted simply as impatience on the part of younger planners awaiting their opportunity to assume influence and responsibility as administrators.

TABLE 3-4.   AGE OF PLANNERS, BY PLACE OF EMPLOYMENT AND ORGANIZATIONAL ROLE

Employment, **Role**	Age			
	26-35	36-50	51+	Total
Public agency: administration[a]	5	9	3	17
Public agency: staff	9	6	2	16
Private firm	7	7	2	16
All	21	22	7	50

[a] "Administration" includes all ranks from section chief up.

However, this interpretation should be considered in the context of the structure of most planning agencies. Commonly, the hierarchy in planning agencies resembles a relatively flat pyramid, with the consequence that any individual planner confronts relatively limited opportunities for advancement within the same agency. Work histories of planners in the sample indicate that many public agency administrators were not promoted from within but, instead, moved into their post from outside the agency. Consequently, redefinition of goals and resentment on the part of lower-level planners may reflect a combination of relatively high expectations encouraged by planning education, present low status in an agency, and limited prospects for advancement within that agency.[13] Finally, something might be said about the relatively older planners who are in lower-level positions in public agencies. Either these people have chosen to remain in these positions, with the mixed benefits of having neither direct responsibility for nor influence on decisions. Or these may be people who have lacked the skills necessary to acquire and maintain administrative positions, in which case seniority without responsibility or influence could clearly lead to resentment.

After this focus on lower-level staff members in public agencies, it is important to recall that most planners, regardless of their positions, tended to redefine their aims from broad-scale environmental change to something more modest and feasible. Here some of the previously discussed findings may be helpful in suggesting the psychological meaning of this redefinition. Earlier, it was noted that planners' initial attractions to planning and the goals which they set for their work were associated with their fields of undergraduate study. The vocational choice literature suggests that choice of undergraduate field strongly reflects personality dimensions. Consequently, it is reasonable to hypothesize that planners' attractions to planning and their goals for practice have deep personal meaning, reflecting whatever influences shaped their personal development. In contrast, as just noted, planners' perceptions of the frequency of unique optimal solutions and their criteria for effectiveness are associated with their organizational role. Yet it is clear that the rewards which either a public planning agency or a private consulting firm can offer its employees are limited. Thus the experience of many planners would seem to be one in which strong personal motives lead people into planning positions in organizations with weak capacities to reward these motives. It should not be surprising if planners feel disappointed or resentful, if they redefine their expectations to fit what they do perceive to be the possible rewards of their jobs, or if they maintain limited personal investment in their planning jobs.[14]

The introductory analysis of the context of professionalization suggested that autonomy is an inappropriate goal for practitioners seeking to be effective in planning. Few planners believe that they have significant autonomy or influence, and yet most still want autonomy. In explaining their plight, they point to specific personal or institutional constraints which impede what would otherwise be the effective exercise of appropriate intellectual expertise. With rare exceptions, there is no recognition that it is the overall environment of planning which limits autonomy and vitiates effectiveness. Nor is there much suggestion that emphasis on purely intellectual expertise itself limits planners' effectiveness and influence.

NOTES

1. Of 16 planners reporting "never" or "rarely" finding single unique solutions, 12 emphasized intellectual strengths. Of 16 planners emphasizing social strengths, six reported finding single unique solutions "always" or "frequently," and five reported finding such solutions "sometimes."

2. Alternative interpretations and conclusions are possible. First, it is possible that planners' statements about their strengths were misinterpreted in such a way as to bias coding in the direction of "intellectual" strengths, in which case the overlap of the two groups would be understated. Effort has been made to minimize this likelihood through several readings of those statements. Second, the fact that many planners emphasizing interpersonal strengths reported finding single unique solutions with some frequency may be taken as evidence that they see the social environment of planning as relatively simple, unless they regard themselves as exceptionally adroit. It is likely that some of the interpersonal experts do see the world as more simple than complex, though it still seems that most of the planners in any way concerned with governance problems fall within this group.

3. The estimate that these groups comprise one third of the sample is necessarily imprecise. As the quotations indicate, these groups do not consistently report any common frequency or frequencies with which they find single unique solutions. They are identified by the content and tone of their comments. Some respondents may share the sentiments expressed by others but not mention them. Thus the estimate of approximately one-third the planners' falling into the latter two groups is based on a sometimes impressionistic—but careful—analysis of planners' comments.

4. The analysis which follows refers to planners' identification of a particular frequency, rather than to their "membership" in one of the four groups just described. Nevertheless, there is considerable overlap. The first group consists of planners reporting finding single unique solutions "frequently" or "always," and the second group consists of planners reporting doing so "rarely" or "never." The third and fourth groups include those reporting "sometimes" finding unique solutions, as well as a few reporting either "frequently" or "rarely" doing so.

5. Projects described as "good" could have any number of characteristics, and, therefore, the percentages for cited characteristics total more than 100.

6. This is the criticism offered by Cohen, March, and Olsen (1972) and Wildavsky (1979), as noted above. Lindblom (1959) has been the most articulate representative of the view that intellectual, social, economic, and political constraints require planners and other social actors to follow a course of "disjointed incrementalism." Etzioni (1968) has reviewed the relative merits of the rationalistic ideal and the disjointed incrementalist alternative and has proposed "mixed scanning" as an alternative which is both goal-oriented and feasible.

7. It should be clear that this latter model of a planning process has been constructed from a pattern of responses offered by a group of planners and does not necessarily represent either a consensus of the sample or the position of individuals in the sample. Nevertheless, it does represent the ranking of criteria for "good" projects mentioned by the sample.

8. Interestingly, seven of the nine in this group are social scientists by training. Implicitly they are saying that a good grounding in the social sciences may make the solution of even complex social problems manageable.

9. It is implied that enforced isolation causes planners not to have influence. It is also possible that the experience of not having influence leads planners to isolate themselves from situations and people who make them feel uninfluential.

10. Responses could include more than one type of indicator of effectiveness. Consequently, percentages for all types of responses add to more than 100.

11. Planners' responses are not associated with such personal characteristics as age, sex, or class origin. Nor are they associated with either field of undergraduate education or type of graduate training. Neither are the responses associated with years of experience in planning practice.

12. There is, indeed, growing concern among planning educators about the role of value judgments in planning and about the integration of the use of methods with the understanding of the values implicated in an issue. One collection of essays which reflects this concern is Clavel, Forester, and Goldsmith (1980). Nevertheless, these matters are still minority concerns, even if they may be spreading. In addition, there is still little understanding of either what this value-informed practice would look like or how students might be taught to engage in it. Finally, the

emphases and teachings of traditional planning education tend to persist. The net result is that, even though some planning educators have new concerns, much of the "hidden curriculum"—the effective curriculum— still teaches an older view of practice.

13. The Needlemans (1974) describe problems of a similar nature in the planning agencies which they studied. They observe that some of the apparent irrationalities in the organizational structures of planning agencies reflect efforts by top administrators to supplement limited material rewards with a number of symbolic and status rewards to planners who are valuable to the department and who have strong ambitions.

14. If this interpretation is correct, it is not unique to planners. Weick (1976 and 1979), for example, notes that people are joined to work organizations by "loosely coupled bonds." For reasons similar to those outlined here for planners, people tend to make limited investments in organizations according to their perceptions of the ability of the organizations to reward them. Hummel (1982) argues that the type of frustration which many planners experience reflects the essence of "the bureaucratic experience." Bureaucratic employees, he contends, are to varying degrees normally deprived of control over both what work they will do and how they will do whatever they do. They are left with simply their energy, to be used without their control in what is effectively other people's work. Crucially, Hummel emphasizes, the experience contributes to the dissolution and fragmentation of workers' personal identities.

REFERENCES

Clavel, Pierre, John Forester, and William Goldsmith, eds. *Urban and Regional Planning in an Age of Austerity.* New York: Pergamon, 1980.

Cohen, Michael D., James G. March, and Johan P. Olsen. "A Garbage Can Model of Organizational Choice," *Administrative Science Quarterly, 17* (1972), pp. 1-26.

Etzioni, Amitai. *The Active Society.* New York: The Free Press, 1968.

Hummel, Ralph P. *The Bureaucratic Experience.* New York: St. Martin's Press, 1982.

Lindblom, Charles. "The Science of Muddling Through," *Public Administration Review, 19* (1959), pp. 79-88.

Needleman, Martin, and Carolyn Emerson Needleman. *Guerrillas in the Bureaucracy.* New York: John Wiley, 1974.

Weick, Karl E. "Educational Organizations as Loosely Coupled Systems," *Administrative Science Quarterly, 21* (1976), pp. 1-19.

Weick, Karl E. *The Social Psychology of Organizing.* Second edition. Reading: Addison-Wesley, 1979.

Wildavsky, Aaron. *Speaking Truth to Power.* New York: Little, Brown, and Company, 1979.

4

PLANNERS' CLIENTS AND CONSTITUENTS

The general statements of planners about their expertise and autonomy take more specific form in response to questions about planners' working relationships with lay citizens. Here planners were asked in what ways citizens should be involved in the planning process, whether there are skills required in this process which only planners possess, and to what degree citizen participation should be facilitated by the support of an advocate planner. In each case, planners were required to give voice to assumptions about what distinguishes the expertise of planners from the abilities of laypersons and about how much autonomy from laypersons planners should enjoy. Together, these questions concern the major components of an issue central to planners' acquisition of professional status: public accountability. Planners' assumptions about exclusive expertise reflect their beliefs about the degree to which planners should or can be intellectually accountable to the lay public. Their assumptions about the autonomy to which they are entitled reflect their beliefs about the degree to which they should be politically accountable.

The following comment expresses a common ambivalence toward citizen participation which runs through planners' statements about the public:

> I don't believe that we know what is best for them [citizens], but I don't believe that they know what is best for them, for the community as a whole.

CITIZENS AS ADVISORS, BUT ONLY LIMITED PARTICIPANTS

The planners were asked what they considered to be the proper role for citizens in the planning process. Almost three-fifths (57 percent) of those responding argued that citizens should play a minimal or advisory role, whereas a minority (43 percent) supported a role of active participation for citizens.

At an extreme, several planners who wanted to minimize citizens' participation described their participation as an obstruction to rational decision making. One veteran planner said that he was willing to listen initially to whatever citizens wanted to say but then wanted to send them away, so that he could do the real work. He emphasized that he was angered by citizen groups who believe that their interest in a project is any substitute for his expertise about the project:

> I am interested in their opinions and then want them out of projects. I am annoyed by citizen groups who stop projects who have no economic interest in the projects. The citizen participation pendulum has swung way too far. [Citizen groups tend to] replace the logic with volume [of their voices].

Further, another planner emphasized, if planners were to listen to every citizen with an opinion about a project, there would be no time for any substantive work:

> I have attended so many public hearings. My impression is that democracy is very good. I believe in it, but it slows down the process. Citizens' involvement is very, very important. I have attended public hearings. I have the feeling that people here have no confidence in technical people, technical knowledge, and they question technical proposals. It's good, but if you waste time responding to nonsense, you get slowed down. . . . Too much democracy becomes anarchy, and we have to be very careful of the limitations of both. Citizen participation is good, because we are paid by them, but if we go beyond their comprehension, the process gets slowed down.

A local planner emphasized a theme reiterated by a number of planners: citizen participation is implicitly a statement of mistrust of planners' intentions and abilities:

> In theory, in school, you hear that's great, citizen participation. But they're a pain in the ass. You have some people who are professional citizens, who have a chip on their shoulder. But this is an elitist position. I just wish they'd trust me. I don't enjoy working with citizens at all.

Many planners express mixed feelings about citizen participation. On the one hand, it is consistent with the tenets of democratic decision-making. On the other hand, a majority of citizens tend to act in ways which are inconsistent with principles for reasonable decision-making. For example, citizens tend to be apathetic, aroused to sporadic participation in planning processes more often by opposition to something than by support for something, self-interested, parochial, concerned with immediate situations, and unable to view issues in either a broad societal perspective or a long-term perspective. These perceptions of citizens are expressed by several planners:

> Well, we can say that citizens should be involved, which is not always the case, because not everybody cares. In this field we all think they should be involved, but some people are not the type to get involved. They go along with the crowd.

> For example, we've been holding meetings on the general development plan. At the first meeting they had 110 people; at the second and third, 40 and 30 people. People just don't seem interested. Consumer interest groups will not be more representative of the citizenry than traditional special interest groups. They are advocates. They will have a tendency to be as narrow-minded and imperceptive of general feelings as traditional groups: mild fanatics about things of concern to them. There is no way of their reflecting general needs. This creates a problem: who do you turn to if you want general citizen input? No citizen group is altruistic, but I don't know how you get around this problem. I guess there is no general public good. There is just competition among interest groups.

Responding to these difficulties, a number of planners propose a model planning process in which planners accept the opinions of the various interested citizen groups and then interpret these opinions in two ways. First, valid statements are separated from falsehoods. Second, the valid statements are analyzed in the perspective of the types of information needed to develop a reasonable recommendation for the solution of the problem in question. Thus, several planners, while relegating citizens to an advisory role, nevertheless, set forth a model for systematic consultation with citizens at different stages of the planning process:

> [Planners] need to know citizens' needs in order to make decisions. Probably one of the best combinations I have seen is where an initial feeling out takes place, talking with people. Then you go to the drawing board, then go down to meetings with people, and then discuss. You've got to know what they want and then give them alternatives. Particularly at the local level, [they can] help to develop the information base on which decisions are made, help to

flesh out the environment. For example, in Health Systems Agencies, citizens would provide an integral perspective which would complement the perspective of the service provider.

I think citizens should be afforded the opportunity to provide comments and feedback to activities or plans which planners work on which obviously affect citizens and their way of life. And this process should start early in the planning stages of the project.

These statements contrast in tone with those of other planners, the minority who advocate active participation by citizens in the planning process. In this view, citizens are not merely advisors who are consulted at the discretion of the planners, but the citizens are important movers of the planning process. An administrator in a county planning agency explained:

They ought to have a role in telling us their perceived needs. The process should be open for those who want to participate. The opportunity should be there. . . . If nobody chooses to participate, I think the planners should search for people. I think they need to be able to vote. They need to be there early on the plan and on the decision.

Another county planner added this comment:

I see them as reviewers, as initiators, and implementors. If they can't help implement, it can't be implemented. I see them as constrainors. There they have shown up noticeably.

A transportation planner reported on a successful experience with this kind of citizen participation:

I see them getting involved at the earliest stages, reviewing work that is done, being involved in the evaluation of alternatives. We have found citizen involvement to be useful. For example, there is a need for a highway between A and B. [We then ask citizens,] "What do you think the alternative should be?" For new projects the process works.

A few planners portray a still more activist role for citizens, in which their work is central and planners serve as technical advisors to them. A planner who had worked at several levels of government began by noting that "It depends on the citizen and on the planner." He continued:

If you get a planner who is fair and has a certain sensitivity, and if you have an informed citizens' group, and you get into a hot issue, the planner should merely be a tool of the group. If you get a citizens' group which is not well informed, the planner has to be chief cork and bottle washer, but he has to have a sensitivity about how to deal with people, based on guiding the group along with a certain awareness.

A long-time county planner argued that planning

ought to be a democratic process with citizens' committees. The role of the planner ought to be a technician, technical assistance to these committees. We want them to come up with alternatives, elaborate on those alternatives, and make a selection from those alternatives.

A local planner made a simple statement about citizens:

They should be doing the planning. They should have technical assistance and should be taught some of the jargon. They should be doing the planning with input from professionals.

Finally, a few planners contend that citizens need to be generally active and politically vigilant. One argued strongly that citizen participation in the planning process, in itself, would give citizens little influence, insofar as many decisions are made outside this process:

Citizens don't at this time have any real role in planning. Citizen participation is a farce. Ninety-nine per cent of the time decisions are made before issues are taken to the community. . . . Sunshine legislation will not alter communities' having a say, because 99 percent of decisions are made before these meetings occur.

Therefore, another planner argued, citizens need to understand that "there are already role players involved" in promoting interests in the political arena "before the public get wind of it":

The proper role is for people to understand that their environment, no matter how stable, is never stable, and so they ought to be always initiating some activity for themselves, gather information, be vocal, organize.

Planners' view of the appropriate role for citizens are associated somewhat, though not with statistical significance, with planners' places of employment.[1] Planners in public agencies are especially likely to advocate an advisory role for citizens, whereas planners in private firms are somewhat more likely than not to suggest a participatory role for citizens. These differences correspond to the normal relationships between planners in these organizations and their clients or constituents. Planners in public agencies tend to work in isolation from citizens and have contact with them primarily in ways prescribed by statutes. Planners in private firms have direct contact with the clients who hire them and have an incentive to maintain relatively close contact, so that these clients might hire them again in the future.

Thus the majority of planners regard the proper role of citizen as one of advisor-on-call. For these planners citizen participation represents a mixed blessing. On the one hand, various statutes and regulations require the involvement of citizens in the planning process, and this participation is consistent with democratic tenets. In addition, citizens may have considerable information about their communities. On the other hand, however, when citizens do get involved in the planning process, they tend to raise issues which planners do not regard as central to the problem at hand, and they demand from planners scarce time which could be used more effectively in rigorous analysis of the problem and formulation of possible solutions for it. Furthermore, although citizens may provide copious information, many planners feel that they have to spend time carefully scrutinizing this information for its validity and usefulness. Many planners express a tension between their belief in citizen participation in a democratic political system and their experience that this participation drains valuable time and energy without evident results.

A DIVISION OF LABOR BETWEEN PLANNERS AND CITIZENS

Citizens' Strength: Parochial Information

Regardless of how planners feel about citizen participation, citizens do participate in the planning process, and planners attempt to make what they consider the most appropriate use of citizens in this process. Either explicitly or implicitly, planners work out a division of labor, in which they do what they consider themselves most qualified to do as trained practitioners and citizens do what laypersons may be best able to do. To elicit these perceptions of differences between the competences of planners and lay citizens, planners were asked which tasks in the planning process citizens were most capable of carrying out and which they were least capable of carrying out.

Planners offer a uniform profile of citizens' competence, irrespective of how the planners feel about citizen participation.[2] Planners agree that citizens are most capable of providing information about their communities. Seventy-nine percent of planners responding to the question mentioned citizens' usefulness in providing local information. Planners find this information particularly useful in identifying problems and needs. Thus a planner who had worked in several parts of the country argued that citizens' information about their community is essential for planning:

> A well-informed citizenry . . . can be very helpful in helping the professional understand a neighborhood, can point out those things which from a planner's experience we might not know. . . . There may be planners who are looking at data who may not understand what they are looking at with the data: for example, a statistical description of housing prices. There is something which is qualitative which is not apparent in the numbers. There is a need for interpretation of quantitative data. Neighborhood groups can provide guidance on customs of the neighborhood, et cetera. . . . My perceptions of neighborhood needs are not necessarily different from those of people telling me about it, but their telling me about it has the effect of telling me that maybe we don't know what we are talking about.

In turn, statements of problems and needs can be translated into formulations of planning goals. Here, too, citizens' perceptions are useful to planners. Forty-eight percent of planners responding to the question mentioned citizens' value in formulating goals.[3] A consultant observed that citizens "can best describe what they envision." Another consultant shared the belief that citizens are most capable of "evaluating their communities, evaluating their needs, gaps between needs and present levels of services, setting goals, development of aspirations." A county planner argued that citizen participation is essential to formulation of goals, or else planning will be unimaginative:

> Citizens have to force the consideration of all possible alternatives— which is not always done. The planning staff will often take the easy choice.

Once goals have been set and alternative strategies developed, citizens may be helpful in evaluating the desirability or feasibility of alternatives. Thirty-eight percent of planners responding to the question said that citizens could contribute to this assessment. A regional planner argued that what citizens are best at is "just evaluating whether what is proposed is good for them or not." A colleague of hers elaborated that:

> Early on they can provide a sense of what is acceptable and what is not acceptable to the community. They can make the planner more knowledgeable about opportunities. They are useful in reviewing the alternatives which are developed. Depending on the project, they can evaluate cost-effectiveness.

A county planner recounted pleasantly surprising experiences working with citizens groups in evaluating alternatives developed by planners:

> I think citizens should be afforded the opportunity to provide comment and feedback to activities or plans which planners work on which obviously affect citizens and their way of life. . . . I am very impressed with the way that local citizens that are going to be affected by a project are able to identify problems with it or weaknesses with the logic of the approach or the program and how it will affect them personally, which I think that the planners sitting back in their offices are not always able to see.

The proportion of planners mentioning the value of citizens' contributions diminishes with each successive stage of the planning process. Thus, as indicated above, whereas more than three-fourths of the planners value citizen information about local communities and their needs, just less than one-half envision citizens involved in formulating goals for solving problems, and just over one-third believe that citizens can contribute anything to the evaluation of alternative possible solutions. This assessment of citizens' capabilities is consistent with the general view that citizens should be consulted occasionally as advisors with general information while planners do the sophisticated and final work in defining and solving problems. Consistently, planners identify as citizens' weaknesses abilities required for the later stages of the planning process.

Even the information which citizens provide planners needs evaluation before it is used. For the strength of citizens' information represents also its weakness. Citizens are experts on what takes place in their own back yards, but they have difficulty seeing these conditions in the perspective of a larger area, such as the city, the county, or the region. They are quite sensitive to immediate developments in their communities, but they have difficulty seeing these events in a long-term perspective. Thirty-eight percent of planners responding to the question about citizens' shortcomings pointed to problems of this nature.

Some planners complain that citizen groups tend to be unhelpfully parochial in providing information. They are least capable of "trade-off evaluations that affect the larger community." "The large-scale issues are more difficult for citizens to get involved in than local issues." A county planning official sympathetic to citizen participation noted, nevertheless, that

> There is a certain amount of disinterestedness needed in decision-making. You need to see the big picture, the long-range picture. That is what they can do least well. If it is going to be next door or tomorrow, that is hard for them to do.

A regional planner concluded,

> If a planning issue has many dimensions, has a whole lot of externalities. . . . planners are in a better position to identify all these issues and to trace out their impacts.

Here planners are appealing to traditional claims of planners to expertise as interpreters of the public interest. They see themselves as receiving local, self-interested information from many neighborhoods. But they consider this information of limited usefulness until they, as trained planners, are able to evaluate it and place it in a perspective of what is in the interests of the citizens of the jurisdiction as a whole.

Related to the complaint about citizens' parochial focus is a concern, referred to above in passing, that citizens tend to fixate on present problems and cannot think about long-term lines of development. Citizens concentrate on present conditions, have difficulty imagining that some problems may go away without significant outside intervention, and have difficulty picturing other, possibly more serious, problems which may arise in the future. In addition, when evaluating a proposed course of action, they focus on the apparent immediate consequences and have limited ability to think about longer-range future implications of the proposal. These concerns were expressed by two planners skeptical about citizen participation:

[They are least capable of contributing on] anything which has long-range implications. I don't think a community, because it has self-preservation interests, can make proper decisions for the interests of a larger community, the whole metropolitan area. . . . I think the planner is more aware of the larger implications than the neighborhood itself.

They are least able to—and this is one of the weaknesses of citizen participation—they are least able to see the long-term comprehensive benefits of a project. They are most concerned with how it affects one area directly. They are better able to identify the weaknesses than they are the benefits.

In this case, planners are appealing to another traditional claim of expertise, an exclusive ability to understand the future implications of present actions. In particular, planners have special training in forecasting, which enables them to see present events as part of longer developmental trends and which enables them to anticipate a problem. Thus, planners receive present-oriented information from citizen groups and must place it into a dynamic time perspective before the information is useful in the planning process.

Citizens' parochialism and their present-orientation limit their ability to participate effectively in either the planning process or, more significantly, the process of political decision-making of which the planning process is a part. A regional planner argued that citizens are least capable of contributing to "decision-making":

I don't think they have the perspective of all the viewpoints that have to be taken into account. I don't think they understand how decisions are made. I think it is the role of the planner to meld all these perspectives and account for them but make the most rational choice.

A long-time local planner contended that, in his experience, citizens

were not interested in planning decisions. They were fascinated by the political process. But they couldn't translate their experiences into decisions about the parcel of land. People identify issues which you need to respond to. The professions are accountable [for analysis and recommendation]. Citizens couldn't recognize alternatives or weigh alternatives in a large perspective. Citizen consultants get bored at that level.

The implication is clear: citizens' narrow picture of conditions gives them a special strength as a source of information but disqualifies them from having deciding influence in the planning process.

Planners' Strength: "Technical" Skills

Even in cases where citizens have relatively broader views of conditions, nevertheless, there are certain skills required in the planning process which citizens simply lack the training to contribute. These are called "technical" skills. The most frequently mentioned shortcoming of citizens (cited by 55 percent of planners responding) is "technical" skills. This is essentially a definitional statement: by definition, "technical" skills are those skills which distinguish specially trained planners from lay citizens. At the same time, planners differ in the examples which they provide, and some planners express a characteristic uncertainty about whether there are distinctive technical skills separating trained practitioners from laypersons.

In describing citizens' weaknesses, some planners quickly refer to "technical kinds of analysis" without much elaboration about the distinguishing competence of trained planners. The following comments are typical: "The more technical it is, the less possible it is for the ordinary citizen to get involved." "To get involved in all the technical things is beyond the ability of the average citizen." Yet even here there is some doubt:

> It is difficult for citizens sometimes to understand or be involved in the technical aspects of what we do. But I am not sure they need to. I don't understand all the technical aspects.

Other planners are more specific about what "technical analysis" involves. A health planner argued that with

> technical issues that involve more complex evaluation, a certain amount of simplification of complex issues has to occur for the general public. For example, with the sub-area councils in health planning the consumer is trying to get a handle on all those supply and demand issues, et cetera. When citizen groups get involved at that level, they become highly dependent on technical staff.

A private consultant offered other examples of expertise which planners would have but which citizens would lack:

> technical aspects. The public doesn't have expertise and time. The

mechanics: what type of building material, actual siting considerations. For example, how many personnel in a medical clinic.

A local planner suggested a definition of "technical" skills by distinguishing questions of what should be done from questions of how something should be done. Citizens, he suggested, can contribute answers to the "what" questions, but the "how" questions are technical questions. Citizens are least capable of working on "the technicalities. They can tell you that they want a road somewhere, but they can't tell you how."

A number of planners are less concerned about refining intellectual definitions of "technical" skills or offering indisputable examples of these skills than they are about the social function of a distinction between "technical" and other skills. They are centrally aware that the existence of "technical" skills serves to distinguish a specialized training and expertise of planning practitioners from other practitioners and lay citizens. The following, representative responses are not specific about the content of "technical" skills, but they clearly link planners' exercise of such skills with privileges which should accrue to professionals:

> [What citizens are least capable of doing is] the real analytic task and probably the real design task. . . . This is what you as a professional are supposedly trained for. This is your unique abilities, what the average citizen does not have.

> [Citizens are least capable at] technical analysis, but I have often found an interesting insight in non-technical analysis of technical analysis. I have seen some intelligent analysis of grandiose schemes which planners have developed. But also the technical area is still an area of the planner's expertise. While the citizen should be cautious of planning, he should still be aware that the planner is an expert.

Throughout the discussion of planners' "technical" skills there is a contrast between the cognitive content and the affective content of responses. Affectively, planners are united by an unwavering desire to draw on any claims to expertise necessary for dominance in the process of formulating plans. This desire is bolstered by a consideration of the social and economic benefits of a public perception that planners do possess exclusive expertise. Yet cognitively, even when the social and economic stakes are explicated, planners express uncertainty that their skills are specialized or esoteric. This cognitive uncertainty, in turn, gives rise to affective doubts about whether planners reign over an exclusive "technical" domain. These doubts trouble but do not unseat planners' desires to dominate the planning process.

The complex relationship between the cognitive and affective messages is illustrated by the responses of the 20 percent of the sample who contend that planners have no exclusive skills. This group is evenly split between advocates of active citizen participation and proponents of limited citizen advice-giving. A typical representative of this group reflected on his past experiences with citizen groups:

> We have had citizens who have participated in very complex aspects. We have had engineers who worked with Bendix. Their weakness is the fact that sometimes they can't stay with the process. There is nothing they can't do.

A county planner sympathetic to citizen participation reinforced this viewpoint:

> You see different individuals being able to do different things, and I don't know that there are particular things about the steps that you go through in the process that any citizen or groups of citizens that are generally knowledgeable couldn't do an adequate job. I don't think that by definition there is any skill which may not be available in the community. I think that planners put together many skills at once. I don't think there is anything profound about this, so that citizens could participate in any phase of the process. A different question is whether citizens have the interest or the time.

A planner favoring the restricted use of citizens as consultants argued that an aura of mystification surrounds "technical" skills and suggested that education and incentives could enable citizens to exercise any skills:

> To some extent—it may sound a little crazy—if [citizens] were paid for their time, they might be willing to do the more tedious things. I hesitate to say the technical areas, because I don't believe that the technical areas are all that technical. Professionals tend to make people believe that. If there were not that mystique of technology, I think we would all be better off.

An advocate of active citizen involvement in planning argued that planners should provide citizens with any necessary education to carry out tasks in the planning process:

> I don't think there are many particular things in the classic planning

cycle from goal identification to data gathering to analysis to plan formulation, et cetera, [which citizens are not capable of doing]. There is probably no stage that they are not relevant in and if properly motivated and provided with information could probably participate. If planners were really good at education, they would educate [citizens] to be planners, and then planners would not have a specific job.

In summary, then, planners tend to believe there is a proper division of labor in the planning process. Above all, planners have responsibility for organizing the activities and the information collected in planning. Citizens, by and large, should take the role of providing information about their communities, their needs, and their problems. At the same time, planners must reinterpret citizens' parochial and present-oriented information in the broader and long-range terms necessary for use in planning. Planners use this information to finish the work of formulating the planning problem and then move on to articulating goals and possible alternative strategies for reaching these goals. To a lesser extent than earlier, citizens may participate by offering comments on goals and alternatives proposed by planners. However, planners must apply their technical methods to an analysis of needs and alternatives in order to prepare final recommendations.

This portrayal of a division of labor in the planning process rationalizes comments made by planners. It represents the affect of wanting control over the planning process more accurately than it reflects cognitive uncertainties about real differences in skill between planners and lay citizens. In this division of labor planners are receptive to public comments and suggestions, particularly in the early stages of the planning process, but most planners believe they should have autonomy in making the final selection of goals and recommendation of alternatives.

ADVOCACY PLANNING AS A MIXED VALUE

Advocacy planning was proposed in the 1960's as a response to perceived shortcomings of a centralized planning process.[4] Two arguments were forwarded in support of the concept of discrete communities' being represented in the planning process by their own, partisan, advocate planners. Sociologically, it was argued, cities had become too complex for a small group of planners in a single planning office to understand with sophistication. Accordingly, in order to collect the information necessary to assess needs and to make recommendations about these needs, community groups should be represented by advocate planners who would make special efforts to present the communities' perspectives to the planning department. Politically, it was argued, any recommendations about the allocation of scarce resources among groups with competing interests were inherently political decisions. Therefore, each community with special interests should be represented by an advocate planner who would offer the most competent support for the position of the community in an explicitly political planning process.

In ensuant discussion of advocacy planning, some planners agreed with either the sociological or political analysis of difficulties with centralized planning but dissented from the recommended remedy of advocacy planning. It might be possible, they suggested, to modify the organization of the conventional planning process to incorporate more viewpoints into this process. Thus planners debated the relative merits of "inside" advocates, who would represent community views while employed by the planning department, and "outside" advocates, who would represent community views in the employ of community groups (Kaplan, 1969). While Community Action Programs made it possible for community groups to hire advocate planners (Marris and Rein, 1973), some planning departments hired their own "district," "neighborhood," or "community" planners (Needleman and Needleman, 1974). Each type of advocate planner confronted a special set of dilemmas. Yet, at the heart of the debate over advocacy planning, as the Needlemans demonstrated, was a tension between "old" and "new" planning. The "old," or traditional, planners believed that conscientious technically oriented planners in a local planning department could, in fact, understand and plan for a city. They regarded the "new," or advocate, planners' closer ties with community groups as unprofessional because political. In addition, implicitly, the new model suggested that traditionally trained planners could not adequately serve the city for which they presumed to plan. Crucially, the new model suggested that citizens who had not studied planning had expertise about cities and

planning which trained planners lacked. Thus the debate over
advocacy planning was a debate over both the political and
intellectual authority of trained planners.

For and Against: Who Needs It?

Planners in the study sample were asked for their views about
advocacy planning. At best, their support could be said to be
mixed. Of these responding, not quite half (46 percent) favored
advocacy planning without reservation, one-third (33 percent) had
mixed feelings, and one-fifth (21 percent) opposed advocacy
planning completely.

Those favoring advocacy planning offered two basic arguments.
The more frequently cited justification refers to a weakness of
citizens. Citizens either lack expertise to be effective in the
planning process, or for some reason they lack representation in
the process. A conservative expression of this viewpoint came
from a suburban county planner:

> I think it's good. I think it is necessary. It goes back to my feeling
> that citizens need to be guided. But an advocate should guide his
> group. Then it becomes a combination of technical knowledge and
> citizens' requirements, needs being responded to and the possible.

This formulation is conservative in that it portrays citizens as
people who lack information and will need to be dependent on a
trained planner for the satisfaction of their basic needs. At the
same time, the planner gives structure and discipline to their
participation by analyzing their requirements technically and
imposing on them a sense of what is feasible. A similar perception
that citizens lack information and do not know how to participate
in planning, nevertheless, produced a more ebullient endorsement
of advocacy planning from a planner with several decades of
experience in both the public and private sectors:

> When [the idea of advocacy planning] first arose, I was violently
> opposed to it, because I had not thought it through. "Planning
> should be for the whole community." I am not so sure about this
> after participating in the park planning process in the county. I think
> that some ethnic groups need a planner to advise them because they
> are not familiar with the whole process. So I am not averse to their
> receiving advice from a planner about how they fit into the whole
> community. This is a change in attitude on my part because here in

this county we have the [low-income black] group. We needed to understand that community. And we were pleased to have representatives from that group come up and tell us about it, and our park planners have been down there to talk with them, and they have told us their needs.

This planner refers to an "inside" advocate, working for the department of planning. He notes that the quality of the planning process and resultant recommendations were improved by this kind of advocacy of community views.

This latter comment is linked to a second argument made on behalf of advocacy planning: there are limitations to what staff members in a planning department may do without representation from community members. Fewer planners offered this argument, probably because it appears to imply a criticism of planners, although, as the following quotations demonstrate, it need not. A staff member in a public agency summarized general concerns about the potential parochialism of a governmental planning staff:

> I believe in advocacy planning. The complexity really is a problem, and there is no way that, if planners become isolated in some part of City Hall, talking primarily to other planners, there is no way that they can effectively determine the needs of different areas that they are planning for. And I see the advocate planners as being a sort of intermediary or liaison between the ivory tower planners and the people being planned for.

Another public agency employee suggested that agency planners may face both limitations of understanding and political constraints on the positions which they may consider:

> I believe that an advocate planner is good in that groups need someone to translate their ideas into a vocabulary, a translation for the decision-making people. I don't think that the staff planner is fully able to go from one facet to another with total impartiality and empathy for the people he deals with. Sometimes he is politically unable to. He is accepting a very big challenge.

One of the most pessimistic assessments of the capabilities of public agency planners emphasized bureaucratic and political constraints on staff members' work:

> All of us have become so imbedded in the Establishment that we are its lackeys. The people see us that way. I would much rather be free, as I was as a consultant in a small town. I've often thought and

wondered how planners that are being employed by citizen groups are being paid. In the role of advocate, I think you've got to be free. Ideally, you have to be able to speak on behalf of the people. If you can't. . . . Probably all I'm complaining about is that it is harder and harder for me to feel that I am speaking on behalf of the people. The Establishmentarians are running things. About the complexity of things, I don't know. But the advocacy of things of, by, for the people [is crucial]. I don't know how you get the money, and you need protection. Ralph Nader talks about some things which I think planners ought to be talking about.

In this last view, then, advocacy for community groups from outside the planning agency is essential for planners in the agency to receive and to make open use of information about communities with weak links to local decision-makers.

In questioning a need for advocacy planning, other planners raise three objections. The first is, simply, that there are no problems to which advocacy planning would be a solution. One viewpoint defended the citizens:

I would hate to see everyone having their own advocate planner. Planners screw up and fuck up enough as it is. Within the profession and within the general population there is a greater amount of awareness to community issues and planning issues. Citizens are much better informed. The need for advocacy planning is decreasing.

A second viewpoint defended the planners:

I am opposed to building in your own advocacy system. I think it is counter-productive. I think it is up to the urban planner. Your boss *is* the citizen out there in all the diverse groups. You also have to go through the treadmill of the interest groups, the politicians. That's the jungle. But you have to recognize who your real clients are. You may not be able to admit it to your boss. If there is an advocate, *you* are the advocate. You do not go out and hire an advocate and create a fight. Citizen participation is a tool to help you recognize this, but, as far as a straight advocacy system, no.

In short, if well-trained planners persevere in carrying out the traditional planning process, they will be able to recognize and take into account the diverse interests of a heterogeneous population.

A second objection, tied to the traditional view of planning, rejects advocacy planning as a development which would politicize a process of deliberation which is supposed to be technical and dispassionate. A county planning administrator presented this point-of-view in his philosophical framework:

> I really would not want to see it, I guess. It comes from a philosophy of what government is, not what planning is. Government does not provide services. Government governs the community. Raising conflicts—I think you have to be careful about how much you get carried away. There is a lot of wasted energy. And it kind of goes against my grain. Planning should be professional, a rational kind of thing. You try to leave your value judgments outside this process. The community, its advocates, should be inside the government, at the planning process. The planning process should be responsive, but it should be the political process which has the conflicts. I see going to an advocacy approach as being binding and reducing flexibility in the decision-making process. I don't see that a group that can articulate its needs is ignored. I think the key is the articulation if it does not need to be within the chambers of government. I would prefer it not to be. . . . If there needs to be articulation of needs, I would rather that the community hire its own planner, and not be part of the government, but I don't see the need to structure this. To me this is the same thing as having district community members on your council. How can you make a public interest choice?

This is the traditional claim of planners to collect information about community needs and disinterestedly analyze the information and produce recommendations which represent a collective, public interest.

A third objection responds to the problem of planning in a complex society. Communities, indeed, have become complex, these planners acknowledge, but the creation of advocate planners for each discrete interest would be an inappropriate response, because it would only increase the complexity of decision-making. Instead, the proper response would be to simplify planning by assigning responsibility for the needs of all groups to a single, central group of planners. Traditionally oriented planners can manage under complex conditions if only they exert themselves more broadly. This position was summarized by a consultant:

> It seems to me that, with the complexity of the world, we ought to move in the direction of making the world less complex than to move in the direction of building more complex institutions to deal with a more complex world because this compounds the complexity of the world. I don't know if this is possible.

A veteran county planner argued that the increased complexity which advocacy planning would create would not only aggravate the work of agency planners but also break down the legitimate traditional model of comprehensive planning:

> I would think that as our society becomes more complex and we are more sensitive to negative impacts on groups, that we need to maintain the emphasis on comprehensive planning and to add to that from a central place more sensitivity to how it affects people at the local scale. But I would think that individual advocate planners would not be productive in the long run. What it might do would be grind things to a halt and force changes. But it would be a very painful process. I think there are other ways of getting to these changes.

Underlying Concerns About Control

Responses to this question about advocacy planning are peculiar. Planners' positions on the issue are often not readily explainable on the basis of their comments. On this particular issues planners tend to espouse a point-of-view without offering much explanation for the position taken. Yet, even if many of the responses are uninformative cognitively, they seem to be unified by a common affect. In particular, criticisms of the concept of advocacy planning are frequently defensive and express a sense of beleaguerment. Beneath considerable rational discussion of the merits of advocacy planning seems to lie a basic concern about whether planners will be able to maintain control over the process of planning. The following comments, critical of advocacy planning, express some of this feeling and highlight the concern with retaining control:

> I would agree that things are becoming more complex and that it is becoming increasingly difficult for a specific group of planners to recognize the needs of all groups, and I like the idea of advocacy planning. But I would have the caveat that we flip from advocacy planning to adversary planning. . . . I would think that another route would be for those planning bodies that deal with the public to have on their staff some specialists—for example, someone who deals with the housing problems of the aged and handicapped. I have my reservations about a separate advocate planner.

> I don't think this is needed, specifically advocacy planning. I don't believe that much in this, because the whole thing can be transmitted to the people through the planning team itself once the

plans are made. Public hearings can be held, or interested citizens can come to the planning office to discuss these things. But I think it is better served by frequent public hearings.

I guess if a well-educated planner cannot grasp all of the issues, then we've got a problem in the society that can't be solved by just coming up with a new kind of planner who is a Planners' Planner or an advocate.

In all these comments there is a concern for planners' maintaining control over the planning process. Planners already take into account the needs and concerns of diverse social groups, and, insofar as any groups are not heard, minor tinkering with planning agency procedures will suffice. These are the voices of the Needlemans' "old" planners defending themselves against the "new" planners and their public constituencies.

The dynamics of the respective positions on this issue, however, still are not clear. The Needlemans' "old" planners defend their position with tenets for "professional" action (Needleman and Needleman, 1974). Their position is a well-worked and time-honored intellectual position. The possibility that positions on advocacy planning reflect intellectual convictions about the role of citizens in the planning process is supported by an association between responses to this question and responses to the question about citizen roles. Planners favoring active participatory roles for citizens are more likely to support advocacy planning than planners preferring advisory roles for citizens, although the association is not statistically significant.

There is the further possibility that positions on advocacy planning reflect feelings about personal competence as a practitioner. Evidence for this interpretation is provided by an association between responses to this question and responses to the earlier question about perceived personal strength, or expertise, as a planner. Planners regarding their strength as interpersonal or political are significantly more likely to support advocacy planning than planners regarding their strength as intellectual, as Table 4-1 shows. This finding suggests that planners who feel more competent interpersonally and politically favor advocacy planning because it involves relationships in which they feel comfortable. Conversely, planners who feel primarily technical competence may have misgivings about or oppose advocacy planning because it introduces into the planning process stiuations which cause them discomfort.[5] This potential discomfort would help to explain the concern of a number of opponents of advocacy planning that it would threaten their ability to control the planning process. Thus it would appear that part of the conflict between proponents and opponents of advocacy planning, as between "new" and "old" planners, concerns areas of practice in which individual planners feel comfortable. These feelings of confidence in particular types of personal strength become translated into and contribute to statements about the usefulness or propriety of advocacy planning as a part of the planning process.

TABLE 4-1.   POSITION ON ADVOCACY PLANNING AND PERCEIVED PERSONAL STRENGTH

	Position on Advocacy Planning		
Strength	*For*	*Mixed Feelings/Against*	*Total*
Intellectual	10	17	27
Interpersonal	8	4	12
All	18	21	39

$X^2 = 3.03$
$P < .10$
$V = .278$

An interesting additional line of conjecture is suggested by an association between responses to this question and planners' ages, shown in Table 4-2. A majority of planners between ages 26 and 45 either have mixed feelings about advocacy planning or oppose it, whereas a majority of planners 46 and older support advocacy planning. The number of older planners is too small to warrant firm conclusions, but statements from the older planners, all of whom work or have worked in public agencies, suggest that for them experience led to a belief in advocacy planning as a remedy for the limitations of work in central planning departments.

Statements on advocacy planning are consistent with statements on citizen roles and the capabilities of citizens. The majority of planners want to limit any change in the planning process which would increase either the voice or the influence of citizens vis-a-vis

TABLE 4-2.   POSITION ON ADVOCACY PLANNING AND AGE OF PLANNER

Age		Position on Advocacy Planning	
	For	*Mixed Feelings/Against*	*Total*
26-45	12	19	31
46 and older	6	2	8
All	18	21	39

$X^2 = 3.35$
$P < .10$
$V = .293$

planners. The concept of advocacy planning evokes particularly strong and explicit defenses of a traditional model of comprehensive planning by a centrally located department of planning. The vehemence with which this time-honored model of planning is invoked would seem to reflect, in part, the uncertainty and doubt which planners expressed earlier about their expertise. On the one hand, advocacy planning is a special form of citizen participation, in which lay citizens, whatever their own expertise, are assisted and represented by a trained, competent planner. Not only is the work of agency planners made more time-consuming by the need to respond to communities with advocate planners, but the training of the advocate planners means that they will present information with appropriate technical interpretations which will demand a response. Most important, the training of the advocate planners gives them and the communities which they represent legitimate standing in the planning process and forces agency planners to respond. On the other hand, all the pressures which these perceptions of advocate planners engender are met by agency planners' own uncertainties about whether they themselves exercise special skills. Simultaneously they doubt their own ability and assume that other, advocate, planners have exceptional ability. In advocacy planning, agency planners more than meet their match.

Statements about advocacy planning clearly express planners' concerns about their autonomy from their clients or constituents. These concerns can be conceptualized in the framework of

Arnstein's (1969) rungs on "a ladder of citizen participation," ranging from forms of nonparticipation to forms of tokenism to forms of real power. Hardly any of the planners in this sample suggested either of the forms of nonparticipation: citizen participation as manipulation of citizens or as therapy for disgruntled citizens. At the same time, only a few planners recommended any of the forms of real citizen power: citizen participation as a partnership in decision-making, as delegated power in decision-making, or as citizen control over decision-making. Rather, the majority of planners advocated the forms of citizen participation which Arnstein characterizes as tokenism: citizen participation as informing citizens, as consultation with citizens, and as placation of citizens. In the end, most planners want autonomy from citizens. Most planners believe that solicitation of advice from citizens in the early stages of the planning process is sufficient to meet any obligations for public accountability which they may bear. Significantly, few planners consider submitting their proposed final reports to citizens for comments before publication. For most planners the concept of public accountability refers to the process of planning but not to its outcomes. They want to be trusted by citizens, and, despite some doubts about their own expertise, they want to have dominance over citizens in the planning process.

NOTES

1. Planners' views of citizen roles are not associated with such background characteristics as age, sex, or socioeconomic status; with field of undergraduate study or orientation of planning; or with length of employment in planning.

2. For almost every characterization of citizens there are equal numbers of planners favoring the advisory and the participatory roles.

3. Because respondents could mention any number of characteristics of citizens, percentages add to more than 100.

4. Heskin (1975 and 1980) provides an analytic history of advocacy planning.

5. It may be added that position on advocacy planning is not associated with such background characteristics as socioeconomic status or sex; with undergraduate field of study or orientation of planning training; or with length of employment or current work role. An association between age and position on advocacy planning will be discussed shortly.

REFERENCES

Arnstein, Sherry R. "A Ladder of Citizen Participation," *Journal of the American Institute of Planners*, 35 (July, 1969), pp. 216-224.

Davidoff, Paul. "Advocacy and Pluralism in Planning," *Journal of the American Institute of Planners*, 31 (November, 1965), pp. 331-338.

Heskin, Allan David. *The Lessons of Advocacy Planning.* Ph.D. dissertation, The University of Washington, 1975.

Heskin, Allan David. "Crisis and Responses; A Historical Perspective on Advocacy Planning," *Journal of the American Planning Association*, 46 (January, 1980), pp. 50-63.

Kaplan, Marshall. "Advocacy and the Urban Poor," *Journal of the American Institute of Planners*, 35 (March, 1969), pp. 96-101.

Marris, Peter, and Martin Rein. *Dilemmas of Social Reform*, Second Edition. Chicago: Aldine, 1973.

Needleman, Martin and Carolyn Emerson Needleman. *Guerrillas in the Bureaucracy.* New York: John Wiley and Sons, 1974.

Peattie, Lisa. "Reflections on Advocacy Planning," *Journal of the American Institute of Planners*, 34 (March, 1968), pp. 80-88.

5

PLANNERS' PROFESSIONAL CONSCIOUSNESS

Professional status for any group of practitioners requires the demarcation of an area of practice as an exclusive domain. This territory may be informally established by practitioners who distinguish themselves as especially knowledgeable and useful. More formally, the domain of practice may be defined through the institution of statutory licensing procedures.

The professionalization of any type of practice is a political process. For example, if planners want authority in an area of advice-giving, they need to persuade public decision-makers that planners' knowledge is effective and should be accepted. In order to work for this public endorsement, planners need to develop a shared consciousness of themselves as practitioners who are doing similar work and have common interests.[1] This consciousness provides the motivation to organize for public support and helps to define the goals and strategies of a professionalization campaign.

However, planners' expressed ambiguity about their expertise and their complaints about limited autonomy raise questions about their professional consciousness: Do planners see themselves as sharing intellectual and material interests with other planners? How do they feel about organizing with other planners in order to obtain the privileges of "professions"?

This chapter looks for answers to these questions. In this analysis evidence may be framed by a particularly vivid but representative image of almost heroic efforts required of planners as a result of felt self-deprecation and isolation:

> I have met a far greater number of men who were milktoasts and mealymouths and were far more interested in protecting their butts. They were concerned to see how many angels they could get on the head of an eagle, rather than be concrete. The planner has to do it himself. He can't depend on any organization to do it for him. Once

he does that God-damned plan, he needs to fight for it. He should not be wishy-washy. I think they have to be individualists when it comes down to nitty-gritty.

PLANNERS' EXPERTISE: UNCERTAINTY

Shared professional consciousness among practitioners commonly begins with a perception that they practice similar skills. Accordingly, it is important to review what planners said about their expertise. Approximately two-thirds of those interviewed describe themselves as intellectual problem-solvers, who are experts in the application of skills of data collection, analysis, synthesis, and design of solutions for problems. They claim to examine and solve problems with a consideration of future contingencies and opportunities. A minority of approximately one-third emphasize a different type of expertise, either in addition to or in place of the intellectual expertise. They claim to solve problems, but they consider themselves experts in the interpersonal skills of organizing people to agree on definitions of problems and to come together in support of potential solutions for the problems. These groups represent two types of claims of expertise, although their claims are similar in that both groups present themselves as problem-solvers.

However, these claims are weakened by comments which accompanied them. Many planners confess that they are not certain whether they have strengths. Crucial to the discussion of professional consciousness, a number say that they are not convinced that they have skills which are peculiar to planners—which distinguish them from either other practitioners or laypersons. Further, even though almost every planner identifies some intellectual ability as a strength, few can clearly describe just what skills are involved. Finally, even though most planners are involved in interpersonal transactions, few mention having any strength in this area, and few among those who claim interpersonal skills can state articulately what these skills are.

These uncertainties do not help to develop a shared consciousness among planners that they exercise common, clearly identifiable skills. To the contrary, these uncertainties raise doubts whether planners begin with a consciousness of participating in the exercise of a shared expertise.

PLANNERS' ETHICS:
DIVERSITY AND INDIVIDUALISM

A traditional view of a profession is that it is a self-governing collectivity of practitioners who exercise specialized skills within ethical bounds set and enforced by the collectivity.[2] Planners' statements about personal strengths do not provide a description of specialized expertise which could be clearly considered the technical core of a profession. Nevertheless, it is possible that planners consider themselves unified by a distinct ethical direction. In order to examine this possibility, the planners were asked to summarize what they regarded as the major principles of professional planning ethics as they applied to the planners' own work.

A number of planners impulsively answered that they didn't know what professional planning ethics were. Some said that they believed there might be codified ethics, such as the American Institute of Planners' Code of Professional Responsibility, but that they were not familiar with them. Others contended that there were really no planning ethics to speak of: "In planning there is no code of ethics well codified." A few planners argued that the question about ethics is really irrelevant: they contended that it would be easy to identify the tenets of planning ethics but that bureaucratic constraints on planners' discretion are so great that these tenets do not matter. However, the perplexity which these comments attempted to mask is conveyed by the answer offered by a planner with ten years' experience:

> I really haven't thought about ethics as such to be able to answer that right off the cuff. Just do what you think is the right thing to do in regard to whatever situation. I don't think that planning ethics as such are different from what you would call professional ethics. What professional ethics are, I don't know either. Just handle yourself in a businesslike, a professional manner.

Nevertheless, most planners felt the need to present some statement of professional ethics. Some prefaced their response with the statement that they do follow ethics in practice but that their ethics are personal, not tied to the planning profession. An administrator with many years of experience said,

> I don't have a list of ethics, except that it is visceral, almost, just how my fibers respond to it. I'm not a religious person, so I have no

Judeo-Christian ethic to fall back on, but I do things which people consider ethical. How people act is more important than their attitude.

A local planner of less volubility declared simply that "My conscience is my guide."

The content of planners' descriptions of professional planning ethics may be distinguished into two categories: those in which "ethical" practice is equated with technically competent practice and those in which statements of ethics refer to such conventional ethical concerns as equity, human needs, and social justice.

Approximately one-third (34 percent) of the planners responded to the request to summarize principles of planning ethics with descriptions of technical principles which should be followed in "good" planning. These statements emphasized the tenets of traditional comprehensive planning. For example, ethical planning is a systematic problem-solving process:

> I think of it [professional planning ethics] in terms of a body of knowledge, in terms of a way of solving a problem, looking at alternatives, evaluating alternatives, and coming up with a recommendation...I guess it is a planning ethic to evaluate alternatives.

In addition, this problem-solving process should be logical:

> [You] need to make yourself aware of all the information that is available for the decision-making process and put it in a logical format.

Above all, problem-solving should be value free:

> I think at all times I try to be accurate and objective in relation to what I do. We all try to look for solutions which are clear...I guess it is related to being objective.

These principles of planning—systematic collection of information, consideration of alternatives, logical analysis, and rationality—refer to norms which are more properly considered technical than ethical. Although all these principles have ethical consequences in practice, the norm of objectivity directly admonishes planners to avoid making personal value judgments in their work.

Yet these principles are not merely matters of intellectual conviction; they are supported by strong feelings as well, as the following equation of technique and ethics indicates:

> I haven't looked at the AIP ethics recently, but what I personalize is,

if I think through a problem or situation and I see that what is going
on and moving toward a decision will be wrong, I will articulate
that as strongly as I feel justified, based on how important I feel it is.
I will as much as possible stay true to a rational approach and avoid
the political expedient as much as possible and view it within a
societal context as much as possible...I think the basic thing is
approaching it from a rational point-of-view. But a lot of planners
think there is an idealized end-state. I just don't accept that. That's
just something for simple minds to concentrate on.

The last sentences of this statement point up a primary focus
of technical statements of planning ethics: they refer to the
process of planning, rather than its outcomes. In the technical
statements of planning ethics, the process of planning is required
to conform to certain norms—that information be systematically
collected and logically analyzed, for example. Sometimes this
technically "good" process of planning is implicitly tied to "good"
outcomes. In these cases, "good" outcomes are whatever recommendations are the logical consequences of the premises built into
the technically "good" planning process. For example, one county
planner stated:

My principles should be, based on thorough research analysis, to
come up with a result to benefit the people we serve.

More often, technical statements of planning ethics appear to
regard good technique as an end in itself. This interpretation of the
statements is consistent with earlier responses about "good"
planning projects, in which planners emphasized their opportunity
to execute a model planning process over the specific characteristics
of the project outcomes.

The remaining two-thirds (66 percent) of the planners mentioned
some type of ethical tenets in their responses. Their statements
contrasted with the technically oriented statements in two ways.
First, they spoke in ethical, rather than technical, terms. Second,
they referred to both the process and the outcomes of planning.

One major ethical principle related to the process of planning
refers to loyalty to the planner's client. For public agency planners
this may be a specific community group or groups or an elected
official. For private consultants the client is someone who pays for
specific services. Although the financial and political relationships
between public and private planners and their respective clients
may differ, the statements of ethical responsibility to clients are

similar for both public and private planners. A planner in a state agency declared,

> You've got to recognize who your real client is, and that is to whom you owe your allegiance primarily, as much as you can, and still maintain your position and your effectiveness in your position. You have to be perceptive of the wishes, needs, and wants of that clientele. You might not always be interpreting them correctly, but you have to do the best you know how. That's simply what you are really working for.

Here there is an emphasis on collecting information that reflects the values of the client. A private consultant emphasized giving clients sufficient information to enable them to make judgments in their best interests:

> The ethics are to give top quality consultation to the client. There are in the road to development approval innumerable pitfalls. If he is not advised on the process, he can end up losing out. We're being paid substantial amounts of money by people who are expecting the best advice, and we have to deliver this.

Several statements went further. They contended that it is not sufficient for planners to be responsive to their immediate clients or constituents. They have to be concerned for the interests of all groups affected by a possible decision. A county planner emphasized that planners cannot always be certain who their client is and that certain community groups affected by a deliberation may have difficulty contributing their views. He argued that professional ethics require planners to articulate the views of diverse community groups in the process of collecting and analyzing information for planning:

> [Professional planning ethics mean] fairness, in terms of representation of many sides of an issue. There is a professional responsibility to bring to a public dialogue professional preparation of plans of sufficient technical preparation so that you are basing decisions on a credible foundation. There is a necessity to speak for groups that are normally unspoken for—people who are traditionally left out because of income levels, educational background, lack of representation.

A local staff planner insisted that planners should attend to the broader implications of issues in the community:

Basic planning ethics are that you are looking at the good of the larger community, versus the interest of any specific interest group. And also, as a corollary, that you want to bring to bear a more rigorous analysis to the situation than simply "Give me" or "I want"—that you should apply the planning process as a more disciplined approach to your problem-solving.

These latter statements express the traditional ethical claim of planning to serve a "public interest." They hold that, in order for the public interest to be served, many members of the public must be represented in the process of planning.

Here it is possible to draw a contrast between technical and ethical concerns in relation to the planning process. The technically oriented planners emphasize the importance of collecting as much information as possible and analyzing the information logically and without personal bias. The ethically oriented group do not deny the importance of intellectual rigor, but they emphasize a different concern. They stress the importance of collecting information from specific groups with specific interests (either a narrowly defined client or a broadly defined public constituency) and of analyzing this information consistent with the biases of these groups.[3]

Planners emphasizing the ethics of outcomes indicate two orientations. Some believe that an ethical process of planning will lead to ethical outcomes from planning. For example, one of the planners quoted above expressing a concern about the public interest added,

I am sure that through the normal course of business we end up accomplishing the basic principles of equity, respect for the law, seeing that the administrative process, as fairly as possible, achieved the spirit and letter of the legislation.

Some planners indicated that in various ways they make an "independent" test of the outcome of their work. They have certain ethical standards for planning outcomes, and they measure their final products against these standards. For example, several planners mentioned sympathy for "the underdog":

I suppose there is [in my work] a heavy dose of prejudice toward underdog, underprivileged groups. I particularly don't attempt to lend support to those who have [money or power]. I won't try to screw them, but I won't attempt to get involved with them.

Others, such as one administrator, watched for the consistency of outcomes with normative standards of a "good life":

> As I see it, my job responsibility is to provide a framework for the orderly growth of the city, which would benefit not only the present occupants, but also the future occupants of the city. And the way I conduct my administration of this responsibility will determine in the long run the success of that responsibility, and that's through maintaining your professional ethics, your moral code, your posture in dealing with your superiors, as well as the people you serve.

A community planner identified tacit standards which guide the design of the final product in the agency where he works:

> We don't do anything to endanger the health of people. We are conscious environmentalists. The community must be habitable for the people who will live there.

For these planners the "public interest" or the interests of clients can be considered served only if the outcome of the planning process—a proposal on paper or a service or facility on the ground—measures up to such specific ethical standards as equity, personal growth, or health.

Planners' responses to the question to summarize professional planning ethics leave several impressions. The first is the initial inability of many planners to articulate any code of ethics, no matter how trivial. Regardless of whether statements about ethics correspond to actions, it is remarkable that so many planners are unable even to provide the rhetoric of ethical tenets which come so readily from so many other groups of practitioners. More specifically, it is noteworthy that few planners even referred to the American Institute of Planners' Code of Professional Responsibility, and none cited any part of it in describing professional planning ethics.[4] The second important impression is the discomfort which planners experience with their difficulty in identifying ethical principles which guide them. This discomfort suggests that many planners doubt that they follow clear ethical directions in their work. Third, a relatively greater proportion of planners focus their ethical concerns on the process of planning rather than on the outcomes of planning. Either they assume that a "good" process will lead to "good" outcomes, or, as responses to the question about "good" projects suggested, they may be more concerned about the quality of their participation in the process than the quality of the outcome for those affected by it.

One observation bears special emphasis. A significant group of planners translate ethical issues into technical issues. Instead of describing ethical ends for the products of their work, they refer to technical standards for the process of their work. They express little concern for the interests of groups affected by the issues which they analyze. Whatever the actual ethical consequences of this definition of ethical duty, emphasis on "objectivity" relieves these planners of responsibility for attending to the ethical consequences of their actions. These "ethics" are not concerned with ethics.

The statements about professional planning ethics do not express an image of a cohesive group of practitioners unified by a sense of common purpose.[5] To the contrary, although there are some common themes in the responses, the underlying tone is one of individualism. The explicitly ethical statements express an isolation in the vagueness and uncertainty of the formulations of ethical principles. The technical statements prescribe an isolation in emphasizing the individual practitioner's faithful adherence to norms for logical thinking. Collectively, these statements not only reveal a group of practitioners in some disarray. But they also fail to offer any consistent response to public concerns about the ethics of practitioners claiming expertise in dealing with important social problems.[6]

PLANNERS' VIEWS OF OTHER PLANNERS AS A REFERENCE GROUP: CONFUSION

The responses to the questions on expertise and ethics raise serious doubts about any shared consciousness among planners as a collectivity of practitioners. Still, there may be other ways in which planners feel that they share responsibilities or a sense of purpose with other planners. In order to explore whether planners in some way regard other planners as a significant reference group, the sample were asked to what degree they are influenced in their work by the expectations of the planning profession.

A majority of planners (54 percent) reported that they were "not at all" or only "slightly" influenced by the planning profession in their work. Less than one-third (30 percent) said that they were "completely" or "considerably" influenced by the profession. The remainder (16 percent) were "moderately" influenced.

Analysis of the responses shows that a significant number of planners feel they are working in isolation from any identifiable professional reference group. First, one-third (32 percent) of the planners questioned about being influenced by the expectations of the planning profession declared outright that they did not know what the expectations of the profession were. The following comments are typical:

> To me the planning profession is so . . . in such a state of flux, that I don't know what is expected.

> I'm a little perplexed what the expectations of the planning profession are. I hear them [sic] speaking with many voices.

> I'm not sure what you mean by the expectations of the planning profession. I think such a phrase does not mean a damn thing. I don't think the planning profession has any overall philosophy or guidance.

> I don't know what the planning profession is or what it expects. It has fallen into a morass of corruption.

These statements convey several significant feelings about "the planning profession." The first comment offers a common observation that "planning" appears to be a diffuse activity. As with the second response, it expresses a feeling of perplexity about how to practice "professional" planning in the absence of clear standards. The second statement also introduces a theme dominant in many planners' perceptions of "the planning profession": despite the fact that all respondents were members of the American Institute of Planners, many of them perceived the profession as something belonging to "them," to others. Many planners see "the profession" as something from which they are for some reason set apart. The feelings evoked by the perplexity and the estrangement are expressed in the last two quotations. Both show considerable anger toward an external "planning profession" which cannot give them proper guidance for their work.

Many planners would like to take direction from a professional representative but when they do not find it become resentful toward whoever should have but did not fill the perceived vacuum of intellectual and political leadership. One indication of the desire for professional guidance is the fact that several planners who said that they did not know what the expectations of the profession were indicated that they were "moderately" or "considerably" influenced by these expectations. A general expression of this feeling comes from one local planner with a number of years of experience:

> I am not sure-what the expectations of the planning profession are. I guess it would be hard for me to be guided by them if I don't know what they are. I read that stuff that comes out of the American Institute of Planners, and I cannot relate to that. The AIP as a national organization . . . it seems to me that we [sic] have always been behind what is happening.

A second indicator of the isolation of planners is the number (26 percent) who say that they rely solely on themselves in setting their expectations for work. For example, the planner who spoke of the "morass of corruption" commented, "I have to follow my own conscience." Another planner offered a comment typical of this group:

> I will stand up for what I prefer. I haven't identified that strongly with AIP as such.

Other planners who appear to work in isolation respond to their desire to be guided by a professional collectivity by suggesting that perhaps coincidentally they may be doing what a professional leadership would want them to be doing. Although they rely on personal expectations, they hypothesize that these expectations may be those of "the profession." One local planner explained,

> It is hard to say what are the planning profession's expectations and what are mine. By a set of precepts and principles chiseled on the AIP walls, I would say [I am influenced by the planning profession] "not at all." By a set of basic rules I would say need to be applied to management decisions of which planning is a part, I would say "considerably."

A young public agency administrator offered this relatively sanguine view:

> I don't know what planning is. It is hard to say what the expectations are of something you cannot define. I think my outlook is guided, rather, by some concrete expectation, by my training, and my reading of the planning literature. I have internalized planning attitudes. I don't know if they are listed anywhere. I feel that my attitudes in many ways are attitudes that planners have, but I am not sure I could write them down. Maybe the AIP codes . . . Sometimes

> I go back to the AIP Code of Ethics . . . I use the AIP Code of Ethics as a crutch, to affirm my position. I am falling back on my own moral outlook. It helps to have it written by a profession.

In contrast, other planners report that they do draw guidance from an identifiable reference group. Some planners identify this group as their agency colleagues:

> I never thought about the expectations of the planning profession. I think about the expectations of the Planning Department. The planning profession to me is far too broad to have meaning in my work.

Some planners working in non-traditional fields state that they turn to a small group of colleagues because the nature of their work makes it difficult to find guidance from an identifiable planning profession. One planner with ten years' experience said,

> There is a reference group, but I am not sure that I can indicate what it is. It is not the planning profession, and it is not the AIP. It is to some degree the people with whom I work.

Another elaborated that she "wouldn't stick to the planning profession" but would turn to any "professionals who are involved in the same field, but that is not necessarily planners."

Finally, there is a relatively small group of planners who feel a need for affiliation with a professional organization and who feel that they can identify with other planners across the country. In contrast with some planners quoted earlier, they do not see the planning profession run by "others"; rather, they regard themselves as active movers of the profession as practice changes. This view is aptly expressed by a young planner:

> I feel that what I am doing is not in isolation from the planning profession. I feel comfortable that my profession has norms and certain expectations. I am in an agency that is doing a type of work that is similar to agencies doing work for other metropolitan areas. I like to compare what I am doing with what other people and groups are doing, to see whether the goals and output and thinking are comparable with what other similar people are doing.

The degree to which planners say that they are influenced by the expectations of the planning profession is associated with planners' organizational roles, as Table 5-1 shows.[7] Public agency administrators are most likely to report being influenced by the profession. Lower-level staff members in public agencies and, particularly, private consultants are likely to report little influence. When the ensuing comments are examined, differences among planners in different roles are less pronounced, with the distribution of planners who do not understand what the profession expects fairly even among all roles. Rather, there seems to be some difference in emphasis by planners in different roles. Public agency administrators are most likely to say that they try to do work which would meet the expectations of the profession, even if they are not clear what the expectations are or if they regard the expectations as unrealistic. Public agency staff members are more likely to indicate that they rely on personal expectations or look to the expectations of other staff members in the agency. Private consultants are more likely to indicate that they rely on personal expectations or look to the expectations of their clients. The statements of public agency staff and private consultants are consistent with earlier comments about where they look for indicators of effectiveness in their work. Public agency administrators may be practicing diplomacy when they allege considerable

TABLE 5-1. INFLUENCE OF EXPECTATIONS OF THE PLANNING PROFESSION, BY PLACE OF EMPLOYMENT AND ORGANIZATIONAL ROLE

Employment, Role	*Degree of Influence*			
	Not at all/ Slightly	*Moderately*	*Considerably/ Completely*	*Total*
Public agency: administration[a]	4	4	8	16
Public agency: staff	10	2	5	17
Private firm	13	2	1	16
All	27	8	14	49

X^2 = 11.91
$P < .02$
V = .349

[a] "Administration" includes all ranks from section chief up.

influence from the planning profession—despite the fact that such influence could lead them into conflict, for example, with the expectations of elected officials or other public clients.

It is noteworthy that, again, lower-level staff members in public agencies give signs of being particularly isolated from others. Earlier, they indicated that they had conflicts about their responsibilities with their administrative superiors, and they reported being constrained from above by political considerations. Frequently they turned no further than their agency colleagues for indications of their effectiveness. Here they say that they are hardly influenced by the planning profession and that they rely on colleagues or themselves in deciding how to do their work. It is possible that some of their isolation is a response to their conflicts with administrators. For many this conflict takes the form of a difference between staff members' conceptions of technically good work and administrators' views of politically acceptable work. Kahn et al. (1964), in examining the consequences of role conflicts in organizations, report that withdrawal from communication with others is a common response to persistent conflict. Withdrawal is a way of reducing reception of conflictful, and stressful, directives. They hypothesize that introversion may be a common response to this type of organizational role conflict.[8] Hence it is possible that role conflicts in public planning agencies contribute to isolation of lower-level staff members not only from administrative superiors, but also from a professional reference group.

From all the statements about the influence of the planning profession over personal practice one strong impression emerges. For most planners there is no clearly identifiable "planning profession" which serves as a reference group. Those who do report being significantly influenced by the planning profession refer to it as a source of intellectual guidance but rarely say that it is a cohesive group whose fortunes they feel they share. Nevertheless, many want both intellectual guidance and the emotional support which comes from a sense of belonging to a group. A minority feel that they receive this support. Others are disappointed or become resentful when they do not. Thus a general question about influence by professional colleagues evokes relatively little expression of group solidarity and considerable confusion and hostility.

ATTITUDES TOWARD LICENSING: AMBIVALENCE

Questions about expertise, ethical norms, and influence by a professional group evoke, at best, a weak expression of a shared professional consciousness among planners. Still, there is one other way in which planners may feel some sense of shared work and interest: at the least, they may define themselves negatively through clear ideas about whom they would choose to exclude from the practice of "planning." One common way in which practitioners stake out—and exclude others from—an area of practice is through the establishment of licensing procedures. Planners in New Jersey, for example, were early, successful organizers of efforts to institute licensing for the practice of planning. Leaders of the American Institute of Planning, succeeded by the American Planning Association, as well as the Canadian Institute of Planners, have taken up the issue and have weighed alternative criteria which might be employed to distinguish planners from other practitioners. Planners in the sample were asked what they thought about establishing some type of licensing for planning.

Fewer than one-fourth of the planners (22 percent) unambivalently favored licensing. Two-fifths (40 percent) opposed any type of licensing. The remainder (38 percent) expressed mixed feelings about licensing. These responses show little support for a measure which would set planners off from other practitioners.

A small number of planners were direct in arguing in favor of licensing. They provided good reasons: licensing could improve the quality and stature of planning. The following comments illustrate these concerns. A private consultant bluntly argued for licensing as a way of improving planners' low status:

> Licensing is necessary just to get the respect of the uneducated person. There should be some recognition system to recognize [planners'] expertise.

A local planner described licensing as a strategy necessary for the defense of planners:

> Not to [license] belittle the confidence of the profession. Planners

are a pretty beleaguered group to begin with. All you have to do is pick up TAB [an employment bulletin for planning jobs] and look at jobs and salaries, and this says something about how people see planners. I think the only profession which is in sadder shape is social work.

A planner in a county agency argued that licensing could improve the quality of planning work:

I think licensing as a vehicle to institute a level of quality is a very good thing. You will assure yourselves that the people who do planning have a minimum level of competence. You can not assure quality, but you can assure a minimum.

These are some of the most positive statements in favor of instituting licensing. Even so, none of these planners offered an unqualified argument for licensing. The first planner implied that planners are an unrewarded group of practitioners. They ply their skills but do not receive appropriate recognition from the many uneducated people in society whose lives are affected by planners' work. Licensing is a means of evening relations with an unappreciative public. The second comment suggests that planners now feel belittled, unconfident, and beleaguered by citizens generally and planners' employers and colleagues in particular. The comment implies that planners are in "sad shape" because they have not been willing or able to take appropriate initiatives such as licensing to establish their proper relationship with clients and colleagues. The third planner expressed a concern about the quality of work done by people variously labelled "planners" and suggested that the quality—and, presumably, the status—of planners' work could be improved by setting licensing standards. At the same time, he expressed skepticism about the power of standards to assure quality in work. This skepticism underlies the arguments which many other planners offer against licensing. In all these comments there are hints of self-deprecation, which appears more openly in later comments.

Planners who expressed any support for licensing were asked what criteria they would employ for licensing planners. Among planners who expressed unqualified support for licensing there were a few clear suggestions about requirements. Typically, one planner advocated attention to "either education or experience, along with a practical examination." Several planners talked at length about the relationship between education and experience as requirements for licensing. A planner in a public agency offered the following criteria:

> As much as I hate to say it, I guess I would say a planning degree [should be a requirement], because I know the quality of programs around the nation varies. I am a strong advocate for work experience as well as academic credentials. Perhaps I would put it the way they put it here in relation to jobs. For example, if you have a degree in planning, you can enter at X; if you have a degree in public administration, you might need [to supplement the degree with a certain amount of experience before reaching X] . . . I would like to see testing in specialty areas, probably much like the American Institute of Planners does its testing now. I think that testing is a legitimate function after a period of experience. So it would be the requirement of a degree . . . I am not sure it would have to be a planning degree [sic] . . . plus some experience, so that someone [just] coming out of school could not be an AIP-licensed planner.

A planner who had worked at several levels of government emphasized the importance of experience for licensing:

> You can not come out wet behind the ears as a Master of Urban Planning from any university and be automatically stamped as urban planner, because there is a big difference between theory and working on the job. We need to have well-rounded experience . . . I myself have a strong urban design background. These are the tools you use. But I think you also have to know how to use the political system . . . Urban planning is still more an art than a science . . . If you don't have that feel for cities and an appreciation for people, you can not be a planner.

The specificity of these comments is exceptional. Most planners favoring licensing are vague about what criteria should be set for licensing a practitioner as a planner. Typical is the comment of one planner who declared that licensing was "urgently" needed. He offered the following response when asked what criteria he would establish:

> Degrees and experience. It would be hard to say specifically what. I have faith in the American Institute of Planners. I don't know what subject areas.

Thus a number of planners favor licensing because they would like it to establish a distinct status for planners but have difficulty defining where in practice boundaries should be set. This predicament could contribute to the lack of confidence and self-deprecation hinted at in several statements in support of licensing.

Planners opposed to licensing offered some articulate responses which help further to understand planners' thoughts and feelings about licensing. A public agency administrator opposed to licensing expressed his thinking this way:

> I think it is preposterous. I don't know how the hell you can license somebody when you do not have criteria for what it is or what they do. Some kind of membership is okay . . . I don't think planning is a clearly defined enough discipline to draw a test to say that one guy is a planner and another is not. The value of planning is that it is interdisciplinary. Most of the effective procedures which I see are adopted from management. But there is no body of knowledge, as there is in the field of economics or engineering, and, therefore, you can have people like the planning director I worked for in Pennsylvania, who is one of the most skillful planning directors there is, and he has only a bachelor's degree in political science. That is probably why he is a good planner. He did not muck up his head by going to planning school. I talked with a panel at a university, and I told them that the people I am interested in hiring need to have good research skills and good communication skills. I don't care how good they are technically if they cannot do good research and cannot express themselves in a written and verbal way. That is why I don't think licensing is a good way to measure, because you are not talking about skills that are finely defined.

This planner expressed a common ambivalence about the elusiveness of a definition for "planning." On the one hand, he referred to many planners' interests in interdisciplinary work as an argument against the compartmentalization which licensing would foster. Centrally, however, he contended that planning is too diffuse an activity to define precisely. "Planning" is, he suggested, whatever people called "planners" do, regardless of their training. His statement implies some sanguinity with this situation, although it seems to be just such a situation which leads the group quoted before to call for licensing as a way of securing some boundaries.

Another planner opposed to licensing referred to his feelings that licensing constituted an unwarranted protectionism on the part of planners:

> I think it is more of a protective device for planners, not for the public. Most of these licensing things end up with people being licensed by their peers. And the problem is how to protect the

community. Most elected officials know how to find out what is good by interviews. This will tell more than licensing.

A more strongly worded expression of a similar view was given by a planner with many years' experience:

> It is a way of aggrandizing the planning profession. It reflects delusions of grandeur. It goes back to that viewpoint of mine that planners have an overly important viewpoint of the work which they do. The historical background to this which I see is that "if we don't license planners, the health and welfare will suffer," but I don't see that planners are doing anything that affects health and welfare that intimately. Planning does not have that kind of life and death impact that other fields that are licensed in do.

On the one hand these statements offer the ethical judgment that protectionism is not good for the general welfare. However, in addition, the second statement contends that licensing is unnecessary—and probably unlikely—because planners' work is relatively unimportant. In this self-deprecating comment, this planner suggests that, because planners do not have much effect on the problems regarded as significant by the public, planners deserve the low status which they hold.

A planner with a state agency offered one other objection to licensing, related to what would be necessary for its administration:

> I don't think [licensing] is going to help this issue. I tend to be against it because it will bring more bureaucracy into play.

In short, the risks entailed by an open market in planning would be outweighed by the costs of entrusting control over entry into planning to a bureaucratic agency.

Ambivalence and Limited Tolerance for Ambiguity

Many planners among both the proponents and opponents of licensing appear to agree in seeing planning as a diffuse, vaguely defined activity. Where the two groups appear to differ is in their tolerance for the intellectual uncertainty and occupational insecurity to which this ambiguity may contribute. In this context, the group of planners expressing mixed feelings about licensing offer a particularly useful insight into planners' feelings about licensing. First, they comprise the largest body of opinion about licensing, and their views are, therefore, numerically most representative of the sample. In addition, even though their position on licensing differs from that of others, because they are ambivalent, they give expression to some feelings about licensing and planning which are shared by planners with other positions.

Planners with mixed feelings about licensing find themselves drawn toward licensing for varying combinations of practical and symbolic reasons. The practical benefits of being able to protect work from others are appreciable. Still more important may be the symbolic and psychological rewards: licensing would bring planners self-respect, as well as the esteem of others. However, these planners are uneasy about instituting protectionist licensing to restrict an area of practice. Somehow, it would seem, the quality of a practitioner's work should be sufficient to ensure employment. These planners are not convinced that licensing procedures identify the best practitioners. In general, they are uneasy about delineating an area of practice for planners because they think that planning is too broad (or vague) an activity to draw any clear boundaries around.

These ambivalences come across in statements from two planners expressing mixed feelings toward licensing. The first is a young county planner:

> On the one hand, part of me says yes . . . the part that wants security, more money. Basically it is a union card, a way of keeping people in and out. I wouldn't have a problem with the license. If I wanted it, I could get it. It is a way of raising the salaries of planners. With regard to the quality of planning, it would not have anything to do with the quality of planning, because once people got their license, they would believe that they could do anything they wanted. I don't think they would ever take anyone's license away.

An older planner shared his mixed feelings in this way:

> I'm skeptical about the value of this. If it were a measure that would ensure a higher standard of practice, I would be in favor. But I think it is a measure of job control. I seriously question whether, the way it is now, it is a profession at all. There are not too many areas in which we have knowledge beyond that of a qualified technician, and I cannot see too much interest in developing that. There seems to be more interest in qualifying technicians for a structured set-up than in really increasing professionalism.

These planners are raising two types of questions. The first are ethical questions: whether it is proper to institute licensing as simply a way of cornering some part of the labor market. The meaning of these ethical concerns is explored further below. The second type of questions concern whether it is feasible to establish licensing procedures which will actually assure the quality of practice. The comments here identify two uncertainties: first, whether "good" planning practice can be defined sufficiently precisely to permit standards against which practitioners may be measured; second, whether it is possible to establish administrative procedures which will effectively assure that these standards are likely to be met in practice. These concerns are the focus of a comment by an architect-planner who compared planning with other types of work:

> I have very mixed feelings about [licensing]. Architects are licensed, and it certainly has not guaranteed the high standards of architecture perfectly. The whole health/safety standards in architecture and medicine are largely irrelevant. The kinds of things you would want to test before you license someone as an architect—for example, "Are you really interested in preserving resources?"—are difficult to do. Maybe it would be helpful as an institution to sort out who would and wouldn't be [interested in preserving resources]. But I really do philosophically have mixed feelings about it. I think there are grounds for licensing doctors on the basis of competence. But I am not sure about planners.

In short, in the context of social problems which citizens consider important, it is not certain whether many planners are effectively dealing with these problems, and it is not certain whether licensing procedures would really identify those effective planners.

The emotional meaning of the ethical and intellectual ambivalence which many planners feel about licensing is suggested by one other response. This is a veteran planner with many years' experience:

> The idea in the abstract is wonderful. The practical thing to implement is an incredible problem. It can easily be subverted by another discipline which thinks they can control the market for planners. For example, in New Jersey civil engineers have defined planning [that is, this planner believes that the licensing standards in New Jersey reflect the skills of civil engineers]. Secondly, it is a real problem in administration. I think you could argue that you ought to have some minimum qualifications as a planner. He ought to be able to read and speak relatively well, with a minimum of mathematical ability, expression, and analysis. To the extent that we have lousy

graduate schools, this might weed out civil servants who stay in it their entire life.

So much [planning] is done. I don't say it is an art, but it has so much subjectivity to it, and it is difficult to evaluate. I went through the [AIP] oral examination procedure, and now I hear of the other procedure which AIP is trying, and it is not easy to administer. On the positive side, it would give the public, to some extent, a measure of confidence that they are getting somebody who is not really a problem. And I think it would also be useful to give students in planning a feeling about how they are doing. As culturally biased as it is, it would be a good start.

I have a feeling that if the graduate schools were doing the job decently, the licensing would not be necessary. I understand that a lot of schools have moved in this direction, and they do a relatively decent job. I don't think there would be that kind of concern to limit entry into the profession. It all gets back to the evaluation thing I was talking about. It is all a subjective thing. Licensing would probably be more trouble than it is worth. It could be misunderstood. I would probably tend to stick as much as possible with a direct graduate school education.

I have seen particularly some urban studies programs. There is a tendency to view anyone with a commitment to help the public as good enough to get out of graduate school. There isn't a substitute for the kind of technique which is required for the research and analysis and posing of alternatives in planning. [These urban studies programs are] strong on community coordination and advocacy. But that is only part of planning. I am afraid that people who come out are not really qualified for much of anything, including planning, at a professional level. They don't know basic graphical skills, communicational skills. They are long on dedication to the public good, but they don't have the ability to really carry it out, and they may end up doing more harm than good.

The distinct affective tone to this statement signals that this and other statements about licensing really deal with emotionally charged issues. For example, on the one hand, specific parts of the statement make explicit, well-defined points: that planning requires identifiable skills and that some graduate programs do not teach these skills. On the other hand, the response as a whole is very loosely organized, and it includes contradictory statements: namely, that a licensing examination would be desirable and that licensing should be avoided insofar as possible. This loose, non-logical structure of the statement suggests that the question about licensing evoked considerable feeling about planning and about the respondent's performance. Further evidence of the feelings contained in the statement are several expressions of anger: toward "subversive" other disciplines, toward "lousy graduate schools," and toward people "with a commitment to the public good" who lack rigorous technical skills.

With caution about generalizing from individual statements to a group, it seems useful to examine this statement in the context of the self-deprecation expressed by other planners. Lack of confidence about the substance of planning, uncertainty whether planners engage important social problems, and a sense of being under siege from other groups of practitioners could be expected to contribute to the anger which is expressed in this planner's words. The question about licensing was originally posed in order to elicit planners' expressions of professional consciousness. The perceptions and feelings offered in response combine in a way that makes it difficult to articulate such a consciousness. A majority of planners observe somehow that planning is a diffuse, varied activity which is difficult to define. That is, it is difficult for them to define. As a consequence, for an individual it is difficult to identify a core activity which he or she carries out which is shared by a distinguishable group of others. Under these conditions a positive professional consciousness is unlikely to develop. Recurrent self-deprecatory comments attest to the difficulty of developing a positive identity.

Logically, then, it would seem that, if "planners" cannot be enclosed within definitional boundaries, others cannot be set off from them. Yet this is not quite how many planners respond. Some respond to uncertainty about what planning is by simply insisting that they can establish licensing. Some planners acknowledge that this insistence is primarily psychologically reassuring: boundaries believed to be real are believed to be real. A large number of planners simply express uneasiness. But the last statement quoted above suggests what may be a common response. For this planner—and, apparently, others—anger creates an emotional barrier between the planner and others. Yet this tactic cannot quite succeed. The objects of the planners' anger are just about as nebulous as others' descriptions of planning. Emotionally, some number of planners may set themselves off from *some* others, but the combined uncertainty about the nature of planning and these others leads not so much to a shared consciousness with other planners as to an individualistic isolation from many, including other planners.

Several qualifications to this general picture are necessary. First, the characterization just offered seems to be consistent with the comments of a number of planners, but it certainly does not apply to all planners. Second, even the planners who do tend to isolate themselves in the manner described above are not completely set off from other planners. Most of them continue to perform work which is called "planning"; most continue to call themselves "planners"; and all in this sample at one time belonged to the American Institute of Planners, the professional association of planners. Nevertheless, they would not want to be pressed to articulate what it is that they do and how it differs from what others do, because they are not sure that they know.

Planners' responses to the licensing question are associated with their organizational roles, as Table 5-2 shows.[9] Private consultants are most likely to favor licensing, and those consultants who do favor licensing emphasize the greater economic security which a clear delineation of "planners" could provide. Public agency administrators, in contrast, are most likely to oppose licensing, and none give it unqualified support. Almost unanimously, their responses indicate that the planning work which they do is diffuse and varied, and they indicate skepticism that any licensing procedure could identify high quality work. Public agency staff members are most likely to have mixed feelings about licensing. On the one hand, they seem to recognize the diverse nature of planning activities in their agencies; on the other hand, they tend to feel that licensing planners could give them more secure and better rewarded status in civil service positions. Nevertheless, although there are these differences in emphasis among planners in different roles, the intellectual and emotional themes described above transcend role differences. Beneath statements of support or opposition lies considerable ambivalence about whether, where, and how to draw boundaries around "planning."

USE OF A PROFESSIONAL ORGANIZATION: DISENGAGEMENT AND ISOLATION

Organization for professional status normally rests on practitioners' shared consciousness of common interests. In the case of

TABLE 5-2. SUPPORT FOR LICENSING, BY PLACE OF EMPLOY-
MENT AND ORGANIZATIONAL ROLE

Employment, Role	Type of Support			
	Unambivalent Support	Mixed Feelings	Opposition	Total
Public agency: administration[a]	0	4	10	14
Public agency: staff	5	9	2	16
Private firm	7	2	5	14
All	12	15	17	44

$X^2 = 17.16$
$P < .01$
$V = .442$

[a]"Administration" includes all ranks from section chief up.

planners, however, instead of a coherent group consciousness there
seems to be an ambiguous image of the core components of
planning, skepticism that planners are effective in addressing
important social problems, and troubled uncertainty about how to
distinguish planners from other practitioners. Even though the
planners sampled were members of a professional organization, it
is not clear whether they would feel motivated to use such an
organization to promote professional interests and to acquire
legitimacy as problem-solvers. In order to explore this question,
planners were asked how important they considered it to be for
every professional planner to belong to the American Institute of
Planners.

As noted earlier, subsequent to the study, the American Institute
of Planners merged with the American Society of Planning
Officials to form the American Planning Association, a single
organization of both practitioners and others interested in planning.
It seems likely that statements about the AIP could be generalized
to any organization of planners, insofar as these statements express
expectations of professional organizations or attitudes about them.
However, whether specific evaluations of the performance of the
AIP will be repeated in subsequent evaluations of the new APA is

a matter for speculation. It may be noted that Page and Lang's (1977 and 1978) study of Canadian planners showed some assessments of the Canadian Institute of Planners similar to comments in this study about the AIP. This similarity suggests that responses offered here represent general views of professional associations.

The planners sampled, who were members of the American Institute of Planners, gave, at best, mixed support to the AIP. More than one-third (38 percent) said that they regarded AIP membership as "not at all" or only "slightly" important for professional planners. One-fourth (26 percent) said that membership was "moderately" important. Only a little more than one-third (36 percent) assessed membership in the professional association as either "considerably" or "completely" important for every professional planner.

Both supporters and critics of the AIP share similar expectations of the professional organization. They differ primarily in their estimation of the degree to which the Institute does or can satisfy these expectations. Planners' concerns in assessing Institute membership correspond to issues raised in responses to previous questions. The planners tend to have an ambiguous image of what planning is, and they evaluate the professional association's ability to provide a clear image. They also tend to be uncertain how to draw boundaries between themselves and other practitioners, and they evaluate the organization's ability to identify boundaries.

These concerns are unified by a psychological unrest which accompanies them, and many planners commented on the personal security which membership in the professional organization does or could provide them. Repeatedly, planners echoed the comment of one planner that "It is very important to belong to *some* professional association." An administrator who had been in planning for two decades commented, "I feel a certain confidence in being part of a professional organization."

Planners look to a professional organization to guide them in defining the essence of their work. This concern is expressed by a local planner:

> I feel that every professional needs some organization to identify with. Now, whether this organization in fact really does something for the individual as such is another thing. But I think that every

professional needs some organization to identify with. I think it holds the profession together. AIP tends to hold the planning profession together. In my particular instance, I deviated a little from planning as such, and yet I've still got a tie with AIP which I intend to continue.

A private consultant elaborated on this concern, alluding also to the external concern of distinguishing planners from other practitioners:

I think a professional needs to have a professional organization to belong to. This is part of being a professional, having an organization that establishes criteria for getting into it, that sets planners apart from the surveyors of New Jersey [where this planner sees State licensing criteria as defining surveyors as planners]. I think it is very important to have an organization that will qualify you, that has standards to get into it, that sets standards of excellence just to be a member, and then to use that organization to keep you current of the field. I don't think that AIP does this, at least for me.

For these planners membership in a professional organization is crucial insofar as the organization can give definition to what planners do and provide information on methods which planners may incorporate into their practice. This latter point, technical assistance, is particularly important for a number of planners. Several planners weighted this contribution of a professional association more heavily than others:

I think it is important for an exchange of information, of current methodology. To the extent that the AIP is a repository of this kind of information, I think this is the usefulness of it.

I would continue to be a member because the information which I can get out of AIP is my primary motivation. I don't think membership or lack of membership would make a difference in terms of the kinds of jobs I would do. But in order to give them [clients] the kinds of services which I think I should, I find membership in AIP very useful.

The perceived failure of the American Institute of Planners to provide useful technical assistance led a number of planners to accord it little value or to quit. More than one-fourth (28 percent) of the planners interviewed had dropped their AIP membership in the six to 18 months between the time that their names were selected from the local chapter membership list and the time that they were interviewed. Consistently, those who had left the organization mentioned the failure of the organization to provide them with information useful in their day-to-day work. For most planners the *Journal of the American Institute of Planners* (now the *Journal of the American Planning Association*) was the primary expression of the views of the national organization and the principal vehicle through which technical assistance might be offered. Although assessments of the *Journal* were mixed in the sample, the following types of negative views led some people to quit. Some planners moved into specialized fields where another professional association or journal could be more helpful. However, a significant number of practitioners continued to identify with traditional planning concerns but felt that their interests were not served by the *Journal*. A county staff member commented that he quit because of

> finances, coupled with my feeling that AIP was not meeting my need as a planner. I was a member for five years. I would watch the JAIP come out. I could probably count on one hand the number of articles that had interest to me, personally or professionally.

Some practitioners feel that the organization is dominated by academics who do not understand practice and cannot contribute to improvements in practice. One former member commented,

> I think AIP sometimes gets too academically oriented for its own good. I think that AIP has more members who are academically oriented than it has planners employed in working.

Although this generalization about the predominance of academics in the organization is empirically inaccurate—12.1 percent of the national membership worked in colleges, universities, or research organizations in 1976 (AIP, n.d.)—the perception refers to the tone of articles in the *Journal*.

Private consultants in particular seem dissatisfied with both the national journal and the local chapter leadership. One of the planners who was quoted above as saying that the professional association could be useful as a source of technical information had the following conclusion:

> My negative reaction about the AIP is that to a large extent it is dominated by public employees and has a point-of-view that does not reflect the real world.

Empirically, the statement about public employees in the Institute has some validity. In 1976 slightly more than half (52.9 percent) of the national membership were public agency employees, whereas private sector members comprised approximately one-third (30.7 percent) of the membership, with the remainder associated with academic or research institutions or miscellaneous organizations (AIP, n.d.). This comment represents the view of some consultants that public agency planners tend to be concerned with ways of meeting statutory requirements of public programs, whereas private consultants are expected to do actual problem-solving in complicated situations.

The comments reflect the diversity of the activities of planners. This heterogeneity is one of the sources of planners' uncertainty whether "planning" can be clearly defined. The affect of the responses to this perception is consistent with that expressed in connection with the role of a professional reference group and licensing. Planners express a combination of insecurity and hostility. They feel insecure working in a world in which they face complicated and conflicting expectations, and they feel hostile toward the professional organization which they believe should have but has not provided assistance in simplifying the tasks of planning practice. As a result, they feel still less confident yet about their ability to carry out future planning assignments. This general feeling comes particularly frequently from private consultants. They perceive that their economic well-being is directly tied to the quality of their work, whereas public agency planners' job security is shielded from the quality of their work by civil service regulations. Significantly, the level of personal identification with the professional association is low. The association is widely viewed as something external to the world in which planners practice. It is also regarded as either unreformable or not worthy of efforts at reform. Even though the respondents belonged to the American Institute of Planners, few made any reference to "us" or suggested that "we in the AIP" should act to make the organization more helpful or useful. This personal isolation is a theme which emerges in an examination of a second expectation of the professional association.

As the planner who referred to licensing in New Jersey indicated, planners also expect a professional organization to demonstrate to others how planners differ from them. Planners want the professional organization to represent them to others on public issues. A local agency administrator expressed his disappointment with the Institute in these terms:

> Apart from the *Journal*, I get absolutely nothing out of AIP. I am not sure that they have effectively stood up for anything, lobbied for anything, pushed for clarification of public issues.

Most pointedly, many planners expect the professional organization to serve as a political instrument to demonstrate for them their power vis-à-vis others. The psychological salience of this expectation is expressed in the statement of a local staff member:

> It's too bad that [AIP] is not doing what it should do. It should be rumbling up on the Hill, getting us money, prominence, instead of all that other piddly crap. We need a big father figure there, a big lobbyist to tell us what to do. Maybe we need a non-planner there, because our purposes are very noble, and they should be protected. Other professions are usurping our responsibility. We need a real florid non-academic. I want a sign from Carter that he is still a planner . . . We are really getting coopted.

This statement is more explicit than others, but the psychological themes are typical. At the same time that planners insecurely work on complicated problems, even if the professional association cannot give them special tools for solving the problems, at least they would like the organization to hold off critics and give planners room and authority to figure out solutions. Many planners would like the political support of a figurative father. As this planner notes, many planners feel that their purposes are noble and that they would threaten the purity of their work by involving themselves directly in politics. Without the protection of a powerful organization, planners, because of the high-mindedness of their work, risk being coopted by devious politicians. The images in this quotation are singularly vivid, but the themes are common.

Thus there is an ambivalence among planners. On the one hand, they feel isolated from others by insecurity about their competence and hostility toward an organization which does not give them tools. On the other hand, they would like the support of this organization in defending them against others who would appear to criticize them for their shortcomings. Indeed, some planners are prepared to organize for this latter purpose, for some of the same reasons that they would push for licensing. A staff member in a state agency observed about the American Institute of Planners:

> It is quite deficient as an organization, but it is the best we've got. A professional organization, its strength lies in its membership. If every planner strived for membership, then the Institute would better reflect the planning profession, and it would begin to be a better voice for the profession and improve the image and role of planning.

Yet, beneath these expectations too there lies a doubt, a feeling that a professional organization of planners has a difficult task to carry out, if it is to define the domain of planning. Perhaps the organization should not be expected to be able to do more than individual planners can in this regard. Perhaps, indeed, it is irresponsible for planners to expect an organization to act for them. One administrator criticized the AIP sympathetically:

> The AIP does not seem to present the practicing professional with very much in terms of useful information. They have made passing attempts to get down to the practical, day-to-day situations. But I am not sure that any professional organization like this can do that. Planning is very difficult to define. No matter how AIP is organized, it is probably not the fault of AIP, but the fault of the profession. It is difficult to define why people are in it, what they want from it, what they get out of it, so that any group that represents this body of peculiar individuals has a hard road ahead. The local groups are useful to only a handful of people. I do not see the local groups being helpful. I don't know how it can. It is more a social thing. On the national level, I don't see how they can have an impact. They do not have a clear constituency.

This statement is an individualistic refusal to delegate intellectual responsibility. If individual planners cannot define for themselves what it is that they do as planners, it would be irresponsible to ask others to do so for them. As a specific example, it would be inappropriate to have an organization enter the legislative process to seek to enact a licensing statute. This would be inappropriate, even though it would be reassuring to have a "father figure" or a big lobbyist to promote the interests of planners. The individualistic refusal to delegate responsibility must be weighed against the earlier statement that planners' purposes are too noble to be sullied in the dirt of politics. It is possible that the later statement is a rationalization for the earlier one. Because some planners feel that politics is dirty, therefore, they justify their reluctance to organize for action to gain power as intellectually irresponsible.

Those planners who do not support organization create a bind for themselves. They feel insecure about their competence, and they want support from a professional organization. There is an existing organization, but it provides little technical assistance. Many planners feel hostile toward this organization. At the same time, they feel susceptible to criticism from others regarding their competence and their authority, and they would like support from a professional organization in relation to these others. However, for some reason—either because "planning" is difficult to define or because politics is repugnant—they finally cannot justify their own investment in an organization. As a consequence, they must contend with feelings of self-doubt and impending criticism in isolation.

This reasoning brings the discussion of planners' consciousness full circle. Planners begin with an ambiguity about what it is that they do. They practice whatever they do with a feeling of isolation from a reference group of colleagues. They have difficulty distinguishing whatever they do from what other practitioners do. All these uncertainties are deeply troubling. Hence they look to the organization of planners to clarify for them and for others just what their work called "planning" is. Yet they are disappointed with the efforts of the organization. Finally, many feel that perhaps it is inappropriate to expect an organization to resolve personal doubts. Hence they turn further inward, withdrawing from the organization, blaming themselves for their uncertainties, practicing more in isolation, and not finding resolution.

Thus, while many planners want social legitimacy to practice on certain types of problems, their self-image handicaps them in several ways. First, some planners have serious doubts whether they can really be effective in dealing with problems which citizens consider important. Second, the diversity of activities labelled "planning" leads many planners to conclude that "if planning is everything, maybe it's nothing."[10] Third, the conceptualization of "planning" as a series of intellectual activities contributes to isolation in day-to-day work which leads many planners to think of themselves as isolated more generally from other planning practitioners. Fourth, the diffuse character of "planning" activities and the isolation encourage a self-deprecation which, in turn, discourages efforts to identify either intellectually or politically with other planners. Finally, this weak identification provides little motivation for taking organized action to promote social legitimacy for planning practitioners in desired areas of work. And this cycle repeats itself.

NOTES

1. The concept of professional consciousness receives dual treatment in the literature on professions. Although almost all students of the professions agree that a professional consciousness is essential for professionalization, the role which this consciousness is considered to play varies with the orientation of the observer. Those who take the attributional approach to professions invariably include this self-consciousness as an essential characteristic of "professions." Thus for this group of students the possession of a professional consciousness, in combination with a small number of additional attributes, in itself gives a group of practitioners professional status. Those who take the political approach to professions and focus on the degree of autonomy of practitioners vis-à-vis their clients identify this self-consciousness as an essential motivator to acquire autonomy. The complex relationships between professional consciousness and professional status are discussed later in the main text of the chapter. For a classical presentation of the attributional orientation, see Greenwood (1957). For presentations of the political orientation, see Freidson (1970) and Larson (1977).

2. Greenwood (1957) includes the possession of a stated ethical code as an essential "attribute of a profession." Freidson (1970) observes that, whatever the content of or sanctions underlying any statement of practice ethics, the persuasive claim to members of the public that practitioners' actions are governed by a code of ethics is strategically important in securing professional status and privileges.

3. This difference in emphasis implies a difference in views of the planning process similar to that associated with differences in emphasis on personal strengths. Specifically, the planning process suggested by the technical views of ethics corresponds to the process suggested by planners claiming intellectual strengths, and the ethical view of ethics depicts a process similar to that of planners with interpersonal strengths. However, there is no statistically significant association between responses to these two questions. There are two plausible explanations for this lack of association. The first is that many planners, although believing that ethics require a participatory planning process, nevertheless, feel that they themselves lack the expertise to orchestrate such a process. The second explanation, suggested by a careful reading of planners' comments, is that

many planners consider a planning process to be participatory when the ideas of many groups are represented; this type of process is still primarily intellectual.

4. In September, 1981, the AIP Code was superseded by the American Institute of Certified Planners' Code of Ethics and Professional Conduct, which supplemented the former's negative admonitions with positive exhortations.

5. Not only is the content of the planners' ethical statements varied, but also the statements have quite different structures. Marcuse (1976) has identified what he considers to be the principal approaches to ethics presented in the planning literature. With one exception, each of the approaches is espoused by some of the planners interviewed in this study: "subjective approaches," which make ethical judgment a matter for individual choice; "pluralist approaches," which emphasize the importance of representation for all interests; "objective approaches," which emphasize fixed standards, such as technical norms, for action; "egalitarian approaches," which emphasize fixed standards in social terms, such as support for "the underdog"; and "process approaches," which emphasize the way in which decisions are made, such as through informed discussion. In promoting a "structural approach," Marcuse has encouraged planners to develop practical ethics which transcend concerns with "the client-serving, guild-related roles of planners to examine their real effect on the social, economic, and political system in which the planner's activities take place" (p. 272).

6. This conclusion is consistent with the findings of Howe and Kaufman (1979), who surveyed the ethical views of a national sample of the membership of the American Institute of Planners. In contrast with this study, their study asked questions about specific situations involving ethical dilemmas, and their respondents provided more specific answers about what ethical action would be than did planners in this study. Nevertheless, the responses offered were, as in this study, both general (the use of threats and the distortion of information were abjured) and highly variable. Howe and Kaufman conclude that "it is very difficult to establish any single ethical standard that is meaningful to the whole profession" (p. 253).

7. Planners' responses about influence by the expectations of the profession are not associated with such personal characteristics as age, sex, or class background; with field of undergraduate study or orientation of graduate planning training; or with years of work experience.

8. Unfortunately, they suggest, this strategy for coping with conflict often contributes to a vicious cycle which aggravates the conflict and, in turn, increases isolation:

> The characteristic coping style of the introvert thus produces and intensifies a vicious cycle: the more he withdraws, the more he is seen as too independent. He is subjected to more intense pressures to change and to become more responsive; his emotional tensions are increased, and he is

stimulated to further withdrawal. Unless he leaves the organization, his [superiors] are eventually apt to block his coping efforts and put him in a bind from which he cannot withdraw, increasing his vulnerability to the emotional costs of conflict. Thus the introvert's very effort to reduce the conflict may bring it back to him intensified (Kahn et al., 1964, p. 275).

9. Responses to the question are not associated with such personal characteristics as age, sex, or class background; with field of undergraduate study or orientation of graduate planning training; or with years of work experience.

10. This is a title of a provocatively skeptical article by Wildavsky (1973).

REFERENCES

American Institute of Planners. "Membership Survey from 1976 Roster." Washington: American Institute of Planners, n.d.

Freidson, Eliot. *Profession of Medicine.* New York: Dodd, Mead, and Company, 1970.

Greenwood, Ernest. "Attributes of a Profession," *Social Work, 2* (1957), pp. 44-55.

Howe, Elizabeth, and Jerome Kaufman. "The Ethics of Contemporary American Planners," *Journal of the American Planning Association, 45,* 3 (July, 1979), pp. 243-255.

Kahn, Robert L., Donald M. Wolfe, Robert P. Quinn, J. Diedrick Snoek, and Robert A. Rosenthal. *Organizational Stress: Studies in Role Conflict and Ambiguity.* New York: John Wiley and Sons, 1964.

Larson, Magali Sarfatti. *The Rise of Professionalism.* Berkeley: University of California Press, 1977.

Marcuse, Peter. "Professional Ethics and Beyond: Values in Planning," *Journal of the American Institute of Planners, 42,* 3 (July, 1976), pp. 264-274.

Page, John, and Reg Lang. *Canadian Planners in Profile.* Toronto: Faculty of Environmental Studies, York University, 1977.

Page, John, and Reg Lang. *Final Report on Results of Survey-Questionnaires.* Toronto: Faculty of Environmental Studies, York University, 1978.

Wildavsky, Aaron. "If Planning is Everything, Maybe it's Nothing," *Policy Sciences, 4* (1973), pp. 127-153.

6

ORGANIZATION IN THE COGNITIVE MAP OF PLANNERS

UNDERSTANDING ORGANIZATION

Planners' Problems with Organization

When examining strengths as practitioners, planners emphasized their facility in thinking about and finding solutions for a wide range of problems in community and social development. These aims and skills would seem to be valuable for social decision-making. However, many planners subsequently described constraints on their autonomy, and they reported that they were not consistently granted the discretion or the respect which they expected to be commensurate with their skills. Why are planners with this seemingly useful expertise not accorded the autonomy or legitimacy which they expect in practice?

Many planners revealed considerable uncertainty about what they do and expressed difficulty in distinguishing their expertise from that of either lay citizens or other practitioners. For many planners ambiguity about what they do has apparently led to self-deprecation, hostility toward the professional association of planners, and isolation from other planners. Why do so many planners have such a weak professional consciousness, despite the existence of a professional association, an association of academic programs in planning, and several planning journals? What is the explanation for the contrast between many planners' coherent initial images of planning and claims to problem-solving expertise and their subsequent ambiguity about what they do as planners? Is there any relationship between planners' feelings of constraint in practice and their weak professional consciousness? Is there something about the type of expertise which planners claim that may contribute to limited respect and autonomy and to limited professional consciousness?

First, regarding the disjunction between what planners regard as their expertise and organizational constraints on their autonomy in work, one might say that something is "out of place." One interpretation would accept the validity of planners' aims and maintain that the organizations in which planners are employed are inappropriate for the work which they expect to carry out and that the organizations should be changed. This view is supported by planning theorists who contend that the complexity and turbulence of social conditions require new patterns of organization.[1] In this view, planners receive a "double message." On the one hand, they are exhorted to discover creative solutions for complex problems. On the other hand, they are employed in organizations which limit their access to information and enforce norms of accountability which interfere with extended periods of rumination on complicated problems. Working in these bureaucratic organizations, planners are programmed for failure, and what should be surprising would be if they were able to offer any creatively successful solutions for problems.

Yet planners' statements do not support this position. While there is considerable grumbling about the "craziness" of bureaucratic procedures, there is little explicit questioning of the validity of bureaucracy as a model for organization. On balance, most planners appear to respond to organizational constraints simply by redefining their expectations to match the limited perceived opportunities available. Although this reaction may be interpreted as a begrudging acceptance of bureaucracy, planners' suggestions for changing their work setting suggests that many planners unconsciously accept bureaucracy without comprehending how it functions.

In the analysis of the disjunction between planners' original expectations and their sense of organizational constraint, then, a second interpretation seems reasonable: the goals and expectations of many planners are out of place in the work organizations. However, these expectations would seem to be "out of place" in a special sense. The problem does not seem to be that the expectations are simply inappropriate. After all, planners continue to be employed with instructions to apply intellectual and other skills to discovering potential solutions for problems.

Rather, planners' expectations appear to be "out of place" in the sense of not being clearly tied to any specific places or settings with which planners have contact or within which they work. Planners tend to describe their work as if it were purely intellectual. They imply that the world consists of ideas and that the mandate of planners is to give order to these ideas. The "placelessness" of this world-view can be emphasized by contrasting such a world of ideas with another world-view. The stock-in-trade of many planners is maps—maps of the geographic environment. In addition, most planners have filed somewhere in their records one or more organizational charts—maps of the organizational environment in which they work.[2] Further, other planners have developed explicit or tacit analyses of community decision-making—maps of local power structures. These maps all identify and variously locate a number of "places": some geographic, some organizational, and some political. Yet planners' statements suggest that, when acting as planners, they act in a world of ideas, not located in any place.

A second question raised earlier in this chapter was how to characterize the weakness in planners' professional consciousness. Here it is helpful to re-examine the ambivalence which many planners expressed about their identity and relationship to other practitioners. On the one hand, they were confident that they performed reasonably well at work called "planning." On the other hand, they had difficulty explaining how their planning work could be distinguished from the work of other practitioners. On the one hand, they were concerned or angry about the possible incursion of other practitioners into what they considered the domain of planners. On the other hand, they generally had questions about or expressed clear opposition to licensing procedures, which would be the surest way of protecting their domain from other practitioners.

One way to characterize the focus of this ambivalence would be to say that many planners have an ambivalence about delineating their "place" as practitioners. They feel that they have a place in decision-making, but they have intellectual difficulties in defining it. They feel that others are invading their place, but they have intellectual and emotional hesitations about staking out clear boundaries to their place. It appears that a central reason why planners have a weak professional consciousness is that they cannot settle—intellectually, emotionally, or politically—on occupying a clearly demarcated place in the processes of making decisions about problems. In other words, just as planners' expectations about their expertise appear to be "out of place," planners' sense of professional consciousness seems to be weak because it, too, is out of any "place." Planners have difficulty locating themselves and their work in some kind of "place."

Here it is helpful to examine the concept of "organization"—both as a structure and as a process of creating a structure.[3] An organization as a structure may be considered a place. Many planners' statements suggest that they have little or no conscious relationship to the place of the formal organization in which they work or the other organizations with which that organization is linked. Aside from being the object of occasional complaints, it does not seriously enter into their thinking when they go about their work of identifying solutions for problems.

Organization as a process is a way of establishing boundaries around—or defining—a place. Sometimes this process is called "politics." Persons or groups who perceive that they share interests with others may act in such a way as to join together for certain purposes. In taking collective action, they will attempt to be conscious of where—for these specific purposes at a particular time—their organization ends and where other actors—potentially supportive, potentially hostile, or simply irrelevant—begin. Although these boundaries may be difficult to delineate with precision, establishment of some general boundaries is necessary for taking action and distributing the rewards (or costs) of action.[4] Many planners' statements suggest that they have ambivalence about organizing around some purposes for collective action. They may organize ideas, but they rarely consider organizing themselves and other people into groups or formal associations.

Cognitive Maps

Social psychologists have developed a construct to understand individuals' experiences of "place": the "cognitive map." Originally formulated by Tolman (1948) to explain the behavior of rats in experimental situations, the construct has been applied to human behavior as well. The construct was developed in order to explain how it is possible for people to make their way coherently through complex environments when they can have direct contact with only some small part of the environment at any moment. It was hypothesized that people can act effectively in complicated environments because they carry in their heads an abstract image of the larger environment, analogous to a street map. This "cognitive map" refers to spatial, temporal, and social elements in someone's world which are meaningful to that person and which that person would want to take into account in acting. Neisser (1976) has described a cognitive map in the following way:

> I will . . . use the term "orienting schema" as a synonym for "cognitive map" to emphasize that it is an active, information-seeking structure. Instead of defining a cognitive map as a kind of image, I will propose that spatial [and other] imagery itself is just an aspect of the functioning of orienting schemata (p. 111).

Thus people are assumed to carry within their heads a mental model of the world which helps them locate themselves in space, time, and social meaning. What people actually experience and the meaning which they attach to this experience depend crucially on this cognitive map. People "see" other people and objects which are located by their maps, and they somehow fail to "see" any others which are excluded. In the process of locating phenomena for experience these maps make certain people and objects more likely to be discovered and certain other people and objects less likely to be discovered. The effect of the cognitive maps is to "sensitize" people to certain types of phenomena while simultaneously rendering people "insensitive" to certain others. The shape and contents of the maps change with experience, and people and objects may move into and out of "visibility" on the maps.

The construct of a cognitive map has been applied empirically to the analysis of the actions of political elites (Axelrod, 1976) and members of organizations (Weick, 1979). In these studies the underlying assumption is that people's mental maps of the environment guide their actions in the environment. People act in ways which are appropriate to the "places" which are seen through their cognitive maps; in the environment portrayed by the cognitive maps actions taken appear to be rational. Failures in action may be the result of an inadequacy of such resources as political support, skill, time, or money. In addition, failure may be attributed to an inaccurate cognitive map of the environment of action.

Questions about the accuracy of someone's cognitive map are commonly couched in terms of whether that person sees "the real world" as it actually is. What comes to be regarded as "the real world" reflects individuals' selective cognitive maps of the environment. Because people act on their perceptions of the environment, the dominant perception of "the real world" will reflect a shared commitment by a number of persons to some particular view of how the world is. Implicitly, this view will reflect a consensus about how the world "logically" should be. This negotiation of a view of "the real world" is a process which Berger and Luckmann characterize as "the social construction of reality" (1967).[5]

There are three significant ways in which someone may be said to hold an "inaccurate" view of "the real world." First, the environment may, in fact, be extremely complex, such that no one may hold an especially accurate cognitive map of the environment. For example, the national economy may be extremely complicated, with no theories offering much assistance in understanding its operations.

Second, someone may hold a view of the world which, in the process of abstracting concrete phenomena into conceptual categories, simplifies excessively. As a consequence, subtle but potentially powerful phenomena in the environment may be ignored. What is overlooked may reflect intellectual biases. For example, someone trained as a sociologist may tend to develop a cognitive map which makes it easy to "see" formal relationships in organizations but which makes it difficult to "see" psychological dynamics in relationships among actors in the organizations. Or someone trained as an engineer may tend to develop a cognitive map which makes it easy to "see" the characteristics of physical materials but which makes it difficult to "see" either formal organizational relationships or psychological dynamics within organizations.

Third, someone may be popularly considered to hold an "inaccurate" cognitive map when that person's map sensitizes him or her to phenomena regarded as relatively unimportant or nonexistent by the cognitive maps of a majority of others. For example, someone may see the possibilities of using solar energy technologies in new housing developments, while most others may see only oil, gas, and coal as "practical" sources of energy. The "inaccuracy" of this particular cognitive map and this person's ineffectiveness in promoting the views highlighted by the map may reflect a minority status in society. The interests supported by this viewpoint may be perceived as—and may materially be— inimical to the interests of a large number of others in society. In this case it is inappropriate to characterize the cognitive map as "inaccurate" by any "objective" standard, and it would be inappropriate to ascribe any ineffectiveness of the actor holding the map solely to the map itself. There are conflicts of interests about issues, and this person may be overruled by the political resources of others.

A primary characteristic of cognitive maps is that they are selective. They do not portray every single detail in the environment, because the number of details is infinite and because the surveillance of an infinitely detailed environment prior to action would require an infinite amount of time and, presumably, would lead to failure. Rather, cognitive maps are abstractions which are intended to assist action by focusing actors' attention on details most likely to be important in choosing effective actions. In each of the three types of inaccurate, or ineffective, cognitive maps the source of ineffectiveness is their inappropriate selectivity.

The discussion of planners' problems with organization suggested that planners' cognitive maps may be selective in a way which contributes to ineffectiveness. Many planners may have expertise in the intellectual and technical aspects of a problem but may be inattentive to the organizational environment in which decisions about the problem are made and to the politics of decision-making. Similarly, they may be relatively more concerned with intellectual definitions of their expertise and relatively less sensitive to the organizational and political processes of establishing a secure domain for practice. These possibilities pose two questions regarding planners' cognitive maps. Do planners' cognitive maps differ in their selectivity? Why may some planners focus on substantive problem areas without looking at the organizational or political environment of these problem areas?

In exploring for answers to these questions, the following section examines psychological dynamics which may underlie the development of cognitive maps. At the same time, the analysis is not meant to "psychologize" views of the world by reducing all perceptions of values to intrapsychic issues. In particular, the discussion is not intended to suggest that conflicts of material interests reflect simply the playing out of psychological conflicts.

Cognitive Style

A conceptual link between cognitive maps and psychological dynamics has been provided by the construct of "cognitive style." A cognitive map was described as an abstract mental structure through which information about the environment may be organized. The specific content of mental images of the world reflects interactions between various external phenomena and this internal organizing structure. The characteristics of the mental images are influenced by the characteristics of the cognitive map. These latter characteristics have been described as "cognitive style":

> Cognitive style, emphasizing the structure rather than the content of thought, refers to the ways in which individuals conceptually organize their environments (Goldstein and Blackman, 1978, p. vii).

This construct has been developed to account for the apparently different ways in which individuals mentally structure information about their environments.

A study of differences in cognitive styles among students is particularly useful here in exploring relationships between cognitive maps and psychological dynamics. Hudson (1966) discovered in a study of liberal arts and physical science students that the two groups tended to be distinguished by different cognitive styles, which he labelled "divergence" and "convergence." The divergent cognitive style of liberal arts students is characterized by a tendency to "look" outward from a stimulus object when thinking about it, to associate with it a large number of other objects, many of them not directly related to the stimulus. In contrast, the convergent cognitive style of physical science students is characterized by a tendency to "look" for a single appropriate association to any stimulus object and to seek this association among immediately proximate objects. Simplistically put, when asked to find a solution for a problem, the diverger tends to look widely and open-endedly at some particular problem, whereas the converger tends to focus quickly on a "single correct" solution to the problem. As an example of this difference, Hudson observed that, whereas the convergers tended to score higher on traditional, forced-choice intelligence tests, the divergers tended to offer more, as well as more unconventional, responses when asked to offer mental associations with some object.

Hudson's findings indicate that certain types of cognitive styles tend to be associated in individuals. Thus individuals who tend to have a predominantly convergent cognitive style tend also to think alike in a number of other similar ways. The same is true for divergers. For example, Hudson found that people with a convergent cognitive style are likely also to have a cognitive style with the following characteristics. They have a tendency to compartmentalize topics from one another (p. 85). They tend to react to controversial issues with stereotyped views (p. 85). They appear to dislike ambiguity (p. 86). In contrast, divergers tend to analyze objects in general categories (p. 56). They have relatively more flexible responses to issues (p. 65). In considering something, they may be more likely to reason by analogy or association than by Aristotelian logic (p. 92).

Hudson makes an important observation in examining the thinking of these two groups: differences in typical patterns of cognitive style appear to be consistently associated with typically different content of images offered by the two groups. He finds that

> The convergers are more likely to omit people, and have a special taste for deserted "lunar" street scenes. Conversely, the divergers tend to populate their pictures, even when humans are irrelevant to the action (p. 54).

Although Hudson studied adolescents, not adults, this thematic description of typical cognitive maps suggests a link to an earlier concern about the cognitive maps of planners. "Lunar" maps, devoid of people, seem analogous to cognitive maps which clearly show substantive problem areas but which reveal little about the organizational context or the politics of problem-solving in relation to those areas. In contrast, the freely populated maps seem analogous to cognitive maps which portray the human actors whose motives, interests, and relationships constitute the organization and politics of problem-solving. These analogies are only suggestive, but they provide two anchors to Hudson's research in this discussion of cognitive maps, cognitive styles, psychological dynamics, and planners. First, Hudson's findings point to links between cognitive maps, cognitive styles, and, as indicated below, psychological dynamics. Second, there appear to be similarities between Hudson's described types of cognitive maps and two possible cognitive maps which planners may hold. Consistently, there may be associations between planners' cognitive maps and the two cognitive styles which Hudson describes, as well as psychological dynamics which he finds associated with these cognitive styles. At the same time, Hudson's generalizations about his study population should be considered with caution in relation to the study population of planners.

Hudson's description of different propensities to "see" people suggests that there is a meaningful relationship between an individual's style of cognition and the content of the individual's cognition or, put differently, that there is some relationship between cognitive style and cognitive mapping. The hypothesis which Hudson offers for this relationship concerns psychological dynamics. He finds that typical personality characteristics tend to be associated with people with typical patterns of cognitive style, ánd he suggests that the personality characteristics are analogous to the characteristics of cognitive style.

For example, Hudson describes the students with a convergent cognitive style in the following way:

> Convergers are more likely to approve of being obedient, and having a low opinion of themselves; and to disapprove of being independent of their parents. They are more likely to approve of accepting expert advice, and having set opinions; more likely to disapprove of being highly imaginative, and of artistic sensitivity. They are more likely to approve of mixing well socially, and being a good team member, of being personally neat and tidy, and of being very well mannered; and to disapprove of "arty" clothes and bad language. Convergers also seem more likely to disapprove of being highly strung; and more likely to approve of having a "stiff upper lip" (p. 67).

A careful examination of the characteristics of the cognitive style of these convergers suggests a number of congruities between personality characteristics and cognitive style characteristics. For example, two characteristics of the converger stand out: "his concentration upon the impersonal aspects of his culture" and "the caution with which he expresses his feelings" (p. 84). As noted above,

> his reactions to controversial issues are often stereotyped, and . . . he is prone to compartmentalize one topic from another. Both habits of mind serve, presumably, to minimize the uneasiness which ambiguous or conflicting ideas create; and both may be seen as defenses against anxiety (p. 85).

He "enjoys the security which rigid systems of belief engender" (p. 85). In short, "The converger's restriction affects his thinking as well as his personality and interests" (p. 85).[6]

Hudson offers analogous comments about congruities between the personality characteristics and cognitive style characteristics of divergent thinkers. Moreover, he goes so far as to speculate about relationships between parents and children which nurture particular personality and cognitive traits (pp. 123-137). What is most important here is that he provides empirical evidence that psychological dynamics are related to—and appear to influence—cognitive style, as well as the content of imagery about the social world.

This discussion of cognitive maps, cognitive styles, and psychological dynamics possibly associated with cognitive maps helps to focus earlier questions concerning planners' experiences of place, organization, and politics. First, what do the cognitive maps of planners reveal? What "place" do planners see themselves in? How do they regard bureaucratic organization as a place or political organization as a process? Second, are planners' cognitive maps congruent with salient features of the cognitive maps of influential actors in the social world where they work?[7] Third, what types of cognitive styles characterize planners' cognitive maps? What types of psychological dynamics are associated with planners' cognitive styles or their cognitive maps? A description of planners' cognitive styles would provide material with which to begin to explain how planners come to have certain cognitive maps. Evidence and hypotheses about the psychological dynamics of planners associated with particular cognitive styles would assist in such an explanation.

PLANNERS' VIEWS OF ORGANIZATION AND POLITICS

Planners' Cognitive Maps

Responses of planners to questions in this study provide evidence regarding the first · question asked above: what do planners' cognitive maps show? Planners' statements may be constructed into a representation of a cognitive map of the environment of their work. From this evidence, as well as additional evidence provided by another study discussed below, inferences may be drawn about the dimensions of cognitive style and psychological dynamics associated with a cognitive map. These inferences may assist in understanding why planners see what they see.

Many planners use the term "politics" to refer to decision-making which is based upon bargaining among organized interests. This process is contrasted with decision-making which is based upon rational consideration of—generally, the planner's—evidence. In this sense, "politics" refers to both explicitly political relationships among elected officials and interest groups and a variety of types of "office politics" which are common in bureaucratic organizations. Thus the term "politics" includes normal organizational matters.

Most planners interviewed note that the planning process is affected by something which they call "politics," but the meaning of "politics" and planners' reactions to it vary significantly. On the basis of explicit and implied statements about politics and organization, planners were differentiated into two groups, which may be distinguished by the labels "political" and "intellectual."

The political planners, who constitute a minority of approximately one-third of the sample, accept political negotiation as either legitimately democratic, pragmatically necessary for getting support for decisions, or inescapable. This group includes generally the same planners who, when asked what they regarded as their strengths, described some type of interpersonal, organizational, or political skills, either alone or in combination with analytic or other intellectual skills. They see planning as a process which involves creating agreements among actors with disparate interests, and they believe that as planners they contribute to consensus-building various skills of interpretation, communication, group work, and bargaining. These planners observe that planning decisions entail judgments about social values, and they are relatively comfortable making these value judgments.

The following two statements are representative of this favorable attitude toward politics. The first comment, describing needed changes in the environment of planning, refers to electoral and interest group politics:

> I'm a great believer in this: we need the option for decentralizing decision-making. There have to be systems where interests can protest. There should be a strong executive, but there has to be the option for the legislature to oppose the executive. [Arrangements] shouldn't be so formalized that we're locked into one system . . . The citizen factor is crucial. [It is] the most important role of a human being. The citizen role is the most important role, more than his professional role. Planning is not a substitute for good government.

Another statement refers to working relationships within an organization, in this case a regional council:

> [My greatest strength is] probably in the area of coordination and synthesis and understanding what different people mean—finding some language which both can understand and agree on. In an organization like this, it is like a United Nations. You have all sorts of disciplines inside. On the council you have all sorts of disciplines on the outside. Some of them don't use the same words. Some of them use the same words to mean different things. A lot of the air needs clearing [in order to understand] what is being said, what is meant.

These statements may be understood in two ways. On the one hand, they express positive attitudes toward political activity and day-to-day organizational challenges. In addition, the statements sketch out cognitive maps clearly portraying organizational and political phenomena. The first comment shows an environment in which there are citizens, organized interests, a legislature, and an executive, and the planner contemplates alternative ways of organizing their relationships. The second statement describes an organization in which there are many staff members and many council members speaking different languages, and this planner emphasizes the importance of finding common languages which can organize their concerns into shared understandings and which can organize their interests into joint endeavors.

The following two comments provide similar examples of cognitive maps which depict a number of political actors and which look at ways of organizing relationships among these actors:

> The legislation is important . . . In terms of the legislation and the commitment on the part of Congress, there is a need for it. Also the private sector needs to be involved. We need to build more incentives for private enterprise to be involved.

> If there were less friction between the county executive and the council, better lines of communication between the county executive, state representatives, and national representatives, we would be taken more seriously with our federal programs. We could expand quicker and get results faster. Even if it meant trade-offs between politicians, it wouldn't matter. It would still mean benefits for people.

Again, here is a positive attitude toward organization and politics, a recognition of numerous distinct political actors, and an acknowledgment of the importance of incentives and tradeoffs as a means for organizing action.

In contrast, the intellectual planners, comprising a majority of two-thirds of the sample, differ from these planners considerably. Although they may at some point refer to "politics" in planning, they do not assign it a very clear meaning. Mainly they are clear that they do not like it. "Politics" is a label attached to the behavior or considerations of people who act in variance with what these planners regard as the dictates of rational analysis. "Politics," as vaguely defined as it is, is known as something inimical to planning and something to be eschewed. This group generally includes the planners who, when asked about their strengths, describe themselves as intellectuals who provide rigorous analysis of information and careful synthesis, avoiding any biases. They emphasize that planning should be a rational intellectual process of collecting information about a problem and designing a solution for that problem. These planners resent the intrusion of pressures from elected officials or community organizations into decision-making processes which they believe should be guided by careful weighing of objective information. They regard themselves as competent intellectual problem-solvers, and they believe that they have a reasonable understanding of the types of decisions which would be in the public interest. Even though most planners are sensitive to limitations on their influence in decision-making, the intellectual planners stand out in their complaints about powerlessness.

Several statements, some quoted earlier, represent this antipathy toward politics and organizational concerns:

> The political process . . . gives a whole lot of people an opportunity to participate, but at the same time it results in decisions that are counter to good planning or management decisions. So planning people are faced with having to deal with straw man issues, to accommodate problems that are perceived problems, not real problems. The political issues are based on the pacification of interest groups simply because these groups are vocal. I don't think local officials take heat well. They will work compromises that serve the interests of existing citizens, but in the long run will be shown to be short-sighted. A specific answer is that you ought to build road A from X to Y though people who live there don't want it. There is little way to balance [the interests of a few hundred people who live nearby] against those of the many affected.

> We need a changed attitude or approach in government to allow things to be done in different, newer, better ways. One of the greatest obstacles to the kind of things I would like to do is government agencies. Government itself is set up as an obstacle to private enterprise. The reason [is that] the private sector has gotten away with more than they should . . . for example, the boom in Florida . . . Then the government clamps down, and they go overboard. For example, in areas of rapid development, if there is a tremendous consumer feeling in this county, this state, and in the nation—in the name of consumerism we have all kinds of things springing up which make it hard for things to get done.

Each of these statements explicitly criticizes decisions made on the basis of organized political activity by interested citizens. Each suggests that public decisions should be made on the basis of planners' expertise. One other statement refers to office politics:

> My interest is urban design. But I haven't done too much urban design because I went up in my profession. Because I worked with local governments, I was pushed toward administrative aspects of planning, which I don't like. [I like] architecture and urban design. Landscape architects try to push too many man-made things on architects. I am in favor of natural things.

In this last comment, coupled with a distaste for the personal relationships involved in administration is an expressed dislike generally for "man-made things."

This group believes that power does—and should—come from the cogency of an intellectual analysis. Their statements are noteworthy for the absence of precise references to the bureaucratic organizations or political decision-making processes within which they work. For example, one planner refers simply to "government." They describe troubling difficulty in assessing their work. They say that they do not understand what happens to their work once it enters into bureaucratic decision-making processes. They are not certain who reads their work, what considerations these unknown readers make in looking at their work, and, crucially, why actions which subsequently do take place so often bear little resemblance to their recommendations. To these planners political decision-making is a mystery.

Because intellectual planners expect influence to come from the force of ideas, they have not given much thought to how organizations work. When asked how they would change conditions in order to permit more reasonable planning, they offer responses which express a lack of comprehension of bureaucracy and politics as social phenomena. A few argue that the replacement of specific superiors would transform the planning process; they experience a complex organization as simply the interaction of individual personalities. Some more state that the planning process should be "depoliticized"; they present a complex organization as an abstraction which can be made more or less "political" without any substantial transformation. A large number speak with conviction about the need for planners to have more "power," but they make few concrete strategic recommendations.

The implied cognitive map of intellectual planners is one which scarcely reveals the details of organizations or the actors and relationships of politics. For obvious reasons, then, it is difficult to identify statements which represent this cognitive map. It is primarily the absence of organizational and political images in these planners' statements which provides evidence for a "non-organizational" cognitive map. Yet there is one comment which does depict a world in which many of these planners would feel comfortable:

> The best and the worst things that have happened in the physical environment have happened under despots and patrons. It means that important things have happened in the design aspect of the

physical world when people were in the position to make physical acts of will—the redevelopment of Paris under von Haussman, baroque Rome, Pope Sixtus, Imperial Rome, Greece, all those city planning design achievements, Italian Renaissance, Medicis, Louis of France Versailles. In the Twentieth Century the only reason why in the history of human events we can have a Columbia [new town in Maryland] is that one man [James Rouse, the developer] can put his neck on the line and make it happen. A businessman-merchant. Lots of nice things have happened without imperial power—the Mediterranean hill town, accidental structures, Gothic cathedrals . . . This can't happen again. There has to be control. If people like myself are going to create good environments, we have to have an opportunity to do it. The system has straitjacketed itself, removed itself from the opportunity to create a good environment.

In significant ways this briefly sketched cognitive map bears resemblances to the "lunar street scenes" which Hudson reported finding in the images of convergent thinkers. With the exception of a largely hidden "despot," "patron," or "businessman-merchant," there is no one in this world besides the planner. Although people become despots, patrons, or businessman-merchants only through the exercise of significant power, nowhere is political power visible in this world. There is only the intellectual force of the planner's ideas. Even though the bureaucratic organizations and political coalitions which surround planners actually are densely populated, this cognitive map does not reveal people or organizational structures.

The psychological dynamics shaping such a cognitive map are suggested by the ways in which these planners speak about power. Intellectual planners' limited view of political processes appears to reflect more than a lack of information about these processes. Rather, these planners seem to be deeply ambivalent about the use of power, which is the essence of organizations and politics.

This ambivalence is expressed in statements about two political instruments which could increase planners' power: licensing and strengthening of the professional association. With regard to licensing, a majority of these planners are either ambivalent or negative. While many appreciate the benefits which licensing would bring them, they note that licensing involves an exercise of power. Some planners feel that this exercise is illegitimate because any exercise of power is illegitimate. Others argue that the exercise of power to institute licensing is illegitimate because the intellectual quality of planners' work should be sufficient in itself to bring planners the influence they desire. In effect, they are saying that they would like to be powerful but that they do not want to work for—or with—power.

A similar ambivalence is expressed in statements concerning the American Institute of Planners (or a successor organization) in representing planners' interests. On the one hand, many planners would like a professional association both to provide them with technical assistance and to represent planners' views to others. However, although many planners are disappointed with the AIP on both counts, they offer arguments why the organization should exercise limited power. Many planners reason that, because they themselves are not certain what "planning" is, they should not expect an organization to resolve their doubts for them or to represent them in any way to others. They are saying that they would enjoy benefiting from the work of the organization but do not want to join it because it is not perfect and do not want it to act because they are not perfect. They seem to mean that they would like to have others act powerfully on their behalf but do not want any direct part in organizing power to support these efforts. In addition, they seem to mean that they would like to have others act powerfully on their behalf but believe that they do not merit the support because they are not already powerful.

This ambivalence about power is rationalized in terms of an intellectual individualism: planning is—and perhaps should be—a solitary pursuit. For example, when asked to what degree they are influenced by the expectations of the planning profession in their work, most indicate little influence. They feel uncertain who represents the views or expectations of the "planning profession" other than, perhaps, their office colleagues. When asked specifically about direction from professional planning ethics, a majority say that they are unclear what the ethics of the profession are, and they emphasize that they rely on internal, personal standards in judging work. When asked what they look for as indicators of their effectiveness, a majority of the intellectual planners say that they are not concerned about implementation or recognition from clients but, instead, look primarily for compliments or praise from other planners in their agency. This depiction of planning as an individualistic activity would be more credible, however, if it were not spotted by recurrent expressions of disappointment and resentment about lack of support from and connection with other planners. These planners are concerned that their work involves a responsibility too weighty to carry alone. And yet, as the comments about licensing and the professional organization indicate, these planners are not prepared to offer to share responsibilities with other planners.

Ambivalence about responsibility helps to understand the ambivalence about power, and together they suggest an explanation for the "lunar" quality of these planners' cognitive maps. Referring to power, the intellectual planners say that they would like to be powerful but do not want to be involved in handling power. Speaking of the burdens of individualistic work, they indicate that they would like others to help carry their responsibility but are hesitant to extend themselves to share the responsibility for others' work. The handling of power is, among a number of things, a commitment to sharing responsibility with another. More specifically, it is a commitment to a relationship with another, in which personal fortunes may at least be momentarily merged. This is also the definition of an organization: it is a series of relationships—a place—in which for at least brief periods of time individuals commit themselves to accepting shared responsibility. The intellectual planners want to be powerful without accepting the responsibilities of exercising power. Thus it would appear that this discomfort in accepting the risks of shared responsibility contributes to the "lunar" character of these planners' cognitive maps: other people are indistinct, organizations are only dimly sketched, and "politics" is a patchy fog.

Planners' Cognitive Styles

Some more detailed descriptions of planners' cognitive maps, as well as evidence specifically about dimensions of planners' cognitive styles, may be drawn from a study of planners carried out by Cole (1975). Cole interviewed a sample of 133 planners, most from the Denver area, with regard to their perceptions of their work and with a focus on their cognitive styles. He specifically examined a dimension of cognitive style which may be described as a continuum from cognitive simplicity and concreteness to cognitive complexity and abstractness. With test instruments

Cole characterized planners as relatively concrete in their thinking about the environment or relatively abstract in their thinking.

The meaning of Cole's categories and findings is suggested by associations which have been found between concreteness-abstractness and other dimensions of cognitive style. For example, persons who are more abstract in their thinking have been found to be likely to have characteristics which are related to Hudson's "divergence": (i) a complex cognitive structure with many differentiated categories; (ii) an ability to modify mental set and to be flexible in solving complex and changing problems; (iii) tolerance for ambiguity and inconsistency; (iv) a sensitivity to subtle cues; and (v) a capacity to role play and to think in hypothetical terms. Conversely, persons who think more concretely are likely to have the opposite characteristics, which are related to Hudson's "convergence." More of the meaning of this cognitive style dimension is suggested by other associations with abstract thinking: (vi) independence of social cues related to one's role; (vii) a flexibility with regard to prevailing opinions; (viii) a tolerance for and flexibility in working within low degrees of environmental structure; (ix) an ability to differentiate potential means and ends in problem-solving; and (x) a tendency to reflect before making a judgment and to withhold judgment where information is scarce. The opposite characteristics have been found to be associated with more concrete thinking.[8]

Cole found relatively more planners in his sample to be at the concrete end of the continuum than at the abstract end of the continuum.[9] A comparison of the two groups showed significant differences in perceptions of the political environment of planning. Although most planners say that they experience political pressure in their work and say that they try to work around this pressure, concrete and abstract planners differ in their specific descriptions of the political environment and their responses. One significant difference is that the abstract planners are more likely to state that they feel they have some influence in their work. This finding frames other, subsequent findings by suggesting the hypothesis that differences in cognitive styles contribute to this difference in experienced influence.

Abstract planners describe the planning process in more explicitly political terms than do concrete planners and are more likely to view the political process in favorable terms. Abstract planners are also more likely to work on social problems or to take on advocate planner roles, both commitments likely to increase their direct involvement in political situations. They are more likely to state that interest groups are an asset in finding solutions to problems. They view the participation of interest groups as an important part of the problem-solving process of planning. They actively seek and encourage citizen participation in planning. In contrast, concrete planners see the participation of interest groups as less helpful in planning, and they view interest groups and community organizations as extraneous influences who seek to take from planners control which should belong to them.

Abstract planners are more likely than concrete planners to see themselves as autonomous in the planning environment. Most planners, regardless of cognitive orientation, say that planners should be technical advisors to decision-makers, but planners differ in how they construe that role. Concrete planners say that they prefer to spend their time on analytic thinking, with their specific assignments set by others. When asked what resources they would draw on for influence in a decision-making process, they are particularly likely to emphasize the logic of their research and analysis. When decisions do not go their way, they tend to blame administrators and decision-makers. In contrast, abstract planners are more likely to see themselves as independent intellectuals. They report generating some of their own assignments, and they are more likely to refer to personal values as criteria for evaluating their work. When asked about resources which they use to support their positions, they are particularly likely to mention political relationships with other people in the organization and with elected officials, in addition to the intellectual strength of their analysis. When their positions on issues do not prevail, they are more likely to accept some responsibility.

These findings show a congruence between planners' cognitive styles and their projected cognitive maps. For example, there is the substantial minority of planners who tend to see the world in abstract terms, who mentally organize what they see in many categories, who are flexible in relation to their social role and mental set, who are sensitive to subtle cues, and who have a capacity to think in hypothetical terms. These planners express a positive attitude toward political activity, they see themselves as quasi-political actors, and they describe a planning environment which is well populated: it includes organizational colleagues, elected officials, citizens, interest groups, and political relationships between planners and these other people. In contrast, the majority of planners have a different cognitive style and a different cognitive map. They tend to see the world in concrete terms, tend to be relatively inflexible about their social role and mental set, tend to be insensitive to subtle cues, and tend to have limited capacity to think hypothetically. They are hostile toward politics, they do not see themselves as political actors, and their cognitive maps consist primarily of ideas, rather than people or organizations.

These relationships between cognitive style and cognitive maps may be interpreted in two ways. First, the characteristics of the cognitive maps may be interpreted as products of cognitive style characteristics. These relationships appear relatively straight-forward. For example, a predisposition to see the world in abstract and socially complex terms is likely to produce relatively intricate political maps of the world. In contrast, a predisposition to see the world concretely and simply may produce maps which are simply populated and which consist primarily of fixed intellectual principles.

Second, cognitive maps and associated cognitive styles may both be interpreted as products of psychological dynamics. Here Hudson's work suggests some explanation. People with divergent cognitive styles, similar to the planners whom Cole describes as abstract thinkers, are quick to populate their mental maps, Hudson suggests, because they are relatively comfortable with personal feelings and social relationships. This comfort permits a cognitive style which makes it possible to see political relationships in the environment, just as this comfort supports efforts to affect political relationships. Conversely, people with convergent cognitive styles, similar to the planners whom Cole describes as concrete thinkers, may develop intellectualized and depopulated cognitive maps because of relative discomfort with personal feelings and social relationships. This unease discourages a cognitive style which makes it difficult to see political relationships in the environment, just as the unease inhibits political activities. A relatively concrete and simple cognitive style may provide a psychological defense against anxiety about power and social responsibility.[10]

Interpretation

These two studies of planners help to explain the presence or absence of organizational and political content in planners' cognitive maps in terms of cognitive styles and psychological dynamics. My study distinguishes planners according to whether their cognitive maps view the planning process in intellectual terms or in political terms. The study differentiates planners whose cognitive maps are more sensitive to technical information and less sensitive to political information from planners whose cognitive maps operate in just the opposite way. Cole's study distinguishes planners according to whether their cognitive styles are relatively concrete or relatively abstract. He finds a strong relationship between an abstract way of thinking about the environment and an awareness of and willingness to engage the concerns of political actors in a planning decision-making process. Cole's study suggests that abstract planners tend to feel more influential than concrete planners. His findings point to a similarity between my intellectual planners and his concrete planners and between my political planners and his abstract planners. These similarities help to fill in descriptions of two distinct types of planners who differ in the ways in which they think about the environment, what they "see" in the environment, and how they act in the environment.

Differences in research methodology in the two studies prevent firm conclusions, but inferential evidence supports some tentative conclusions. First, it appears possible to distinguish two groups of planners in terms of the degree to which there is "place" for organizational or political phenomena in their cognitive maps. Both studies suggest that the majority of planners may be categorized in the group with relatively little sensitivity to organizational issues. Second, it appears that identifiable, specifiable differences in cognitive style underlie these differences in the political content of the cognitive maps. Differences in planners' cognitive styles appear to influence their likelihood of attending to the organizational or political context of decision-making. Some of the characteristics of cognitive style which have been found to be associated with either the concrete or abstract end of that cognitive style dimension would appear to be ascribable to planners found to have more intellectual or more political cognitive maps, respectively. Third, my study, as well as Hudson's earlier findings, suggest that some differences in cognitive maps reflect specific underlying psychological dynamics. For example, a concrete, intellectual view of planning may respond to ambivalence about power and social responsibility. Thus there is the possibility that a concrete cognitive style and an intellectual conception of planning serve psychological needs of planners with mixed feelings about the use of power.

ORGANIZATION AND THE PROFESSIONAL SOCIALIZATION OF PLANNERS

Placeless Practice

An examination of planners' cognitive maps bears out earlier impressions that many planners work without a clear conception of the "place" of their work. They seem unfamiliar with bureaucratic organization as a "place," and they seem wary of political organization as a process for establishing a "place." Thus planners speak of the good states of society and the environment which are their goals, and they talk about the mundane problem-solving techniques which they apply from day to day in their work. However, in the cognitive maps of most—the intellectual— planners there is a blank space between the techniques and the goals. As planners' statements indicate, they have difficulty "seeing" how to move from the exercise of their expertise through their techniques to effective changes in the social and physical environment. This blank space, the absence of a link between techniques and goals, makes it difficult for planners either to move effectively toward enacting their broad goals or to understand that difficulty.

What that blank space does not reveal is organizational structure or political process. In general, planners tend to lack an under- standing of the strategic importance of organization as a political means to accomplish a goal. Planners' statements about their expertise suggest that most believe that intelligence directly brings influence and the strategic resources to enact ideas. More specifically, planners tend to lack an understanding of the functions of the bureaucratic organizations within which they work. Few understand that bureaucratic organization has a rationale, whether or not it is one with which planners may agree. Few understand that bureaucratic organizations are governed by incentive systems which influence and constrain the actions of people in roles, even if planners might not regard the incentive systems as fair. Bureaucratic organizations serve certain purposes within a political decision-making process; otherwise, they would disintegrate. Planners tend not to "see" the "place" which bureaucratic organizations occupy in society, and, as a consequence, planners have difficulties acting effectively in them.

Because of these blank spaces in most planners' cognitive maps, planners cannot readily see that working in a bureaucratic setting poses distinct problems calling for specific solutions. Planners tend to lack strategies for working effectively within a bureaucratic and political setting and, more significant yet, ideas about how to reform the organizational setting to make the type of planning which they desire more likely to be effectuated. Planners' statements provide numerous illustrations—by their omissions—of aspects of organization which planners tend not to see. For example, most planners pay little attention to the nature of organizational roles. As a consequence, they have relatively little understanding of the ways in which their own roles in the organizations restrict the range of problems which they may acceptably identify or the types of recommendations which they may offer. Planners tend to be insensitive to conflicts of interest. Consequently, they have relatively little awareness of alternative ways in which any one "problem" may be seen. In addition, they have relatively little understanding of the ways in which alternative definitions of any problem or alternative recommendations differentially favor the interests of various political constituencies. Planners tend not to recognize that the process of implementing any recommendation requires assembling a coalition of bureaucratic and political actors whose cooperation is necessary for recommended actions to take place. Consequently, they have relatively little understanding that they should structure incentives for an implementation coalition into a recommendation for a "problem solution" if that recommendation is to be implemented.

In short, a clear conception of the "place" of planning practice seems to be missing from the cognitive maps of most planners. Although a significant minority appear to see bureaucratic structures and to understand political processes, most planners seem functionally blind to organizational phenomena. These organizational phenomena which most planners do not see are the essence of the planning process. They are salient features of the cognitive maps of influential actors in the social world where planners work.[11] Unable to recognize these elements, planners are not likely to be able to use their expertise with the autonomy, legitimacy, or, even, effectiveness which they expect. Further, so long as planners are ambivalent about involvement in political activity, they will be unlikely to move to establish an area which will be their domain in this world of practice.

The Planner as Entrepreneurial Problem-Solver

Planners provide this general description of their work regardless of the orientation of the planning school which they attended.[12] This consistency suggests two explanations for the insensitivity to organizational phenomena which pervades planners' comments. The first is that their peculiar cognitive maps reflect elements of professional socialization common to most planning schools. Alternatively, it is possible—and likely—that some people who tend to be insensitive to organizational issues select planning as an occupation because it is consistent with their personal tendencies. The conscious and unconscious elements of this choice are explored elsewhere (Baum, 1979a and 1979b). The discussion here focuses on the ways in which the professional socialization of planners may minimize the likelihood that planners will be aware of how organizations function. By turning from an identification of what may be missing from planners' cognitive maps to a description of what is present, one may begin to understand why planners come to claim a personal expertise which they do not acquire the autonomy to exercise. Here one may find a model of "placeless practice."

One key to planners' professional socialization is the contrast which planners frequently draw between the "real world planning" which they actually do and what they had been taught in planning school. What differs most between what planners believe they were taught and what they do in practice concerns their role. The differences in role involve what are considered realistic professional goals and what are regarded as useful planning techniques. Most of the planners were prepared in planning school for the role of entrepreneurial problem-solver. They were led to believe that they could work as free-lance intellectuals who would be employed to provide rational solutions to clients' problems.

Three crucial assumptions are implicit in this model of the planner's role. The first is that "the problem" in planning is the analytic or technical problem on which the planner works. Consistently, academic instruction on the "planning process" focuses on steps of systematic intellectual analysis, guided by norms of rationality. The organizational context in which intellectual analysis is solicited or utilized is usually ignored or downplayed. However, in reality the technical problem with which the planner is concerned may represent one component of a complex political problem. Further, it is often the case that politicians request technical work primarily to justify a decision already made on the basis of political criteria.[13]

These external circumstances point to the second assumption concerning the planner's role. This is the assumption that, in fact, the planner "owns" the problem on which he or she works. The model of the planner as a "problem-solver" implies that someone has handed the planner a problem and asked him or her for "the solution," which will be directly implemented. Commonly, academic instruction on the "planning process" concludes with the formulation of a recommendation, with little or no consideration for whether or how the recommendation may be implemented. In reality, planners are asked for recommendations on part of problems for others who will consider the recommendation in making decisions.

The third assumption about the role of the planner, encompassing the first two, portrays the planner as an entrepreneur, an independent professional, similar to an attorney. Although students may understand that planners work in agencies, it is not always made clear to them how the planner's work is selected in the agencies. The City Beautiful and progressive reform values passed on in planning schools imply that planners will be expected to identify and work on society's physically or socially most pressing problems. Planners' training suggests that they are well qualified to identify these problems and to prescribe strategies for solving them. They need only wait to be employed by clients who will select them for their unique intellectual, ethical, and aesthetic insights in both defining and solving problems. In reality, for the majority of planners employed in public bureaucracies final authority to set the planner's work agenda—whether it be specific or general—rests with a planning director, who must respond to elected officials and political leaders.

The reality of work for most planners is that they are neither entrepreneurs nor problem-solvers. They are aides to others who are problem-solvers. They do not have much authority to decide which problems they will work on. Elected officials, for example, may require additional information in order to make a decision, and they ask the advice of planners in making the decision. But they do not "give" the problem to the planners; they "lend" part of it and demand it back. Usually they ask planners to work on the technical components of a larger political problem. Finally, they do not ask planners to solve the problem. They ask the planners to organize information in such a way as to formulate alternative meanings of the problem to interested actors and to pose alternative means of resolving the problem. The elected officials ask the planners to formulate the problem meaningfully for them, the officials, to solve. In short, most planners serve as bureaucratically employed advisors to political decision-makers.[14]

Yet many of the planners interviewed did not anticipate these conditions when they entered the work of planning. A major reason appears to be the pervasive but misleading use of the language of "problem-solving" in describing this work. Almost every academic discussion of the "planning process" lauds its utility as a means of solving problems. Planners' presentations of their cognitive maps suggest that their academic planning education provides them with two things. The first is a set of goals, and the second is a repertoire of techniques. One recent book on planning theory explains to planners that goals should properly be formulated as solutions for problems: "Problem = Goal + Impediment to the Goal" (Faludi, 1973, p. 82). And, while the title of another recent book, *The Art of Problem Solving* (Ackoff, 1978), suggests that solving problems is not necessarily a science, its final chapter, "On

Keeping Problems Solved," emphasizes that planners are meant to solve problems. Planners become accustomed to this language and the evident expectations which it raises.

Here planners' second acquisition, techniques, becomes important. In planners' cognitive maps there is nothing between their techniques and their goals (which are solutions to problems). Implicitly planners are taught that sufficient exercise of their techniques will enable them to solve problems. There is no place in their maps for the social organizations which make problems complex or which require political methods in addition to analytic techniques for progress to be made toward goals. The tacit immediacy in this view of action receives strong support from a broader Western culture in which techniques are conventionally expected to hold out quasi-magical solutions for problems.[15]

The work of planners is described more accurately as problem-formulation than as problem-solving. Decision-makers expect planners to identify the multiple meanings of problematic situations, so that the complexities of "the problem" may be set out. Decision-makers expect planners to pose alternative courses for responding to alternative views of "the problem," so that the real intricacy of the situation may be at least a little better understood. Then decision-makers may begin to organize some strategy of response. Yet planners interviewed had difficulty understanding a distinction between problem-formulation and problem-solving because the basic language which they had acquired and used to refer to their work was the language of problem-solving, learned, presumably, in their professional socialization.[16] They had been socialized not to see the role which they would be expected to play and what their client would want from them. In this world-view there is no place for organization.

CONCLUSIONS: ORGANIZATION, POWER, AND RESPONSIBILITY

The absence of organizational phenomena in planners' cognitive maps helps to understand many themes in planners' comments, including their weak collective professional consciousness and their ambivalence about power. The characteristics of planners' professional consciousness directly mirror the characteristics of planners' cognitive maps. In their professional consciousness, most planners have difficulty locating the activities of "planners" in a well-defined place, or domain, of practice. In their cognitive maps, most planners have difficulty locating their individual work in the specific context of an organizational structure. Instead, many engage in some kind of "placeless practice." Further, in their professional consciousness, most planners are reluctant to engage in strategic organizational activities which could publicly delineate a common domain of "planning" practice. In discussing their cognitive maps, many planners express strong ambivalence about engaging in organization as political—and powerful—action to secure autonomy for their work. Thus a diffuse professional consciousness reflects an organization-less cognitive map.

In order to understand why organizational phenomena are scarce in planners' cognitive maps, it is necessary to look more closely at a recurrent theme in planners' statements: ambivalence about power. They say that they want to be powerful, but they offer limited support to organized political activities which could serve their interests. They explain that the organized activities would involve an exercise of political power, about the legitimacy of which they have serious questions. Consequently, ambivalent about the exercise of power, they have difficulty acting collectively to establish privately accepted or publicly recognized boundaries for the domain of their practice. A weak professional consciousness appears almost inevitable.

Still, a deeper psychological examination of ambivalence about power suggests further reasons both why planners have difficulties organizing for power and why they feel only a weak consciousness of shared interests with other planners. Psychologists who have studied the personal experience of power have observed that the exercise of power involves the wielder of power in intimate relationships with both allies and the intended objects of power (May, 1972; McClelland, 1975; and Sennett, 1980). Of the relationship with an opponent, May (1972) writes:

> In fighting there is a vivid intimacy, a closeness that partakes of both hate and love, an intimacy held off by hatred but an intimacy nevertheless, and it can blossom into affection or love (p. 151).

People may be ambivalent about initiating the exercise of power for several reasons. For example, they may fear the risks of the intimate power relationship. Although defeat may not mean personal destruction, it may require an acceptance of intimacy with a controlling other party. Sennett (1980) writes about ambivalent feelings which people have about authority relationships:

> In part it is a fear of the authorities as seducers. In part it is a fear of the act of seduction, of liberty yielding to security (p. 15).

In addition, the act of initiating an exercise of power, whatever the outcome, entails an acceptance of responsibility for the welfare of both one's allies and one's opponents. This acceptance of responsibility may feel burdensome to people who feel that the exercise of power would require of them an emotional overextension. Thus some may fear to exercise power because of the risks of victory: continuing responsibility for victorious allies and new responsibility for defeated opponents. Accordingly, as earlier discussion has suggested, planners' ambivalence about power may be interpreted as an expression of an ambivalence about accepting the risks of responsibility for others. This ambivalence about responsibility would also help to explain the weakness of planners' feelings and expressions of collective professional consciousness.

Reluctance to risk responsibility for others thus contributes to powerlessness. Together, reluctance to take responsibility for others and powerlessness seriously constrain planners' actions. A hesitation toward accepting broad social responsibility and feelings of powerlessness contribute to a tendency to define relevant planning problems narrowly. Earlier discussions noted that planners tend to move from broad statements of goals to constrained interpretations of their expertise and their responsibilities in the planning process. This narrow definition of planning problems may be both emotionally and intellectually reassuring. For planners who are reluctant to take social responsibility narrow problems do not require a risky emotional investment, and for planners who feel relatively powerless narrow problems are, nevertheless, manageable. The most significant consequence of this narrow work focus is that planners become distracted from the problems of governance.

Problems of governance inherently require for their solution a willingness to risk broad social responsibility. They demand a commitment to far-ranging definitions of planning problems. Finally, they call for a preparedness to act in powerful ways. The cognitive maps of many planners, shaped by the psychological ambivalences just described, make it difficult for these planners either to see or to act effectively on the governance problems which concern many citizens.

NOTES

1. One early presentation of this theme was by Mannheim (1940). Recent writers who have emphasized the view that complexity makes bureaucratically structured planning ineffective include Biller (1973), Emery and Trist (1973), Friedmann (1973), Michael (1973), and Vickers (1970). Schön (1967 and 1973) has argued strongly that the organization of bureaucracy is inimical to the organization and development of knowledge. His work with Argyris (Argyris and Schön, 1978) provides examples of the ways in which bureaucratic norms stifle creative problem-solving in organizations.

2. Whether these organizational charts accurately map relationships and processes of decision-making is less important here than that they show a number of organizational actors and indicate that they have some relationships.

3. Thompson (1967) and Buckley (1967) are two organization theorists who argue strongly that a distinction between organizational structures and process is artificial. The structure of an organization at any moment reflects the temporary constellation of continually moving actors at one point in time. At the same time, the movements of actors—into, out of, or within organizations—reflects their perceptions of the value of the present structure for them. Organizations differ in the degree to which the structure fluctuates over time, though in all cases the "structure" reflects one "still picture" from a long, ongoing "motion picture" process. This relationship between structure and process should be recognized. However, for purposes of the discussion of planners' relations to "place," a distinction between structure and process is useful.

4. This view of organizations as a process of interaction among "loosely coupled" actors is emphasized by Weick (1979). Significantly, his book is entitled *The Social Psychology of Organizing*, and his emphasis is distinguished from that of an earlier book by Katz and Kahn, entitled *The Social Psychology of Organizations* (1966). That book looks more closely at relations among actors once they have come together at some point in time.

5. The reader is referred to Berger and Luckmann's book for an excellent contribution to the sociology of knowledge. The perspective of this study of planners reflects the perspective of that book.

6. In this study of city planners it is interesting to note one other observation by Hudson about people with a convergent cognitive style:

> Its chief virtue is that the person concerned is able to *zone* his preoccupations, coping with them one by one, rather than having to handle them simultaneously. He can think unhindered by emotional disruption; and then turn to his emotional life, and deal with as much of that as he sees fit (1966, p. 86, emphasis added).

Although this observation cannot be taken as a definitive characterization of all city planners who have interests in zoning, the comment does suggest that some planners may enter work in zoning and derive satisfaction from it for emotional, as well as any "rational," reasons.

7. This second question may be phrased less elegantly as an inquiry whether planners see "the real world" as it actually is. The more elaborate phrasing is preferred in order to emphasize that the rules and regularities of "the real world" reflect enactments of cognitive maps by the relatively more powerful members of society.

8. This brief summary of accumulated research findings is drawn from reviews by Cole (1975) and Goldstein and Blackman (1978). Cole and Hudson use different language in describing cognitive style. Cole does not refer to Hudson's earlier work. Nevertheless, the links between Hudson's categories and Cole's categories suggested in the text are drawn because of evident overlaps in the focuses of the two writers' concerns.

9. Of the 63 percent of the sample who could clearly be placed near either end of the concrete-abstract continuum, 55 percent were basically concrete in their thinking, and 45 percent were basically abstract in their thinking.

10. One alternative interpretation of Cole's findings may be rejected. Although abstract planners in his sample tended to be top-level staff planners and concrete planners tended to be top-level administrators, the association between cognitive style and role is not sufficiently strong to warrant an interpretation of the findings simply in terms of different role expectations or constraints. Indeed, one might have expected tendencies in the opposite directions of those found: namely, that administrators would be more likely to be politically oriented and active, while staff planners would be more likely to be averse to politics and constrained.

11. In the less elegant language used earlier, these are the salient features of "the real world" in which planning is done.

12. Each planner was asked to suggest a label which would describe the orientation of the planning program which he or she attended. Fourteen mentioned "physical planning"; twelve either said "general planning" or offered a general characterization of their program; five referred to "economic planning"; and ten either mentioned "social planning" or indicated that they had studied in a "social" field such as social work or public administration. Other characterizations of programs were scattered

among a number of categories. An analysis of planners' responses to the interview questions showed no statistically significant relationship between any pattern of responses and planners' stated descriptions of the planning program in which they had studied.

13. For case studies and discussion of the ways in which decision-makers makers may employ planners in problem-solving, see Benveniste (1977) and Meltsner (1976).

14. Two qualifications to this description are necessary. The first is that the location of any particular agency planner along the continuum from entrepreneurial problem-solver to bureaucratic advisor will be affected by the planners' political skills. Both Benveniste (1977) and Meltsner (1976) describe the variation in planners' roles in this respect. A second qualification concerns private consultants. In good economic times and in larger firms consultants may take on a role resembling the entrepreneurial problem-solver. Otherwise, the desires of the paying client substitute in the private sector for the desires of politicians in the public sector.

15. For a discussion of techniques in Western culture, see Ellul (1964).

16. John Forester has been helpful in clarifying the role of planners and their use of language. He has been especially concerned about this distinction between problem-solving and problem-formulation. Two papers in which he discusses these issues are "Do Planners and Policy Analysts Know What our Problems Mean?" (1977) and *The Planning Analyst's Questioning: Toward a Communicative Theory of Design* (1978).

Hummel (1977) has identified a second way in which planners' use of the language of "problem-solving" without a recognition of the organizational context of planning creates a problem. He suggests that there is a conflict between the principles of conventional bureaucratic language and the creative requirements of either problem-solving or problem-formulation. Bureaucratic language, he observes, is concerned with describing standard operating procedures. Directives take the form of "if X occurs, then do Y." This is a language of analogy, not a causal language. It is inherently inimical to creative tasks of thinking about problems:

> The "language" through which bureaucracy speaks to us is not designed for problem solving; it is designed for passing on solutions in as precise and efficient a manner as possible (Hummel, 1982, p. 172).

Thus if planners do not recognize the special structures and language of the bureaucratic organizational context in which they attempt to carry out either problem-solving or problem-formulation, while continuing to speak of "problem-solving," they may unwittingly adopt the forms of a language which further hinders their efforts to be useful in the solution of social problems.

REFERENCES

Ackoff, Russell L. *The Art of Problem Solving*. New York: John Wiley and Sons, 1978.

Argyris, Chris and Donald A. Schön. *Organizational Learning*. Reading: Addison-Wesley, 1978.

Axelrod, Robert, ed. *Structures of Decision: The Cognitive Maps of Political Elites*. Princeton: Princeton University Press, 1976.

Baum, Howell S. "Policy Analysis: An Intellectual Attitude and a Cognitive Style." Paper presented at conference on The Role of Policy Analysis in the Education of Planners, Massachusetts Institute of Technology, Cambridge, Massachusetts, 1979. (a)

Baum, Howell S. "Using Holland's Typology to Assess the Personalities and Origins of Urban Planners." Unpublished manuscript, University of Maryland, 1979. (b)

Benveniste, Guy. *The Politics of Expertise*, second edition. San Francisco: Boyd and Fraser, 1977.

Berger, Peter L., and Thomas Luckmann. *The Social Construction of Reality*. Garden City: Anchor Books, 1967.

Biller, Robert. "Converting Knowledge into Action: Toward a Postindustrial Society." In *Tomorrow's Organizations*, ed. Jong S. Jun and William B. Storm. Glenview: Scott, Foresman, and Company, 1973.

Buckley, Walter. *Sociology and Modern Systems Theory*. Englewood Cliffs: Prentice-Hall, 1967.

Cole, David Bras. *The Role of Psychological Belief Systems in Urban Planning*. Doctoral dissertation, University of Colorado, 1975.

Ellul, Jacques. *The Technological Society*. New York: Vintage, 1964.

Emery, F.E., and E.L. Trist. *Towards a Social Ecology*. London and New York: Plenum Press, 1973.

Faludi, Andreas. *Planning Theory*. Oxford: Pergamon Press, 1973.

Forester, John F. "Do Planners and Policy Analysts Know What Our Problems Mean?" Unpublished manuscript, Cornell University, 1977.

Forester, John F. *The Planning Analyst's Questioning: Toward a Communicative Theory of Design*. Working Papers in Planning, Number 9, Department of City and Regional Planning, Cornell University, Ithaca, 1978.

Friedman, John. *Retracking America*. Garden City: Anchor Press, 1973.

Goldstein, Kenneth M., and Sheldon Blackman. *Cognitive Style*. New York: John Wiley and Sons, 1978.

Holland, John L. *The Psychology of Vocational Choice: A Theory of Personality Types and Model Environments*. Waltham: Blaisdell, 1966.

Holland, John L. *Making Vocational Choices: A Theory of Careers*. Englewood Cliffs: Prentice-Hall, 1973.

Holland, John L. *Manual for the Vocational Preference Inventory*, revised edition. Palo Alto: Consulting Psychologists Press, 1978.

Hudson, Liam. *Contrary Imaginations*. New York: Schocken, 1966.

Hummel, Ralph P. *The Bureaucratic Experience*, second edition. New York: St. Martin's Press, 1982.

Katz, Daniel, and Robert L. Kahn. *The Social Psychology of Organizations*. New York: John Wiley and Sons, 1966.

Mannheim, Karl. *Man and Society in an Age of Reconstruction*. New

York: Harcourt, Brace and World, 1940.

May, Rollo. *Power and Innocence*. New York: Dell, 1972.

McClelland, David C. *Power: The Inner Experience*. New York: Irvington Publishers, 1975.

Meltsner, Arnold J. *Policy Analysts in the Bureaucracy*. Berkeley: University of California Press, 1976.

Michael, Donald N. *On Learning to Plan—and Planning to Learn*. San Francisco: Jossey-Bass, 1973.

Neisser, Ulric. *Cognition and Reality*. San Francisco: W.H. Freeman and Company, 1976.

Schön, Donald. *Technology and Change*. New York: Dell, 1967.

Schön, Donald. *Beyond the Stable State*. New York: W.W. Norton and Company, 1973.

Sennett, Richard. *Authority*. New York: Alfred A. Knopf, 1980.

Thompson, James D. *Organizations in Action*. New York: McGraw-Hill, 1967.

Tolman, Edward Chase. "Cognitive Maps in Rats and Men," *Psychological Review*, 55 (1948), pp. 189-208.

Vickers, Geoffrey. *Freedom in a Rocking Boat*. Baltimore: Penguin Books, 1970.

Weick, Karl E. *The Social Psychology of Organizing*, second edition. Reading: Addison-Wesley, 1979.

PART THREE

Conclusions and Implications

7

THE PRESENT LIKELIHOOD OF PLANNERS' ACQUIRING PROFESSIONAL STATUS

What do planners' self-perceptions mean for the likelihood that planners will acquire professional status? This chapter examines the findings of the study in terms of the degree to which planners satisfy the prevailing requirements of professional status. Because autonomy is an anachronistic defining characteristic of professional status, the analysis will focus on the likelihood of planners' acquiring a special legitimacy, or authority, to practice in the area to which they lay claim.

AUTONOMY: IMPLICATIONS FOR LEGITIMACY

Although legitimacy without autonomy becomes a new defining characteristic of a profession, planners' perceptions of their autonomy are important for two reasons. First, planners' aspirations indicate whether they strive for the type of autonomy traditionally accorded professions or whether they might accept a different view of the relationship between practitioners and clients. Second, the degree to which planners now practice with autonomy provides an indication of the public respect for and prestige of planners and has implications for the likelihood that planners will practice their expertise with a special legitimacy.

Limitations on Autonomy

The pervasive theme in the planners' discussions of their autonomy is that they enjoy little of it. They complained repeatedly about their powerlessness. These complaints express planners' aspirations: they felt that they have little power, and they believed that greater autonomy is necessary for them to be effective. They wanted greater autonomy in defining the problems on which they work and in setting the solutions for these problems. They wanted their recommendations to be implemented without discussion or negotiation.

There was little recognition in the discussions of power that there may be tension between autonomy and either effectiveness or legitimacy. The crux of the argument for greater autonomy is that liberation from the nonrational constraints of organizations and political processes is essential for planners to be able to identify and recommend rational solutions to problems. Only a minority of planners in the public sector recognized a value in citizen participation in planning, either for intellectual content or for political support. Planners in the private sector noted the importance of client participation in decision-making for client satisfaction, but many consultants complained about their clients' whims. The model to which most planners aspired is that of autonomous practitioner—the entrepreneurial problem-solver.

Planners' aspirations to autonomy may be self-defeating; legitimacy to practice planning may be accorded only to practitioners who are prepared to work with citizens and make themselves publicly accountable. Nevertheless, an examination of the reasons for planners' limited autonomy helps provide an indication of the public evaluation of planners' efforts.

The planners interviewed described four sources of limitation on their autonomy.

The Complexity of the Social World. Planners observed that the problems on which they work are complex and difficult to solve. Some planners asserted that, given sufficient time and support, they could find solutions to any of these problems. Many others were less sanguine. The constraints posed by this condition are not matters of policy: they are not limits to planners' autonomy enacted by citizens. Simply, they are part of the social world in which citizens and planners live and work. This complexity and the uncertainty which accompanies it are the primary arguments for insisting that planners collaborate with affected parties in defining and solving problems. Crucially, these conditions plead against autonomy for planners as an obstacle to their effectiveness.

Constraints of Bureaucratic Work. Planners reported that bureaucratic norms of hierarchical accountability directly limit their autonomy within the organizations in which they are employed. A staff member in a public planning agency may do extensive analysis of a problem and develop an elaborate justification for a recommendation, only to have the work modified by administrators to meet criteria of political acceptability—or even rejected. This limitation does reflect public policy. Citizens have never established planners as an independent arm of government. In the public arena they have been employed as advisors to members of the executive and, more recently, the legislative branches of government. Planners acquire legitimacy as advice-givers by working with elected officials who have been authorized by voters to make decisions on their behalf (Gilbert and Specht, 1974; Rein, 1969). Planners' subordination to the officials who employ them provides them with continuing legitimacy to render advice.

Some planners have acquired legitimate autonomous influence with public constituencies (Benveniste, 1977; Caro, 1975). These planners have combined a demonstrated expertise in solving public problems with organized support of citizen groups independent from the planners' ostensible employers. However, these planners are exceptional because of a second, indirect constraint of bureaucratic work, which affects planners' autonomy by limiting their ability to demonstrate problem-solving expertise. The division of labor in bureaucratic agencies fragments both intellectual and political responsibility for problem-solving. Several planners may each work on a part of a larger problem. In turn, the planners together may have responsibility for only relatively technical components of the larger, political problem. This division of labor tends to give individual planners narrow tasks, insufficiently important or visible for members of the public to recognize them as a basis for giving planners autonomous influence in decision-making.

Unlike the first constraint of bureaucratic work, this indirect constraint on planners' autonomy is in no obvious way a deliberate product of public policy. The bureaucratic division of labor reflects officials' ideas about reasonable ways to organize and control the work of formulating and solving problems. This specific division of labor may be self-defeating for officials, insofar as it may fragment intellectual responsibility without providing for significant coordination, not only among planners, but also including elected officials and affected citizens.[1] Nevertheless, the complexity of and uncertainty surrounding social problems require some division of intellectual labor, and effective problem-solving would lie in the direction of public accountability of planners in a way that would limit the autonomy of individual planners.

Citizens' Constraints on Planners. The planners complained about a number of actions deliberately taken or tacitly endorsed by citizens to constrain the influence of experts like planners. Most generally, planners complained about the political process. Decisions are made through a convoluted process of bargaining, in which many apparently peripheral interests are linked to the planning issues at stake and principles of rationality are jettisoned for considerations of political expediency. Not only is this process one whose rules are difficult for most planners to understand, but also most planners are prohibited or discouraged from entering the process.

A more specific complaint of planners was that this political process has not given them the types of support which they need in order to do good planning, regardless of their role in decision-making. Most tangibly, planners felt that they lack economic resources. Many planners believed that planning department budgets are insufficient to pay staff members to spend time enough to develop thoughtful solutions for problems. In addition, many planners felt that low levels of funding for public programs which planners recommend using in solving problems represent, in part, a rejection of the intention of planning. A less tangible type of support which planners felt that they are denied is political. Planners believed that elected officials give little value to planners' work. Many planners felt that elected officials see deference to planners as a surrender of the officials' prerogatives and would never consider proposals which contravened their perceived political interests. Other planners contended that officials would accord them greater support if the benefits of planning were better understood. Accordingly, the third, least tangible type of support which planners felt lacking is intellectual. Many planners were convinced that neither members of the public nor their elected representatives appreciate the potential benefits of planning for decision-making.

Planners' most specific complaint about the constraints of the political process is the numerous laws and regulations which specify in advance how planners shall work and what they may recommend.

This group of constraints represents the wishes of citizens to limit the autonomy of planners vis-à-vis elected officials. Citizens want planners' work, whatever its benefits, to serve public interests as these interests may be interpreted by elected representatives. In order for planners to be effective and influential in the political decision-making process, they must make themselves accountable to members of the public, at least through their representatives.

Planners' Self-Constraint. There is one final type of limitation on planners' autonomy, about which the planners did not complain: their own insensitivity to organizational issues and their ambivalence toward the exercise of power. Paradoxically, this is the one constraint which planners can control. Yet it is their lack of awareness of this limitation which gives it such strength. Consciously or unconsciously, they limit their influence by misperceiving the environment of their work and by restraining themselves from attempting to act powerfully in the environment. In the process, they also limit their effectiveness in solving problems. A better understanding of organizational processes in planning would improve planners' effectiveness. In addition, such an understanding would make planners more sensitive to citizens' desires to have planners accountable to them. Planners would see that citizens are not prepared to grant legitimacy to planners who seek autonomy without accountability.

Implications: Limited Legitimacy

To assess the constraints on autonomy to which planners refer, it is helpful to turn to the planning theory literature. The traditional model for planning is comprehensive rationality. Given a problem, a planner should collect a great deal of information about the problem, identify a large number of alternative possible solutions, and systematically measure each alternative against explicit criteria in order to identify a single optimal solution. Various critics of this model recommend different substitutes but agree on its shortcomings (Etzioni, 1968; Lindblom, 1959). The critiques hold that the comprehensive rational model of planning assumes an intellectual and political autonomy which planners do not have. The critiques suggest that, in the absence of such autonomy, planners who want to be in any way effective must be sensitive to the organizational and political settings in which they work and in which decisions are made.

Interestingly, the first three constraints cited by planners constitute the basis of this critique of planners' pretensions to purely rational intellectual problem-solving. First, the world in which planning problems arise is too complex to permit comprehensive analysis. Second, the bureaucratic role in which planners work provides limited resources for analysis and binds planners to presenting analyses in relatively brief periods of time. These constraints prevent exhaustive or extensive analysis. Instead, the critiques suggest, planners should consider making limited analyses of those features of problems which are most significant for the actors who will influence decision-making. Third, the political decision-making process constrains the acceptability of certain proposals. Hence, the critiques suggest, planners concerned about having their proposals accepted should not try to examine a plethora of possible alternatives in search of a uniquely optimal solution. Instead, they should survey a small number of alternatives that combine the criteria of optimality and feasibility for the actors involved in decision-making.

This is a familiar debate in planning. Yet the planners interviewed displayed a paradoxical attitude toward the arguments. On the one hand, in their complaints they identified each of the constraints on their autonomy. On the other hand, either explicitly or implicitly, most continued to espouse the comprehensive rational model of planning. After identifying constraints on their autonomy, they neither reconceptualized their role nor considered how to overcome the constraints; rather, they denied the consequences of the constraints. They would strive still more assiduously to play the role of autonomous rational intellectual problem-solver. Here the fourth constraint on planners' autonomy, the constraint which they did not cite, is significant: since planners have difficulty seeing the organizational environment of their work clearly and have difficulty acting in it with power, they can continue to overlook constraints on their autonomy and to strive for autonomy. At the same time, because they have problems making use of the power accessible to them, they would have difficulty modifying present constraints.

The legitimacy of professional status is likely to be accorded planners to the degree that they are willing to make themselves publicly accountable for their work. Planners should be willing to sacrifice pretensions of autonomy to achieve effectiveness in their chosen domain. They have limited autonomy. They recognize the constraints on their autonomy. And yet they continue to act as if autonomy is both attainable and consistent with effectiveness. This private perception and the public impression it makes are likely to limit the legitimacy accorded planners in their problem-solving work.

EFFECTIVENESS: A BASIS FOR LEGITIMACY

Even if planners were willing to work within constraints, they must be able to do effective work. Legitimacy to practice in defined domains will be granted to workers who can demonstrate their effectiveness in solving problems regarded as important by members of the public. Because public assessment of effectiveness in problem-solving is a matter of perception, an examination of planners' own perceptions of their effectiveness is useful here. Planners' perceptions, communicated through work with elected officials, clients, and constituents, affect public perceptions of planners' effectiveness. At the same time, planners' perceptions reflect public assessments of planners' effectiveness.

The Ambiguous Nature of Effectiveness in Planning

One of the few efforts to conceptualize "effectiveness" in planning practice (Kaufman, 1976) identifies three elements which should be incorporated into a definition of effective planning: first, "an achievement element—the ability to induce, modify, or prevent an action; to achieve decision-making impact"; second, "a normative element—actions or effects that are socially beneficial"; and, third, "a constraints element—some conception of what a planning agency can realistically be expected to achieve" (p. 8). This conceptualization focuses on planners' ability to affect the environment in a way that will benefit their clients or constituents and recognizes that any standards for evaluating these efforts should take into account limitations on planners' influence. Evaluation of planners' efforts would require three types of information: which outcomes the planners attempted to achieve, which outcomes they actually accomplished, and what constraints they worked under.[2]

To make this conceptual framework useful in assessing planners' effectiveness it is necessary to characterize clearly the types of effects on clients or constituents which could appropriately be considered possible outcomes of planners' efforts. Planners' work involves problems of governance. As a collective enterprise, then, "planning" has both substantive and procedural concerns.[3] Substantively, planning is an effort to solve problems in fields such as housing, health care, and transportation. However, it is difficult to find solutions for these substantive problems without at least implicitly confronting and designing some solutions for procedural problems. Groups disagree about solutions to problems, they disagree about how to define problems to begin with, and, crucially, they disagree about what rules to follow in resolving these disagreements. Thus the challenge of planning is not simply to solve substantive problems in ways which contribute to clients' needs. The challenge is also to help define and regulate relationships among groups with conflicting interests and world-views and to help establish constitutional decision-making procedures. The outcomes of effective governance efforts would be both substantive programs and, underlying them, the establishment of new, consensually accepted procedures for creating programs.

The planners interviewed described their intended outcomes in terms of broad goals for change in the social and physical environments. With rare exceptions, their goals referred to substantive problems, rather than procedural problems. Consistently, planners spoke of efforts to find solutions to problems in such areas as housing, transportation, and health care. Few suggested that conventional planning and decision-making procedures themselves might preclude the solution of substantive problems or in any way aggravate these problems. Thus most planners were prepared to be measured against high-level goals, but only of a substantive nature.

However, in describing the actual outcomes of their efforts, many planners were modest. They gave relatively little attention to their initial, high-level goals. Unpretentiously, they were less concerned with fashioning their short-term work products into a strategy to meet their long-term goals than they were with simply having the products in some way used. Utilization of work, *per se*, becomes an acceptable outcome. More significantly, many planners did not even concentrate on this utilization of their work. Instead, they turned to internal standards to evaluate the outcomes of their efforts. Many derived satisfaction from engaging in an intellectually stimulating project, whatever its ultimate fate. Public agency staff members in particular redefined their intended outcome to be simple praise or compliments from agency colleagues, regardless of the quality of the effort expended or its effects.

It is evident that many planners redefined the goals which they aim for in day-to-day work. They tended to abandon the espoused high-level outcomes for smaller accomplishments. These redefinitions bring their expectations into line with what they see as the actual outcomes of their efforts. Many planners felt that the most common and most predictable outcomes of their efforts are intellectual satisfaction and colleagues' support. Measured against the initial high-level goals—at least without any consideration of external constraints—these outcomes are disappointing. Measured against the redefined goals, these outcomes, as well as the goals, are not important to many people other than planners. Interestingly, in the process of redefining goals these planners have moved, at least tacitly, from a concern with substantive problems to a concern with procedural problems—specifically, in what ways or places planners may have some control over the planning process. Yet, even in these terms, planners did not express clearly articulated procedural goals, and their accomplishments are either scant or inconsequential.

Constraints on Planners and Their Professional Consciousness

In order to evaluate the planners' gloomy assessments of their effectiveness, it is necessary to examine the third component of an effectiveness measure: constraints on planners' efforts. Most of the constraints described above are considered legitimate by a majority of citizens. Therefore, these constraints must be taken into account in evaluating planners' effectiveness. The following discussion examines the ways in which the characteristics of planners' work roles both limit planners' accomplishments and make it difficult for planners to present a clear assessment of their effectiveness to the public.

Ambiguity of Advice-Giving Roles. The institutionalization of planning functions has been a gradual historical development (Kaufman, 1974). Today the great majority of planners work as employees in public bureaucracies.[4] Planners' roles as advice-givers in bureaucratic organizations are inherently ambiguous and subject to conflicting expectations. Several characteristics of the advisor role significantly affect planners' control over their work.

First, as advisors, they are the full-time employees of the client. Where they are not protected by civil service regulations, they work at the pleasure of elected officials. Consequently, planners are subject to changing perceptions of priority problems, changing views of acceptable solutions to problems, and, as elections take place, changing styles and patterns of communication with their clients.

Second, planners are generally asked to render advice on problems but are expected to leave the actual choice of a solution to the elected officials who are their direct or indirect clients. However, officials differ in their reliance on planners' recommendations in making final choices. These differences reflect variations in officials' leadership styles and in planners' abilities to negotiate for themselves positions of influence with their clients.

Third, "the problem" which is given to the planners is usually only some primarily technical component of a larger political problem with which the official is concerned. However, the degree to which the planner is confined to rendering technical advice depends on the relationship which he or she negotiates with the client. Significantly, the official—or his or her administrative subordinate—may not always directly explain to the planner the relationship between "the problem" on which the planner is asked to work and the actual problem which concerns the official. Thus, the planner's ability to help solve a client's problem depends not simply on technical competence, but also on political acumen.

For these reasons, not only do planners have limited control in defining expected outcomes of their efforts, but, in addition, their clients' expectations—and the constraints which they impose—fluctuate ambiguously over time. Consequently, it is difficult for either planners or their clients to identify a single advice-giving role with a well-defined expected outcome and definite constraints, in the context of which planners' effectiveness may be assessed

The bureaucratic role also hinders planners' development of a clear assessment of their effectiveness in an indirect way. An incongruity between planners' ideal role model—in which the outcomes which they originally expected are attainable—and the actual role which most planners play—in which these outcomes appear unattainable—contributes to difficulties in describing the central components of planners' work and, thus, evaluating planners' effectiveness at this work. The tacit role model which most planners learn in their formal training portrays them as intellectual problem-solvers who work as independent consultants. This model is plausible—and attractive—because it is patterned on the traditional role of autonomous professionals. However, the model does not fit the conditions of work for planners employed as bureaucratic advisors to elected officials.

Employers generally want advice which is sensitive to the political constraints on short-term actions. Planners who aspire to the autonomy of the role of independent consultant are likely to have difficulty accepting the role of bureaucratic advisor. The incongruity between the two models is likely to be confusing for many planners, who seek to understand and describe what they do in one set of terms while really acting in some significantly different ways. For them it is an extremely perplexing matter to identify realistic standards for the outcomes of their efforts. The incongruity between ideal and actual roles is likely to be demoralizing for other planners who want to see themselves as autonomous and yet who would be discouraged to acknowledge that they play a subordinate role at work. For them it may be a degrading experience to formulate standards for work outcomes which accurately reflect their roles. Both of these responses further limit the likelihood that planners will be able to specify expectable outcomes which are reasonable in the context of clear constraints on their efforts. Consequently, it will be difficult to assess their effectiveness as practitioners.

Fragmentation of Problem-Solving Responsibility. Fragmentation of problem-solving work in the planning process creates difficulties in measuring the effects of planners' work. When decision-makers become concerned about a problem, they ask for advice from a number of sources. Usually a planner is assigned responsibility for a technical component of the problem, with another type of advisor examining the political facets. Particularly in relatively large planning agencies, the technical components of problems may be allocated to several staff members, each working in an area of specialty. Further, in most jurisdictions the planning department, which does only planning, is organizationally separate from operating agencies, which implement programs, which may receive reports from the planning department, and which also do their own planning. On top of this, solutions for problems may require drawing resources from several levels of government, each of which may employ planners engaged in parallel or similar planning efforts. Besides this, private groups with interests in problems do their own planning and stand ready to supply information to or otherwise influence the decision-makers or any of the agencies or individuals with responsibility for planning which affects the decision-makers.

Thus, arriving at a solution for decision-makers' problems involves the assembly of analysis, standards or specifications, and recommendations from diverse sources. An individual planner may play a relatively small part in a complex division of labor. A planner may work on a task which is so narrowly defined and which is so indirectly related to final decisions as to hinder drawing a clear connection between the planner's efforts and broad social goals and solutions to problems. Because of the uncertainty of links between planners' activities and eventual outcomes, planners have difficulty setting reasonable standards for expectable outcomes from their efforts. This task is complicated by the ways in which constraints on a planner's responsibilities fluctuate from case to case. The fragmentation of problem-solving responsibility thus creates another obstacle to assessing planners' effectiveness.

Intangibility of Advisory Problem-Solving. These hindrances to evaluating planners' effectiveness are further complicated by a problem in language which makes it difficult to find an appropriate vocabulary for describing planning work. Planning is representative of a growing number of intellectual occupations. Observers of this growth who identify it with "post-industrialism" have emphasized a contrast between its mental component and the primary manual component of manufacturing, or industrial work (Bell, 1973; Hirschhorn, 1975). The mental character of these work activities is particularly difficult to describe because the conventional language used to discuss work has been developed with reference to industrial work.

The customary vocabulary of "work" refers to the activities of the tangible "production process" in manufacturing. An automobile worker, for example, welds a fender and contributes to the production of a car. The conventional language of a "production process" avails poorly, however, in efforts to characterize intellectual work. Planning and other advice-giving entail creating links between people and information. If anything can be said to be "produced," it is a meaningful relationship among pieces of information or a social relationship among people. This "product" may be called a "solution," "insight," or "coordination." The "production process" which leads to these outcomes consists of mental activity, taking place invisibly inside people's minds. This process may entail also some number of emotional or interpersonal activities, which are similarly invisible. This "production process" may be called "problem-formulation," "diagnosis," or "problem-solving."

Any efforts to describe the work of planning must begin with its intangibility. As a point of departure, it is useful to examine the "products"—or outcomes—of planners' advisory problem-solving. The immediate "product" of advice-giving in the planning process is a set of recommendations regarding possible improvements in the environment. Although a written report or plan may be viewed as a tangible product, it is really only a physical representation of fundamentally intangible mental products. Only if a decision-maker accepts a planner's recommendations and if the recommendations are later implemented will there eventually be some more or less tangible effect from the planner's work. The distinction between this tangible product, such as housing construction, and an intangible product, such as a recommendation for housing construction, helps to clarify some confusion between planners and their clients about what should be expectable outcomes for planning efforts. Planners tend, at least initially, to consider that they should have responsibility for the tangible products, even though planners are frequently vague about how they will bring these products forth. Planners' clients tend to consider planners responsible for only the intangible products. Many planners subsequently may come to focus on some kind of intangible product, either in addition to or in place of the tangible product. Still, even if both planners and their clients were to agree that planners' expected outcomes should be these intangible products, it is just their intangibility which makes them difficult to characterize, to measure, and to evaluate.

This same linguistic elusiveness characterizes the planning process as a "production process." Textbooks on planning consistently describe planning as a "problem-solving process" (for example, Faludi, 1973; Gilbert and Specht, 1977). Most of the literature on planning "methods" focuses on the creation of the intangible products and describes numerous intellectual procedures to be followed in solving problems. One recent work (Faludi, 1973) discusses the ways in which the organization of a planning agency can be made to resemble most closely the synaptic connections which are presumed to occur in the human brain during the mental problem-solving process. Many writings on the "problem-solving process" suggest that planners follow a series of clearly identifiable intellectual steps in this process (for example, Puget Sound Governmental Conference, 1974). A small part of the literature (for example, Gilbert and Specht, 1977) refers to interpersonal tasks which may help to convert the intangible products into tangible products.

These descriptions give an appearance of definiteness to the "problem-solving process." Yet this rationalization of the planning process is misleading in two ways. First, although a planning report may contain section headings corresponding to the prescribed steps in the planning process, the thought process which goes into preparation of the analysis embodied in the report normally skips without obvious order from step to step in response to new information and new insight. The order of a report belies the disorder of the process which produced it.[5] Second, important parts of the planning process are both nonrational and, often, unconscious. The intellectual activity of the planning process entails mental manipulation of imaginary future events, an assessment of their likelihood and desirability, and an identification of the imaginary future events which are likely to make the more desirable imaginary future events probable realities. This process involves a complex blend of conscious and unconscious, rational and nonrational activities.[6] The same may be said of the interpersonal activities involved in encouraging the adoption and implementation of recommendations.

Not only do planners occupy ambiguous, fragmented, and varying roles as advisory problem-formulators, but the intangibility of both the "products" and the "production process" in their work makes it difficult to find useful language to describe either expected or actual work outcomes. It is also difficult to discuss various constraints on planners' actions. Consequently, planners experience problems both in articulating the central components of their work and in identifying incongruities between their expected and actual roles. Crucially, both planners and their clients have difficulty identifying the complexities of the planning process, ways in which this process constrains planners' work, and reasonably expectable outcomes for planners' efforts. As a result, evaluation of planners' effectiveness becomes more problematic yet.

Newness of Planners to Professionalization. Nevertheless, despite all these difficulties, it is noteworthy that planners do not even have access to a public rhetoric which they might use to mask their private bewilderment. In this respect they contrast with other groups of practitioners, such as social workers and teachers, who are regarded as professionals even though their work is no less varied and no more tangible.

In order to understand such contrasts, it is necessary to move away from the characteristics of and constraints on planners' roles to the social and political context in which planners seek professional status and in which their effectiveness is assessed. Here a look at medicine may be instructive. Medicine is frequently presented as the prototypical example of a profession (Freidson, 1970; Larson, 1977). Medicine is regarded as having a well codified body of refined technical knowledge which provides the foundation for specialized practice. Medical ethics explicitly ensure that specialized medical skills will be used for the public good. There is a public impression that any physician could easily recite a series of technical and ethical principles which undergird his or her practice of medicine.

This public impression was created as a political strategy to obtain status and autonomy for medicine, but the public image conceals a divergent private reality, which resembles planners' uncertain views of "planning." "Medicine" is a heterogeneous conglomeration of specialty groups held together by various measures of esteem and interest (Bucher and Strauss, 1961). Further, the practice of medicine is frequently much more an art than a technology. This private view of the "profession of medicine" is familiar to members of the profession but concealed from the public.

Planners, among others, tend to believe the public view of medicine as a prototypical profession and turn to this image as a standard against which to measure planning in determining whether it meets the formal criteria for a profession: consensus and clarity on technical skills and ethical tenets. Because planners are relatively new to the enterprise of acquiring professional status, they are likely to compare themselves to this fictitious image of medicine, against which they will find themselves wanting.

Indeed, planners indicated that they do expect to be able to see themselves and to present themselves to others as a group of practitioners unified by common, clearly identifiable methods, ethics, and outcomes. The ambiguous and fragmented organizational roles of advice-givers, as well as the intangibility of planning activities, make the construction of such an image difficult. Yet, planners, observing the model of medicine, do not understand that it is normal for the reality which underlies this type of image to be pluralistic and diffuse. In addition, because planners are generally insensitive to organizational processes, they are likely to overlook the importance of political organization and rhetoric in any process of professionalization.

In forcing themselves to identify and describe only what is common to the work of all planners, planners have prevented themselves from acknowledging and trying to characterize some of the differences as well. Significantly, it is the perception of differences which so perplexes planners in defining "planning" and in constructing a collective consciousness around a definition.

Crucially, so long as planners do not recognize both the reality and legitimacy of pluralistic models of planning, they will continue to be unable to develop reasonable standards for outcomes for these different models, and evaluation of their practical effectiveness will remain difficult for both them and the public which employs them.

The Public Image of Planners: Confusing and Unimpressive

Planners' likelihood of acquiring professional status depends on a public evaluation of their effectiveness. Conceptually, an assessment of planners' effectiveness is beset by a number of problems. It is difficult to set goals for expected outcomes, to measure actual outcomes, and to identify constraints which are meaningful to an assessment of planners' effectiveness. However, a favorable public assessment of planners does not require the clearing of a single "correct" conceptual path through this thicket of problems. More simply, such an assessment requires that planners present some cogent image of their performance which persuades members of the public to conclude that planners are usefully effective.

Planners tend not to recognize that a public presentation of their practice might differ from their private perceptions. Consequently, they project a public image which contains ambiguities and uncertainties which they experience privately. The planners interviewed have limited autonomy in their work and, as a result, had difficulty establishing expected outcomes which seemed realistic. On the one hand, they made broad claims to "problem-solving." They linked these aspirations to "problem-solving" to significant changes in the social and physical environments. On the other hand, planners often tacitly redefined their expectations to correspond to acceptance of their work or, less, acceptance of their intentions. In addition, planners had difficulties measuring the actual outcomes of their efforts. Connections between effort expended and subsequent actions were often difficult to trace. Moreover, actual outcomes might be so disappointing in comparison with original expectations that planners had difficulty identifying these outcomes. The intangibility of planning work compounds these problems in describing outcomes and being certain that planners' efforts have specific outcomes. Finally, although planners experienced broad limits on their autonomy, they tended to be of two minds about whether to accept these constraints as inevitable or changeable. In the first case, standards for expected outcomes would have to be lowered. In the second case, planners would have to hold themselves accountable for their own apparently poor actual outcomes.

The resultant public image of planners may be, at best, confusing and, at worst, unimpressive. It may be confusing because, on the one hand, planners raise high expectations of broad "problem-solving" and, on the other hand, planners speak of relatively modest contributions to the process of problem-solving. The image may be unimpressive because of many planners' apparent downward redefinition of their goals and the somewhat disparaging affect with which they describe their efforts in contributing to these modest goals. In either case, problems with language may hinder the communication of the complexity and the difficulty of planners' work.

The clients who work directly with planners—both public decision-makers and the employers of private consultants—have their own special perspective on planners' work. The clients tend to hold themselves responsible for deriving solutions to problems and expect planners to contribute information and analysis to the process of formulating problems and rendering advice on their solution. Clients appear to be satisfied with the effectiveness of many planners, although the clients' expectations are often limited to relatively narrow assignments. If clients believe that planners confront constraints to their effectiveness, the clients tend to think of limits in time, budgetary resources or, perhaps, planners' own intellectual abilities. Clients do not see themselves as the constraints which planners frequently believe them to be. Finally, clients, just as planners, may not appreciate either the complexity or the difficulty of planners' work.

There is no definitive evidence regarding how clients and other members of the public ultimately evaluate planners' effectiveness. For example, there is no national survey of opinions regarding the usefulness of planners' work. However, there is considerable indirect evidence from which inferences may be drawn. The most forceful evidence is the current social status of planners. Planners report, accurately, that a minority of citizens are aware of the efforts of planners and that a minority of citizens regard planning as offering direct benefits in solving important problems. There is scant public interest in instituting licensing of planners in a society which would hardly consider abolishing the licensing of physicians, attorneys, or teachers.[7] When governmental bodies want advice about courses of action open to them, their first choice may not be to turn to planners, who will assess the rationality of many alternatives. Instead, these bodies may turn, for example, to attorneys, who may do substantially the same type of work which a planner would do but who bring independent professional status and who are considered in some way more "practical" than planners. This public assessment of the relative usefulness of planners and other practitioners is suggested in salary differences. For example, in 1977 the average income for attorneys was approximately $36,000, whereas the average income for planners was $19,500 (Levin, 1979, p. 30).[8]

In addition, indirect evidence about public assessments of planners' effectiveness can be found in current attitudes toward planning programs and government generally. In the present public mind "planners" are linked with the seeming multitude of public programs which cost vast amounts in taxes and accomplish apparently little. In part, this criticism expresses the anxieties of moderate-income workers who are seriously punished by inflation. In part, the criticism of public programs reflects the convictions of both taxpayers and the intended beneficiaries of programs that, whatever the cost, the programs do not work. The former attack on "planning" and public programs may be transient, more an immediate response to a constricting economy than a considered assessment of the effectiveness of planners' efforts. However, the latter attack on "planning" and public programs combines both these temporary concerns with more serious examination of the results of the programs. This group of critics may not recognize the difficulties involved in attempting to solve many complexly related problems with both limited money and limited understanding. They may not recognize that the solutions of the social problems which distress them require confronting problems of governance as well as substantive issues. However, growing complaints that "government does not work" do express a tacit suspicion that problems in governance underlie the gamut of tangible problems which call for immediate relief. Crucially, regardless of whether citizens appreciate the centrality of governance problems, citizens, nevertheless, appear to expect "planners" to solve an array of pressing social problems and appear also to find "planners" ineffective in doing so.

Planners' claims to be "problem-solvers" apparently open them to expectations which are difficult to fulfill. Because planners are not very specific about the types of outcomes which it would be reasonable to expect from them, they become the objects for the projection of many people's expectations about problem-solving in the social and physical environments. Further, planners' failure to address directly problems of governance conveys an oversimplified view of the challenges of problem-solving and encourages exaggerated expectations. Simultaneously, despite planners' real contributions to problem-solving, their vagueness about the actual outcomes of their work, as well as their own disparaging assessment of these outcomes, discourages a public appreciation of their accomplishments. Problems with language make it difficult for planners to describe and for members of the public to understand the complexities of planning work as a context for evaluating planners' effectiveness. Consequently, members of the public may develop not only a low assessment of planners' effectiveness, but also confusion about the appropriate boundaries for the domain of planners' practice. These conditions are not likely to contribute to professional status for planners.

PUBLIC ACCOUNTABILITY: A CONDITION FOR LEGITIMACY

Ethics as a Weak Proxy for Accountability

The traditional image of a profession portrays a group of specialized practitioners who govern the exercise of their expertise by a self-imposed code of ethics. This code ensures that the practitioners' skills will be used in the service of the public. For traditionally organized professions, which practice with autonomy from their clients, the espoused ethical code is a proxy for direct public accountability. Practitioners understand what is in their clients' interests in ways in which the clients cannot, and practitioners accept ethical obligations to hold themselves and their colleagues accountable to standards of their clients' needs. Because professional autonomy has come under challenge, espousals of ethical tenets have diminishing acceptability as a substitute for direct public accountability. In this context, planners' statements about their ethics are informative as an indication of how planners would attempt to respond to clients' or constituents' requests.

The planners interviewed described their ethics in terms of the process of planning, rather than its outcomes. They implied that, if planners adhered to ethical principles in each step of their work, the products of their efforts would inevitably be "good." A substantial minority of planners formulated ethical questions in technical terms. They stated that planners have a responsibility to collect and analyze information in a thorough and rational manner. Presumably the products of such work would be "good," and members of the public would benefit accordingly. In contrast, the majority of planners elaborated explicitly ethical, or social, principles in describing their ethical codes. First of all, they contended, planners should be loyal to their client or constituent. This loyalty requires collecting sufficient information to understand what the client's interests are. In addition, however, planners should be concerned for identifying problems and remedies which represent the public at-large. The interests of immediate clients or constituents need to be placed into the broader perspective of the "public interest." This is planners' traditional—and strongest— ethical claim. Planners contend that they have special expertise which enables them, better than any other practitioners or their clients, to identify courses of action which are in the interests of the greatest number of people in society. Their expertise is inherently ethical. Thus, if citizens permit planners to conduct a planning process in which they are continually attentive to the public interest, all may be assured that the outcome of this work will serve the majority of citizens.

This assertion is the ideal expression of the traditional ethical plea of professionals. These planners claimed as their client the entire society, and they maintained that they understand better than anyone else what is in the interests of the whole society. However, the affect with which planners made these ethical claims raises questions about the content of planners' ethics in practice. Most planners had difficulty summarizing any code of planning ethics. Many were embarrassed at this difficulty and doubted that they are guided by any collective ethics. Many planners invoked individual codes of ethics.

Even if these doubts are not expressed directly, they are communicated indirectly to the public through a failure to articulate a clear code of practical planning ethics.[9] These doubts about planners' ethics provide citizens with little assurance that planners are a group of practitioners who govern their practice by collectively accepted and enforced ethical tenets. These doubts raise serious questions for citizens regarding whether planners' ethical espousals should be accepted as any type of proxy for direct public accountability. These questions about public accountability, in turn, create considerable uncertainty whether citizens will accord planners legitimacy to practice in a claimed field of expertise.

Planners' Resistance to Citizen Participation

Because of this uncertainty it is crucial to examine what the planners said about their direct contact with and accountability to their clients and constituents. Here, in planners' descriptions of their actions in practice, their concerns for the interests of their clients and for the public interest become clearer. When planners spoke of accountability to these interests, they envisioned an accountability which is limited in two ways. First, as with their ethical espousals, they were concerned more with the process of planning than with its outcomes. Most planners said that citizens should be consulted as advisors on-call. They can provide planners with vital information about their communities, their perceived interests, and their problems. Nevertheless, citizens tend to be narrow-minded and short-sighted, and what they say usually needs to be re-interpreted by planners with technical training and a broader understanding of the "public interest." Then this information can be used to formulate problems to be solved in the ensuing planning process. In the early stages of this process planners may ask citizens' opinions in order to ascertain that planners understand the citizens' communities accurately. However, as the planning process advances, fewer and fewer planners were inclined either to consult citizens or to submit work to them for their comments. Most planners regarded the work of formulating final recommendations as their sole prerogative, subject only to consultation with parties with direct control over their income or status.[10] In this way, then, most planners considered themselves to be accountable to the public. They consult with citizens during the planning process—particularly in the early stages—and then take sole responsibility for the final product. By implication, a process in which planners are publicly accountable in this fashion produces outcomes which should be regarded as accountable to public interests.

This account points to a second way in which planners took a limited view of public accountability. They thought of accountability in intellectual, not political terms. The relationship between planners and citizens just described is one in which planners are willing to consult citizens for information about local conditions. This is intellectual accountability, in which planners want to make their descriptions of community needs consistent with citizens' perceptions. However, the majority of planners rejected more active participation by citizens in the planning process, including participation guided by an advocate planner or the exercise of veto power over recommendations for solutions of community problems. This would be political accountability, in which citizens would have effective power in decisions made in the planning process. By implication, because planners are concerned with the "public interest," when planners are intellectually accountable to citizens, political accountability is unnecessary.

Citizens increasingly regard both intellectual and political accountability for both process and outcomes as conditions for the bestowal of professional status. Citizens who are disturbed by the bureaucratization, commoditization, and politicization of services want to wrest back some control over the practitioners whom, directly or indirectly, they employ. At least as important, the very effectiveness of practitioners, regardless of whether they are accorded professional authority, depends on their accountability to members of the public. Particularly the governance problems with which planners are concerned require active collaboration between planners and affected members of the public in all stages of formulating and solving problems. Both the intellectual and social complexities of the problems require extensive participation in order for likely solutions to be discovered and implemented.

Planners do not satisfy these conditions. Insofar as they are concerned with public accountability, they offer intellectual accountability for parts of the planning process. Most suggest, as traditional professionals have argued, that their clients or constituents should accept these measures as either proxies for or guarantees of other types of accountability. By and large, planners still aspire to the autonomy sought by traditional professionals. This pretension reduces the likelihood that citizens will grant planners the legitimacy which accompanies professional status.

CONCLUSION: POOR PROSPECTS FOR PROFESSIONALIZATION

Citizens bestow the legitimacy of professional status on a group of practitioners when the citizens perceive these practitioners to be effective and publicly accountable in contributing to the solution of important problems. In thinking about their expectations of "planners," citizens are concerned about both substantive problems and problems of governance.

Practitioners who would satisfy citizens' expectations in dealing with these problems must meet three requirements. First, these practitioners must directly recognize and work on these problems. Second, the practitioners must be demonstrably effective in their work. Third, the practitioners must make themselves accountable for their efforts to the general public. In all three respects planners fall short, and their prospect for professionalization is limited.

First, planners have considerable difficulty delineating a clear domain of practice. Most planners regard themselves as intellectual problem-solvers, but they have difficulty specifying their intellectual skills or explaining how they contribute to the solution of problems. When they do describe the problems on which they work, they refer primarily to substantive problems and tend to overlook the governance problems which concern citizens. In addition, planners are acutely sensitive to limitations on their influence, and they respond to these limitations with private and public self-doubts. Further, the complexity of both the problems on which they work and the process of planning hinders their explaining publicly what they do which is of value.

Second, planners' vagueness about their domain contributes to doubts about their effectiveness. Their ambiguous public image not only fails to establish for them a clear identity as practitioners working on significant problems, but it also leads to an identification of planners with many disliked aspects of government. Because planners do not clearly explain their role in public decision-making, there is often little differentiation in the public mind between planners who may be concerned to find solutions for broad social problems and "bureaucrats" who are responsible for designing and administering specific programs causing immediate irritation. Further, the general claim of planners to problem-solving skills links them with the manifold and increasingly doubted assertions that "government" can solve any social problems. While planners may, in fact, make progress in solving particular substantive problems, they generally fail to respond to public perceptions that "government [as a procedure for solving problems] doesn't work." Whatever else planners do, their failure to confront these procedural problems of governance gives them the appearance of being peripheral to important problems.

Third, both planners' definitions of their expertise and their work roles minimize their public accountability for their work. Planners describe themselves as intellectual problem-solvers whose expertise it is to collect and give logical order to information about the social world apart from the political pressures of that world. Planners' roles, particularly in public agencies, reinforce this view of their work. Planners in public agencies normally tend to have little contact with the citizens who are their agencies' constituents. In part, this isolation represents a response to an abundance of demands for the completion of projects in limited time. In addition, however, most planners prefer to have limited contact with citizens. A majority of planners believe that citizens have only limited information to contribute to the planning process and regard work with citizens as generally unrewarding. Above all, most planners jealously seek to guard their perceived prerogative to make final recommendations about unique optimal solutions for problems.

This resistance to political accountability to members of the public inevitably results in a loss of intellectual accountability as well. Planners who carry out their problem-solving work in the relative isolation of their offices gain a seclusion from day-to-day community pressures but lose a sensitivity to the thinking and feelings of citizens. This sensitivity is further strained when planners believe that citizens' statements must be re-interpreted before they are useful in planning. Intellectual coherence in the planning process may be thereby gained, but intellectual understanding between planners and citizens is lost. Thus planners who work on various substantive problems are not attuned to hear significant but apparently peripheral comments from citizens about the procedures of planning or of government generally. Indeed, planners are predisposed to interpret questions about the meaning of procedures as an indication of citizens' lack of understanding of a rational process of problem-solving. Planners' typical response to challenge is to withdraw further into intense, isolated work, with the results that, not only may they misunderstand their questioners, but they also may become subject to growing misperception by others.

The immediate consequence of this isolation is that planners are unable to recognize that citizens are concerned about governance problems and expect planners to provide solutions to those problems. The ultimate consequence is that members of the public do not perceive planners as practitioners who are relevant to the solution of important, bothersome public problems. Citizens do not consider planners as candidates for the authority of professional status.

NOTES

1. This position, set forth in the contextual discussion of the first chapter, is elaborated by Emery and Trist (1973) and Schon (1973). The issue here is not that a division of intellectual labor is inherently unreasonable. Rather, the specific division of intellectual responsibility enforced by elected officials or bureaucratic administrators may be inappropriate to understanding the social problems under scrutiny.

2. This is a simplified version of the approach taken in assessing "quality" in health care. The "quality assessment" literature first distinguishes measures of "inputs" (for example, a practitioner's credentials), measures of "process" or "outputs" (for example, the amount of time a practitioner spends with a client or what the practitioner does on behalf of the client), and measures of "outcomes" (for example, changes in the client's welfare or well-being). Having made this distinction, however, evaluators and practitioners have some difficulty in deciding whether to focus on output or outcome measures. For example, a practitioner may

work diligently with a client and may perform all appropriate actions, only to find that the welfare of the client does not change. Other influences on the client may counteract the efforts of the practitioner, or the client may act in ways which defeat the practitioner's efforts. A simple focus on outcomes would make the practitioner's performance appear to be of low quality. On the other hand, the practitioner's services may be only one of a number of influences on a client, and a client's well-being may improve for reasons not obviously related to the undeniably assiduous efforts of the practitioner, or even despite certain actions of the practitioner. In this case, a focus on outcomes might overestimate the quality of the worker's performance. These problems are discussed in Brook and Avery (1976a and 1976b), Donabedian (1966), and Greene (1976), and Institute of Medicine (1976).

In that literature one approach to unraveling the complex relationship between outputs and outcomes is to think in terms of "staging." A variety of common health problems are divided into "stages" in their typical histories. Then it is asked for each stage what an appropriate intervention would be and what a reasonable outcome would be for that appropriate intervention. In addition, efforts have been made to distinguish statistically normal outcomes for specific interventions for clients with different personal or environmental backgrounds which may in some way affect the outcome. (For example, it would be reasonable to expect a different outcome from surgery for heart disease for a patient who smokes heavily than for a patient who does not smoke.) In short, there are attempts in this literature to recognize that practitioners may invest significant effort in making appropriate interventions and that, nevertheless, the effectiveness of those interventions on clients or constituents may be constrained by circumstances beyond the practitioners' control. Simply put, the practitioner will still be accorded some credit for energy invested when it is appropriate.

3. Here the collective enterprise of "planning" includes everyone who is involved in some way in preparing for and making planning decisions, not only people who are regarded as planners.

4. It should be added that many planners who work in the private sector work in firms which themselves are bureaucratically organized. Some of this bureaucratization is a reflection of these firms' needs to respond effectively to complex governmental regulations. Some of this bureaucratization represents what is regarded as a reasonable division of labor in large organizations. Whatever the reasons for this bureaucratization, it has effects on planners in the private sector similar to those of planners in the public sector. Although the following discussion focuses on planners in public bureaucracies, many of the characterizations apply as well to planners in large private firms.

5. I have argued in a critique of the rational engineering model of design (Baum, 1982) that strict adherence to the sequence of steps in the prescribed planning process is likely to prevent the discovery of useful solutions to significant problems.

6. I have described this process of imagining the future and reviewed relevant social psychological literature in "Distribution of Ability to Imagine the Future: Implications for the Planning Process" (Baum, 1977).

7. Indeed, many citizens are much more concerned that their barbers or hairdressers be licensed according to publicly specified standards. These citizens feel that maintaining their personal appearance is a more important—or, at least, more tangible—problem than maintaining the appearance of the social and physical environment in which they live.

8. This comparison of incomes does reflect differences in attributed status but should be qualified. Most attorneys work for private firms and earn incomes proportional to their individual or corporate ability to garner business at their customary fees. Most planners work for public agencies and earn incomes which are limited by civil service regulations based, at least at state and local levels, on relatively poor treasuries.

9. This failure has been a source of concern to the leadership of the American Planning Association. As noted earlier, in late 1981 the American Institute of Certified Planners, within the A.P.A., adopted a Code of Ethics and Professional Conduct, to replace the American Institute of Planners' Code of Professional Responsibility. The earlier Code was considered to be too abstract and to consist of only prohibitions, without any clearly delineated set of ethical purposes. The new Code is more concrete and emphasizes positive ethical responsibilities. The authors of the new Code concluded that, whatever the current private uncertainties of planners, a clear public statement of ethics would have two desirable effects: first, persuade the public that, indeed, planners do have a clear sense of ethical responsibility and, second, reassure planners, similarly, that they have an ethical code on which they may rely for guidance.

10. In the private sector this is the client who hires a planning consultant. In the public sector this is usually an elected official.

REFERENCES

Baum, Howell S. "Distribution of Ability to Imagine the Future: Implications for the Planning Process," *Plan Canada*, 17, 3-4 (September-December, 1977), pp. 218-236.

Baum, Howell S. "Services Aren't Goods: Post-Industrial Principles for Policy Design," *Journal of Sociology and Social Welfare*, 8, 3 (September, 1981), pp. 489-512.

Bell, Daniel. *The Coming of Post-Industrial Society*. New York: Basic Books, 1973.

Benveniste, Guy. *The Politics of Expertise*, second edition, San Francisco: Boyd and Fraser, 1977.

Brook, Robert H., and Allyson Davies Avery. *Quality Assessment: Issues of Definition and Measurement*. Rand Paper Number 5618. Santa Monica: Rand Corporation, 1976. (a)

Brook, Robert H., and Allyson Davis Avery. *Quality of Medical Care Using Outcome Measures: Executive Summary.* Rand Publication Number R-2021/3 HEW. Santa Monica: Rand Corporation, 1976. (b)

Bucher, Rue, and Anselm Strauss. "Professions in Process," *American Journal of Sociology, 4* (1961), pp. 325-334.

Caro, Robert A. *The Power Broker.* New York: Vintage Books, 1975.

Donabedian, Avedis. "Evaluating the Quality of Medical Care," *Milbank Memorial Fund Quarterly, 44,* Part 2 (July, 1966), pp. 166-203.

Emery, F.E., and E.L. Trist. *Towards a Social Ecology.* New York: Plenum Press, 1973.

Etzioni, Amitai. *The Active Society.* New York: The Free Press, 1968.

Faludi, Andreas. *Planning Theory.* New York: Pergamon Press, 1973.

Freidson, Eliot. *Profession of Medicine.* New York: Dodd, Mead, and Company, 1970.

Gilbert, Neil, and Harry Specht. *Dimensions of Social Welfare Policy.* Englewood Cliffs: Prentice-Hall, 1974.

Gilbert, Neil, and Harry Specht, editors. *Planning for Social Welfare.* Englewood Cliffs: Prentice-Hall, 1977.

Greene, Richard. *Assuring Quality in Medical Care.* Cambridge: Ballinger, 1976.

Hirschhorn, Larry. *The Social Crisis—The Crisis of Work and Social Services, Part II: Work, Social Services, and the Crisis of Modern Development.* Working Paper No. 252. Berkeley: Institute of Urban and Regional Development, University of California, 1975.

Institute of Medicine, National Academy of Sciences. *Assessing Quality in Health Care: An Evaluation.* Washington: National Academy of Sciences, 1976.

Kaufman, Jerome L. "Contemporary Planning Practice: State of the Art." In *Planning in America: Learning From Turbulence,* David E. Godschalk, editor. Washington: American Institute of Planners, 1974.

Larson, Magali Sarfatti. *The Rise of Professionalism.* Berkeley: University of California Press, 1977.

Levin, Melvin R. "Bumpy Roads Ahead," *Planning, 45,* 7 (July, 1979), pp. 29-35.

Lindblom, Charles E. "The Science of 'Muddling Through,'" *Public Administration Review, 19* (Spring, 1959), pp. 79-88.

Puget Sound Governmental Conference. *A Comprehensive Human Resource Planning Guide.* Seattle: Puget Sound Governmental Conference, 1974.

Rein, Martin. "Social Planning: The Search for Legitimacy," *Journal of the American Institute of Planners, 35,* 4 (July, 1969), pp. 233-44.

Schön, Donald A. *Beyond the Stable State.* New York: W.W. Norton and Company, 1973.

8

STRATEGY FOR PLANNERS' GAINING LEGITIMACY IN PROBLEM-SOLVING

Planners' acquisition of professional status has importance for two reasons. The first concerns planning practitioners. They believe that they exercise a useful expertise, and they want recognition for their accomplishments. At the same time, they feel that their expertise is being challenged by others with different training, and they want a formal or tacit public license to practice in the domain for which they believe they are best trained. Professional status would bring them legitimacy to practice in a specified domain. In addition, it would bring them public esteem associated with presumed effectiveness in solving significant problems.

The second reason why the professionalization of planners is important concerns the general public. "Planning" is concerned with problems of social governance. The procedural problems of governance increasingly hinder the solution of substantive problems. Citizens who are concerned about the obstruction of social decision-making have a stake in the development of "planning." Specifically, citizens concerned about problems in governance need practitioners—"planners"—who can demonstrate effectiveness in solving problems of governance. Although citizens have no intrinsic interest in the granting of professional status, they would grant these "planners" legitimacy to work in the domain of governance.

How would planners need to think and act differently in order to meet the challenges of governance problems and to gain public legitimacy in problem-solving? This chapter presents a model of effective and legitimate planning. The first section describes a way of thinking which is likely to be effective in confronting problems of governance. The second section discusses relationships between planners and lay citizens which satisfy requirements of public accountability. The third section describes a way in which planners may act so as to combine effective intellectual skills with public accountability in working on problems of governance. The fourth section discusses educational programs which may prepare planners who can satisfy these conditions.

INTELLECTUAL EXPERTISE: INCREASING PLANNERS' SENSITIVITY TO ORGANIZATIONAL ISSUES

A Model of Organizational Sensitivity

Planners' expertise, if it is to be effective in dealing with problems of governance, must include a sensitivity to organizational issues. The cognitive dimension of organizational sensitivity may be described in two ways. First, it is possible to identify a number of intellectual questions which a planner should ask about the organizational context of any problem under scrutiny. Second, it is possible to discuss the cognitive processes which a planner should go through in order to find answers for these questions.

Most discussions of the planning process focus on the intellectual questions about the organizational context, and these questions may be readily summarized. The following formulations are Meltsner's (1972), although others (for example, Bardach, 1977; Cox, 1974) have framed similar questions. Meltsner writes,

> For each policy [planning] alternative the analyst [planner] explores a series of conditional statements: if we recommend X, Y will support it and Z will oppose it. Before the analyst can do this, however, he needs a way of linking his alternatives to their relevant political environment (1972, p. 860).

In order to make these connections, a planner needs to construct scenarios of probable outcomes related to the selection of specific alternatives.

To begin a scenario one must define the problem area containing the issues raised. It is necessary to identify a set of actors who are concerned about the issues and whose preferences are likely to affect a decision on the issues. It is useful to characterize actors by their past positions on the issues and by their likelihood of influencing future decisions. This examination should consider actors' motives and priorities. In addition, the study should clarify what the actors believe about the present and desired states of the world affected by the issues at stake. Crucially, an examination of the actors should identify the types of resources which they can call on to satisfy their motivated preferences. These resources may include money, information, position, time, organization, the ability to manipulate symbols, and skill in using any of these other resources. With this information a planner can identify decision sites which will affect the outcomes of issues and may identify the likely positions and resources of actors at each site. Meltsner concludes,

> After organizing his information in the form of a set of political maps, the analyst then predicts or estimates likely outcomes. He converts a static picture of politics into a dynamic one by estimating which actors will be politically effective, which will exercise power. More importantly, he identifies the possible areas of policy consensus and conflict (1972, p. 863).

The planner looks for likely exchanges among interested actors. Where the planner favors particular outcomes, he or she would seek to develop a proposal leading to these outcomes by means of exchanges likely to be acceptable to interested parties.

All this is rather simply stated. The questions identified are clear and reasonable. Planners should examine the political context of a decision. Yet these questions and this requirement are easier to state than to answer and satisfy. They call for the collection of certain types of information. But, more than that, crucially, they require that planners go through particular cognitive processes in looking at issues and selecting and organizing information into a scenario which is useful for decision-making. These cognitive processes are the essence of organizational sensitivity. It is necessary to understand these cognitive processes in order to understand how planners may find reasonable answers to the intellectual questions.[1]

In examining alternative possible solutions for problems, a planner must understand the consequences of particular courses of action and must be able to identify the means to desired goals. The nature of the organizational sensitivity required for this analysis can be discovered by examining the characteristics of the organizational environment of decision-making conceptually. For this purpose, it is helpful to refer to the "causal texture" of an environment, a concept first developed by Tolman and Brunswik

(1935) and adapted for use in social analysis by Emery and Trist (1965 and 1973).[2]

Tolman and Brunswik suggest that an environment may be thought of as having a "causal texture" with two dimensions: the quality of causal relationships between present actions and future outcomes, and the clarity of indicators of the relationships between means and desired ends. Their work suggests that the intellectual tasks of planning may be complicated by problems in either of these dimensions. First, the causal relationships between present actions may not be—in the context of the current understanding of social relationships—very consistent. At one extreme, means may be "good," in that their enactment leads relatively frequently to a desired goal and only infrequently to a specifically unwanted outcome. At another extreme, selected means may be "bad," in leading relatively frequently to an undesired outcome and only infrequently to a desired goal. Second, even if there is some understanding of consistent cause-and-effect relationships, it may be difficult to identify unambivalent indicators of the existence of good means to desired ends. At one extreme, cues may be "reliable," in relatively frequently identifying good means and relatively infrequently identifying other actions which could lead away from the desired goal. At another extreme, cues may be "misleading," in frequently identifying actions which are likely to lead away from a desired goal and only infrequently identifying good means to the goal.

Emery and Trist have argued that the organizational environments of most planning decisions are "turbulent." They are complex, dynamic, rapidly changing, greatly uncertain, difficult to decipher, and intricately interdependent with other settings. Planners or other actors seeking to act strategically in this type of environment confront two types of problems, corresponding to the dimensions of causal texture. First, there are few good means to desired outcomes because so many actions are contingent on so many others, some contingencies the result of unmanaged uncertainty and others the product of deliberate strategic maneuvering by other actors. Second, there are few reliable cues to the few good means because so much is unknown, some ignorance a reflection of the many contingencies, some the product of deliberate strategic obfuscation by other actors, and some ignorance a product of limited-human cognitive ability.

The organizational sensitivity required for a planner to answer the intellectual questions about action in such a turbulent environment involves a special mental strategy. Mental strategy has been discussed earlier as cognitive style. This section will identify specific cognitive style characteristics which may be useful for understanding a turbulent organizational environment and answering the questions set forth initially. The dimensions of cognitive style described here represent the most commonly formulated categories of cognitive style (Kogan, 1971). The identification of specific cognitive style characteristics with organizational sensitivity is based on Cole's (1975), Hudson's (1966), and my own research, as well as research reviews by Cole and Kogan.[3]

Cognitive Style Requirements

The following cognitive style characteristics appear to be most useful for understanding the organizational context of planning decisions:

(1) Both field-independence and field-dependence: The dimension of field independence-field dependence involves the degree to which an individual interprets the events in a field of experience independently of the immediately present phenomena. In a turbulent environment a field-independent cognitive style would seem more useful than field-dependence for planning because of the complex relationships between actors, organizations, and their boundaries. However, there is some empirical evidence that field-dependent persons "are more sensitive to social stimuli than are field-independent persons," have greater interpersonal skills, and are better at achieving consensus in group discussion (Kogan, 1971, p. 253). In short there is not an unequivocal hypothesis about this dimension of cognitive style.

(2) Mixed scanning: The dimension of scanning involves variations in the extensiveness of intensity of an individual's attention. In a turbulent environment broad scanning with a relatively broad central focus would be most useful initially because this cognitive style would permit the detection of general links among actors in an extensive environment. Subsequently, a narrower scanning of significant actors and connections would be useful for delineating details. This "mixed scanning" has been advocated by Etzioni

(1968) as necessary for understanding turbulent environments.

(3) Broad categorizing: The dimension of breadth of categorizing involves variations in the inclusiveness or exclusiveness of units of an individual's conceptualization of experience. In a turbulent environment broad categorizing would be most useful for planning because it would permit the intellectual association of relatively divergent phenomena which may be related parts of a problem or related parts of a solution. Empirically, broad categorizing is associated with tolerance for deviant instances as potential solutions for problems, as well as the inclination to risk not reacting to change (Kogan, 1971, pp. 257-258).

(4) Low conceptual differentiation: The dimension of conceptual differentiation involves variations in the degree to which an individual divides up the experienced environment into separate conceptual categories. In a turbulent environment low conceptual differentiation would be more useful than high differentiation for planning because the former would permit the mental association of many ideas despite superficial differences among them. Empirically, low conceptual differentiation is associated with exploratory behavior and creativity (Kogan, 1971, p. 260).

(5) Cognitive complexity: The dimension of cognitive simplicity-complexity involves the degree to which an individual experiences phenomena in relatively concrete or relatively abstract terms. In a turbulent environment cognitive complexity would be most useful for planning because it would permit perception of the world with complexity and integration of information about the world in an abstract form. Empirical evidence about the behavior of cognitively complex people shows that they are predisposed to find diversity, conflict, and contradiction in the environment; they are confident in judging incongruent information; they pay attention to inner psychological states; and when they confront tasks where new information is relatively ambiguous, they tend to be suspicious of finding consistency (Kogan, 1971, p. 275).

(6) Reflectiveness: The dimension of reflectiveness-impulsivity involves the degree to which an individual selects hypotheses, organizes information, and ponders various possibilities before offering an answer to a problem. In a turbulent environment reflectiveness would be more useful than impulsivity for planning because of the importance of considering carefully the ambiguous

complexity of a situation before making a decision to act.

(7) Sharpening: The dimension of leveling-sharpening involves variations in the degree to which an individual blurs and merges similar memories and perceived objects or distinguishes present experiences from past experiences. In a turbulent environment sharpening would be most useful for planning because it would permit an appreciation of changes in a complex environment.

(8) Flexible control: The dimension of constricted-flexible control involves variations in the degree to which an individual is susceptible to distraction from an object of concentration. In a turbulent environment flexible control would be more useful than constricted control for planning because flexibility would permit intellectual wandering to actors or phenomena which do not appear central but which may be quite useful in problem-solving. Empirically, flexible control over attention is associated with creativity (Kogan, 1971, p. 284).

(9) Tolerance for incongruous or unrealistic experiences: The dimension of tolerance for incongruous or unrealistic experiences involves variations in individual willingness to accept perceptions divergent from conventional experience. In a turbulent environment tolerance of ambiguity would be most useful for planning because it would permit the acceptance of possibilities which initially appear unfeasible but which may become future realities.

There is a consistent theme in this survey of cognitive style characteristics; in order to understand a turbulent organizational environment, planners must be able to think in ways which consider the complexity, ambiguity, and variability of the environment. Thus the cognitive dimension of organizational sensitivity for planners involves not simply an intellectual concern for a particular set of questions but, further, a type of cognitive style which permits the mental processes necessary for discovering creative and realistic answers to those questions. This formulation of organizational sensitivity in terms of certain cognitive processes provides a new notion of expertise. In addition to an examination of the products of planners' efforts—answers to a set of questions—there is an examination of the mental processes required to bring forth those products.

Effective planning requires that this organizational sensitivity be reflected in actions. Planners who think in terms of organizational issues must act in ways which respond to these issues. Moreover, the terms of planners' public intellectual and political accountability should reflect and support this sensitivity. In this way, planning as a collective enterprise can respond to problems of governance.

PUBLIC ACCOUNTABILITY: INCREASING CITIZEN PARTICIPATION IN PLANNING AND GOVERNANCE

A Model for Citizen Participation

Public accountability is essential for planning because citizens want it and because the complexity of planning and governance problems requires it. This section identifies a set of functional requirements for citizen participation which both meets citizens' desires for accountability of planners and satisfies the requisites of effective planning. The specific arrangement for citizen participation in any particular situation will depend on the nature of the problem under consideration and the decision to be made, along with the interests, skills, motives, and resources of planners and affected citizens.[4]

Functional requirements for citizen participation may be drawn from the characteristics of cognitive style just identified as most useful for planning in a turbulent environment. This approach contributes to a model of citizen participation which makes planners both intellectually and politically accountable to the public. A planner need not have every appropriate cognitive attribute if someone in a working planner-citizen group has the characteristic. In most situations the intellectual and interpersonal requirements for effective planning are too great for any individual—planner or community member—to be able to do all necessary work alone.[5]

Intellectual Accountability

The characteristics of cognitive style specified in the preceding section suggest that planners and citizens should be organized to think collectively in the following ways:

(1) Both field-independence and field-dependence: The planning process should include both individuals who are intimately in contact with the situation which is the subject of planning efforts and individuals who are able to move back mentally and view the

situation within the context of broader social, cultural, political, and economic environments. The ways in which these cognitive requirements may be satisfied in the organization of participation in the planning process are typical of the means of satisfying all functional requirements. It is possible that one or a few individuals may be able to contribute the requisite capacities (here, a combination of field-independence and field-dependence), although it is likely that many individuals may be necessary. All participants must be able to communicate with, understand, and come to some agreement with one another.

Discussion of other functional requirements will emphasize participation needs distinctive to each requirement, with two assumptions underlying the discussion of all requirements: first, that cognitive requirements may be satisfiable by one or a few or, usually more likely, many participants; and, second, that all participants must be able to communicate and come to some agreement with each other.

(2) Mixed scanning: For breadth, the planning process should include many people with different experiences and perceptions of the situation under scrutiny. For narrow focus, the process should include a sufficient number of persons to permit a detailed look at many different aspects of the situation.

(3) Broad categorizing: The planning process should include individuals who can see similarities among many apparently disparate aspects of the situation in question. This goal may involve the inclusion of one or a few individuals whose thinking is "divergent" (Hudson, 1966). In addition, or alternatively, it may involve the inclusion of many individuals with divergent perceptions of the aspects of the situation under scrutiny.

(4) Low conceptual differentiation: The planning process should include individuals who can identify similarities among superficially different aspects of the situation which is the subject of planning. This goal could be achieved by including one or a few individuals who can identify broad similarities among many aspects of the situation. Otherwise, many individuals could be included each of whom sees some similarities among a few of the aspects of the situation.

(5) Cognitive complexity: The planning process should include individuals who are able to recognize complexities in the situation

in question. In addition, the process should include individuals who can view the situation with sufficient abstraction to be able to integrate these complexities mentally into a unified image of the situation. The recognition of complexities may require that many individuals with different experiences participate in the planning process.

(6) Reflectiveness: The planning process should include individuals who are able to reflect on the situation under scrutiny and information about it before deciding on a formulation of the problem or a course of action to solve it. Participation of many individuals necessarily requires reflectiveness in the process of reaching consensus about the planning situation, although reflectiveness does not inherently require many participants.

(7) Sharpening: The planning process should include individuals who are able to recognize changes in different aspects of the planning situation. This goal may be achieved either by including one or a few individuals who can identify even relatively small changes or by including many individuals each of whom is sensitive to changes in some part of the situation.

(8) Flexible control: The planning process should include individuals who can be distracted from their focus of concern to apparently peripheral but possibly relevant aspects of the situation in question. This goal may be achieved either by including one or a few individuals with flexible attention control or by including many individuals each of whom is attentive to particular different aspects of the situation which may be useful in planning.

(9) Tolerance for incongruous or unrealistic experiences: The planning process should include individuals who are able to recognize and accept aspects of the planning situation which may be inconsistent with conventional or consensual beliefs about the situation. This goal may be achieved by including one or a few individuals with a tolerance for incongruity or by including many individuals with different perspectives on the planning situation.

Political Accountability

This discussion indicates that effective planning requires not only the intellectual accountability of planners in sharing with citizens responsibility for cognitive tasks, but also planners' political accountability in sharing leadership for organizational and group process tasks. Moreover, the variety of tasks suggests that different types of leadership are necessary. Whereas, traditionally, planners have attempted to exercise all types of leadership themselves, this discussion indicates that different types of leadership require different abilities and should be formally or tacitly assigned to different participants.

Planners have tended to think about their work in terms of one kind of leadership, plan-preparation leadership. Assigned to prepare planning documents, they generally see all tasks and other types of leadership subsumed in this responsibility. However, there are other types of leadership which others may exercise which do not undermine this responsibility. There are various types of intellectual, or cognitive, leadership. As noted earlier, most planners regard themselves as intellectual experts and assume that they are uniformly competent in all intellectual tasks. However, although the cognitive styles just described are not discretely separable in a process of thinking about a planning situation, nevertheless, participants in such a process may come to recognize different individuals as distinctly capable at particular types of tasks. For example, someone may be acknowledged as particularly helpful in "putting things into perspective"; another may be recognized for "being able to find the hidden parts of the problem which help solve it." Each of these abilities, with its role, constitutes the basis for an implicit form of cognitive leadership. Cognitive leadership may be exercised in part by planners and in part by lay citizens.

In addition, organizational or group process leadership require special abilities to facilitate communication and agreement among people who not only see different aspects of a situation but also use different cognitive processes to view the situation. The importance of this leadership rests in the contribution which it makes to reaching decisions about the perspective which will be reflected and represented in the plan. This leadership provides assistance in devising acceptable procedures for decision-making in a planning process. Crucially, the ability of cognitive leaders to exercise their leadership depends on their ability to get support from participants whose activities are guided by the organizational leadership. Simply put, cognitive leadership rests not on any intrinsic logical superiority, but on the ability to persuade people that a particular viewpoint is valid. Most planners appear to feel stronger or more competent at intellectual than interpersonal tasks. Therefore, it may be appropriate to delegate organizational leadership either to planners who feel strongest at interpersonal tasks or to citizens with organizational ability.

The responsibility of planners for plan-preparation leadership is neither usurped nor undercut by any division of leadership accompanying a division of cognitive and organizational labor among planners and citizens. Although it is possible that an individual planner might exercise all types of leadership—though without necessarily performing all tasks—it is neither likely nor incumbent that this be the case. This formulation of distinct types of leadership in the planning process provides a response to planners' thinking about justifications for traditional divisions of labor between planners and citizens. For example, planners tend to argue that citizens should play a limited role in a planning process because their views are parochial and short-sighted. Here it is suggested that the ability to take a broad view—socially, spatially, and temporally—of a situation is one characteristic of cognitive style. Planners who are especially competent in this regard may take cognitive leadership here, although their ability to exercise this leadership rests on support from organizational and group process leadership. Similarly, many planners argue for a limited role for citizens on the ground that planners have distinctive technical training. Here it is suggested that planners may have technical skills which best suit them for certain types of cognitive leadership, but their ability to exercise this leadership, once more, rests on support from organizational and group process leadership.

Planners might express some concerns about this model for participation. First, there are legal constraints on the options which any group of planners, however composed or organized, may consider, and there is the possibility that the participants suggested here may recommend a course of action which conflicts with these constraints. Clearly, no decision made by participants should contravene the formal responsibilities of planners for preparing plans. However, these responsibilities may be subject to broader interpretation than planners have traditionally allowed.

Second, there is potential tension between selecting courses of action which planners regard as intellectually superior and selecting courses of action which a majority of participants favor. However, the discussion of cognitive style has indicated that, although planners may have special training and expertise, accurate perception of turbulent environments requires the contribution of many perspectives from many people. Moreover, planners' experience has shown that many proposals which they have developed without consultation with affected citizens have not met ready adoption and implementation.

Third, the planning process sketched here involves more time and energy than conventional processes. However, this model has been formulated on the premise that present planning efforts face diminishing effectiveness and legitimacy in the absence of a direct assessment of the types of expertise necessary for understanding the organizational environment of planning decisions. Such an assessment requires that planners think in new ways about both the characteristics of the planning environment which need attention and working relationships between formally trained planners and lay citizens. Both the intelligence required for understanding governance problems and the legitimacy of efforts to work on these problems require the type of public accountability of planning activities outlined here. Some planners may lose some of their accustomed autonomy, but most planners stand to gain effectiveness and legitimacy.

EXPERTISE IN PRACTICE: REDEFINING PLANNERS' ROLES

A New Model for Effective Practice

Expertise entails both a way of thinking and a way of acting. This section presents a model of organizationally sensitive planning which is concerned with social governance: the planner's activities permit a cognitive sensitivity to organizational issues, and the organization of participants in the planning process makes the planner accountable to members of the public. These themes converge in attention to the ways in which planners work with citizens.

There is no ideal role for every planner. The role which a planner takes at a particular time should depend on the characteristics of the situation and on the planner's attributes and resources. The role model presented here is a composite in two respects. First, it combines the characteristics of three observed planning roles. One is the Needlemans' (1974) "bureaucratic guerrilla," a planning agency staff member who is expected to intercede between the agency and citizen groups and to represent the views and interests of citizens in the planning process. Another is Meltsner's (1976) "entrepreneur," an agency staff member who combines political skills with technical skills to advocate for positions in the bureaucratic planning process. The last is Tennenbaum's (1978) "entrepreneur-planner," who is concerned with finding a position in a public agency or private organization which will provide a base for shepherding the implementation of a particular policy or proposal.[6] The role model is a composite also in that it represents a combination of types of expertise which should be available in the planning process through the collective efforts of at least one planner and a group of citizens.

The role model may be most easily summarized as a combination of a technically competent planner and a politically astute organizer. The model incorporates responsibilities from working with citizens to include their viewpoints in the formulation of problems to working with citizens and relevant decision-makers to implement possible solutions for problems. It is not likely—and even less desirable—that a single planner will carry out all tasks which this model entails. Rather, it is simply necessary that a planner with plan-preparation responsibilities be aware of the various tasks involved in the planning process and identify and work with some others who can, together, carry out all tasks. For example, a technician need not be also a political strategist but should, at least, understand and support the role of political strategy in relation to technical work. Similarly, a planner who works for adoption of a proposal need not also work for its implementation but should, at least, understand and support the role of those who do work for implementation.[7]

Formulating Problems and Negotiating Ground Rules

Planners' work begins with someone's request that they look at a "problem." A request may come to a public agency staff member from an administrator or, through the administrator, from an elected official. A private consultant may be hired by a client. A community group may draw the attention of public agency planners to certain local concerns. In each case, a planner is asked to give attention to substantive concerns of a group of citizens.

Initially, a planner should work with the citizens to help them articulate their concerns—what they include within their view of the problem and what they exclude from consideration as part of the problem. The planner will discover readily that citizens disagree about how to define the situation under scrutiny. Planners need to recognize and respond to different parties' definitions of the situation in their own terms. For example, one group may formulate issues in technical economic terms, but this frame of reference may be difficult to understand and unacceptable to a group which is concerned about social equity. In confronting different definitions of the situation, planners need to recognize that these definitions represent different languages used to describe the social world.

Further, differences in language may represent differences in interests. Because the formulation and bounding of a problem amounts to the blaming and acquitting of various parties, planners will find that articulation of issues leads quickly to an identification of interested parties.[8] There may be conflict among these parties about the definition of problems to be considered for planning. At one extreme, parties may disagree about whether a problem exists at all. For example, one party may benefit from a situation which others find harmful. Alternatively, parties may agree that a problem exists but may disagree about how to define the problem. They may recognize that different definitions of the problem imply different attributions of responsibility or blame for the problem. Disagreement about the nature of a problem may revolve about conflicts over whose interests are worth considering and, implicitly, who should participate in the process of defining the problem. Disagreement about the terms in which a problem should be defined—for example, technically, socially, economically, or politically—may represent differences about which interests should be implicated, who should be blamed, and where intervention should take place.

Thus efforts to articulate substantive problems and conflicts about their definition may lead readily to the unearthing of procedural issues. Parties may disagree about what language to use in describing a situation. Further, differences in language may be difficult to reconcile because different vocabularies represent different perceptions of interests. In order to reach some consensus about how to formulate a substantive problem, planners must develop some consensus about procedures to follow in resolving differences in language and interests sufficiently to permit action which is considered legitimate by affected parties.

These actions take on a special meaning in the case of a planner working for a public agency, because the agency itself has its own peculiar language and interests. When a planner begins working with a community group, citizens may be concerned about a relatively narrowly bounded problem. The definition of the problem may even be influenced by an understanding of the limited domain of the agency for which the planner works. If the planner encourages citizens to articulate clearly what bothers them, their exploration may have two effects. First, differences between the language which citizens use to describe their problems and the language of planning agencies and public programs may become evident. Planners must help citizens translate their concerns into language which is comprehensible to planners and "appropriate" to the planning process. For example, planners may help citizens who are concerned about housing conditions to identify regulations which might be brought to bear in improving housing stock. Conversely, planners must help citizens to understand the technical analysis of planning documents in terms of the social, economic, and political interests of community members. As in other cases where different groups use different language, planners may confront difficult challenges of finding common vocabularies which permit both citizens and planners to believe that their concerns are expressed understandably but without loss of meaning.

Insofar as planners are able to mediate differences in language between citizens and the planning agency, the intellectual accountability of the planning agency is increased: citizens can understand its activities better and can express their concerns in a way which is likely to be understood in the agency. A consequence of this increased intellectual accountability is a change in the political accountability of the public agency to citizen groups. These groups can begin to make more explicit and more "appropriate" requests of the planning staff and planning commission. Thus the planner is implicitly and unavoidably involved in negotiating ground rules for planning—both directly on a case-by-case basis ,and cumulatively. In order to meet any planning agency expectations that community organizations be involved in the planning process, the planner must satisfy citizen expectations regarding how they will participate in decision-making.

Consequently, a likely second result of planners' articulation of citizens' concerns is a discovery of differences in interests between community members and a planning agency. Planners' work with community organizations encourages citizens to believe that governmental agencies, such as a planning department, have an obligation to respond to problems which communities cannot solve alone. In doing this, planners evidently increase public pressure on the planning department. Both the limited jurisdiction of planning departments and the limitations on resources within their control must qualify claims to serve the entire "public interest" and give the impression of serving selected interests. Thus planners helping community organizations to articulate their interests in a problem situation may find that the domain of the planners' agency is too narrow to fit the citizens' concerns. In order to respond to citizens' interests, planners should encourage their agencies to extend their domains and to collaborate with other agencies which have responsibilities related to concerns of the citizen group. Here both the scarcity of resources available to public agencies, as well as conflicting demands on the agencies, will bring to light potential conflicts of interests between public agencies and particular citizen groups in specific situations. Again, a planner's efforts to help a community group articulate their concerns about a substantive problem may lead directly to procedural concerns. In this case, the planning agency itself emerges as a party to this procedural conflict.

When efforts to articulate substantive problems lead to procedural problems, planners should address these matters directly. Parties interested in a situation may be separated by differences of perception, differences of language, and differences of interest. Paradoxically, reconcilitaion of differences in perception and language may contribute to a heightened awareness of differences in interest. Further, differences in interest may be accompanied by conflicting assumptions about appropriate ground rules to follow to come to agreement about any formulation of a problem to work on—much less ground rules to follow to a solution. Here planners confront the core of the problem of governance: it is necessary to negotiate broadly accepted ground rules for proceeding.

In some cases, normal legal procedures may be acceptable to all or most parties. In these cases, the planner should seek primarily to secure explicit agreement of affected parties to endorse decisions made by these procedures. In other cases, particular groups may be concerned to have certain arrangements for provision of information, influence over decisions, or, at least, a veto over any decision. Different groups may have different views about when they should be consulted or deferred to. Significantly, some groups may disagree about whether, when, or in what way other groups should participate in the planning process.

Planners need to confront these differences and seek to negotiate a framework for making and implementing decisions in relation to the issues in question. This negotiation of ground rules may require an explication of assumptions and differences among affected parties in order to find some resolution, although in some cases an underplaying of differences may contribute to acceptable agreement. In the process of negotiation it may be easier to begin with the development of agreements about procedures which will be excluded and move gradually toward some consensus about procedures which positively must be followed.[9] The negotiation of ground rules involves not only insightful intellectual understanding of actors' points-of-view, but also interpersonal and organizational skills in working with actors who disagree and helping to develop agreements about procedures sufficient to assure the broad legitimacy of decisions reached subsequently.[10]

Solving Problems: Proposal, Adoption, and Implementation

The solution of a problem involves three overlapping tasks: the formulation of a proposal by planners, the adoption of some proposal by relevant decision-makers, and the implementation of an adopted proposal by relevant program staff. Not only do these tasks overlap with one another, but sometimes the same people, including planners, may be involved in carrying out each of the tasks. The following discussion identifies ways in which planners may influence all of these tasks in the solution of a problem.

The development of proposals for solutions for problems raises the same ground rule considerations as those involved in formulating problems. Conflict about solutions involves disagreements about the criteria which should be used for designing and choosing alternatives, the relative costs and benefits of specific alternatives, and who should bear the costs and who should receive the benefits. Parties which have initially defined the problem situation differently will require correspondingly different evidence bearing on the desirability and feasibility of alternative courses of action. For example, some groups may be concerned primarily about economic consequences, others may be concerned about engineering requirements, and still others may be concerned about redress of social inequities. In addition, the process of considering and selecting alternatives is surrounded by real uncertainty, and interested parties are likely to make assumptions about consequences on the basis of their past experiences and biases.

For a proposal to be adopted and implemented, it must anticipate the technical and political concerns of decision-makers and other actors whose support or cooperation will be necessary for the enactment of the proposal. In some cases, the actors who are important in adoption and implementation are the same as those who are concerned about the identification of problems initially. In other cases, those who are asked to adopt proposals must be convinced that a problem is important and worth their effort in solving. In most cases, those who implement decisions must be convinced that a problem is sufficiently important for them to disrupt their accustomed routines in order to work on it. The considerations which are important in defining a problem and in formulating a solution for the problem may be similar to the considerations which are important to decision-makers in considering whether to adopt a proposal. However, the considerations which are important to program staff members who are involved in implementing decisions may be distinctly different. They may be concerned about economic matters, they may be concerned about political issues, but they are certainly concerned about the effect of any new program on their ongoing organization.

Thus planners confront the challenge of developing some agreement about criteria to be employed in considering potential solutions for a problem, as well as about the nature of evidence which must be included in the analysis of alternatives. In order to do this, planners should consult not only parties who are immediately concerned about the design of solutions to a problem which they perceive, but also parties whose support or acquiescence will be essential to adoption and implementation subsequently. The latter parties may be particularly difficult to consult and instill with a sense that a potential intervention is important when they are not immediately affected. This process of identifying courses of action which may be broadly perceived as both desirable and feasible requires planners to supplement technical analysis with analysis of political issues which affect this large array of actors. The legitimacy of the selection of possible solutions depends on planners' ability to respond to these political issues.

Adoption of Proposals. The formulation of problem-definitions involves the planner in the negotiation of ground rules for participation in planning, and this responsibility continues with the identification of possible solutions for problems, the adoption of proposals for solutions, and the implementation of proposals. Having assumed the role of facilitator of citizen participation and at least tacit advocate of certain citizens' positions, the planner must work within the bureaucracy of the planning department— and, where warranted, other agencies—to assure a hearing for the citizens' position and some inclusion of the citizens' position in the planning process through implementation. The role of intellectual representative of community views almost inevitably involves the role of political representative of these views. In this role the planner must seek to influence other staff members and significant decision-makers.

A strategy for influencing decision-makers hinges on their intellectual dependence on planners as advisors. Although decision-makers tend to regard themselves as political experts and engage advisors for technical assistance, planners must be aware that the boundaries between technical and political issues are subject to either explicit or, more often, tacit negotiation. This negotiation involves not simply the respective responsibilities and roles of planners and formal decision-makers, but, more broadly, the ground rules of the planning process.

To be effective in this negotiation, planners must be competent in a complex negotiation of differences in language. They will already have met with citizens to translate their concrete social and political concerns into more abstract and technical formulations of problems and programmatic remedies. This translation is necessary to permit planning staff members to make the systematic technical assessments of problems and programs expected by decision-makers. However, in order to make these technical calculations meaningful to the decision-makers who must consider the adoption of proposals, planners confront another challenge of translation. They must recast the technical calculations in terms which simultaneously represent the initial concerns of citizens and are sensitive to the combination of technical and political matters which concern decision-makers. Whereas planners, as technically trained practitioners, are normally concerned about identifying information which is scientifically precise and theoretically correct, decision-makers, as political actors, are normally concerned about identifying information which is practically useful and likely to be effective, regardless of its conceptual underpinnings. Planners' presentations must anticipate and respond to these latter concerns in the vocabulary of decision-makers in order to be persuasive with them.[11]

Using this language, planners must attempt to negotiate for themselves a favorable location of the boundary between matters considered technical and within their domain and matters considered political and within the domain of decision-makers. Planners may consider two alternative but complementary tactics. First, planners may seek to expand the domain of technical considerations into the realm of what decision-makers regard as political considerations. The planner may attempt to define many of the decision-maker's seemingly political considerations in terms of technical issues, with regard to which the planner is uniquely suited to render a judgment. More generally, a planner may portray the issues for decision-making in terms which the planner is considered especially trained to understand. This approach is not simply technocratic obfuscation but has legitimacy insofar as the planner's positions accurately represent the views or interests of citizens.

An alternative tactic is to supplement requested technical information with explicitly political information designed to appeal to the decision-maker's perceived self-interest. Here the planner would attempt not to enlarge the range of issues defined as technical but, rather, to expand the perception of his or her expertise into the political domain. For example, requests to planners typically emphasize advice on technical questions, such as the costs and benefits of alternative courses of action. Decision-makers normally are concerned about the costs and benefits to only certain parties, and they will read planners' analyses with these interests in mind. The planner should respond to such a request for advice by including information about costs incurred and benefits enjoyed by the citizens with whom the planner is concerned, in addition to the costs and benefits of those about whom the decision-makers are concerned. Further, the planner should give attention to developing and presenting measures of effectiveness for alternatives which reflect the interests of the citizens with whom the planner is concerned. Finally, concerns with cost-effectiveness should be supplemented with discussion of equity, or the distributional effects of alternatives. Planners should be explicit about who will bear costs and who will enjoy benefits of alternative courses of action.

This tactic has two effects. One is to indicate to decision-makers that choices may be more complex than initially imagined. The other is to present decision-makers with information which may have significant political meaning to them. Decision-makers are concerned about how a particular choice will affect their support from citizens who vote, and the effects of this tactic should increase planners' influence with decision-makers.

In general, planners may influence the adoption of proposals by emphasizing their relationships with a citizen constituency. Insofar as planners have worked with community members, the planners develop their own political support for the positions which they present. This political context of their work becomes incorporated into the content of any of the informational messages which planners communicate to formal decision-makers. Coalitions between a planner and citizen groups add to planners' analyses the additional information that community members are concerned about the outcomes of decisions which they perceive as affecting their interests. Citizens may lobby actively for the adoption of specific proposals. This relationship increases the likelihood that planners' analyses combining technical and political considerations are seriously considered in the process through which planning proposals are adopted.[12]

Implementation. Most conventional planning positions dictate a division of labor between a planner with plan-preparation responsibilities and others who directly oversee implementation of plans once they are adopted. Few planners are able formally to supervise implementation without changing jobs.[13] Nevertheless, there are two ways in which planners should be involved in the implementation process.

First, planners should recognize that actions taken in preparing a plan are inextricably tied to the subsequent implementation of that plan. A distinction between preparation and implementation of a plan is artificial. Both the content of a proposal adopted and the context in which the proposal is adopted affect its implementation, including the likelihood that the manner in which it is implemented will correspond significantly to the principles adopted. In a setting in which different groups have conflicting views about what constitute problems and what might be desirable solutions for problems, any adopted proposal is certain to receive support from some groups and to confront opposition from others.

Moreover, the process of preparing a plan, a process in which the planner works and consults differently with different interests, already prepares various actors to support, pay little attention to, or oppose the plan which is eventually adopted. As planners develop and lobby for a recommendation, they set the groundwork for support for and opposition to the recommended course of action. Therefore, a planner who is concerned about the implementation of a particular recommendation should anticipate the likely positions of significant actors early in the process of preparing the proposal. The planner should prepare scenarios of possible responses to different alternatives before making a final recommendation.[14]

The structuring of incentives into a proposal is an extremely sensitive and complex matter. Not only does implementation require the solving of particular political problems, such as whether staff members in one agency will cooperate with staff members in another agency. In addition, implementation requires the solving of practical problems, for instance, what sequence of actions by whom in what relationship with a client is necessary to improve the well-being of the client. Solutions to problems of this kind are beclouded by large areas of ignorance and uncertainty.

For example, it may be unclear what specific actions by program staff members may be necessary for them to implement effectively a proposal to which all of them give the highest support. Further, it may be unclear how to structure a program to permit the commission and correction of mistakes—learning— once a process of implementation has begun. In many areas it may be appropriate to regard a program as an informed experiment. Yet it may be difficult to structure a proposal so as to provide such an experiment with the requisite political reassurance for decision-makers, organizational and psychological support for staff members, and material and psychological support for clients—even if everyone involved has apparently good intentions.[15] Consideration of these issues requires that planners concern themselves with the ways in which organizations work.

Thus the components of a planner's proposal implicitly establish a system of incentives to which numerous actors will respond. Consequently, once a proposal is adopted, efforts to implement the proposal give rise to what Bardach (1977) has characterized as "implementation games." In general, members of organizations whose jurisdiction and power are likely to be increased by the proposal may be expected to support implementation in a way consistent with the principles of the proposal. Others whose jurisdiction and power are threatened may be expected to implement the proposal reluctantly or to act in ways which subvert the spirit and possibly also the letter of the proposal. In addition, organizational pressures of time and obligations to already existing programs may lead people whose support is necessary for implementation to give limited attention to the new program unless compelled to participate actively. For example, a program which has performance standards which are easily measured and which are accompanied by enforceable sanctions is more likely to be attended to than a program which has vague standards and no clear enforcement mechanisms. On top of these things, sheer uncertainty about how to accomplish certain mandated—and supported—tasks complicates implementation. Unless a program allows for and encourages some experimentation, responses to an implementation order may be ritualistic and even destructive.[16] Therefore, a planner who is concerned about implementation of a recommendation should explicitly identify the incentive system in alternative proposals and incorporate into a recommendation incentives most likely to bring about implementation consistent with the recommendation.[17]

There is a second way in which a planner may be involved in implementation without changing jobs. The planner may consult with and provide technical assistance to organizations or actors who have formal or informal responsibility for implementation. Some of this consultation may be explicitly requested, particularly if planners make it clear that they will provide technical assistance within the limits set by other responsibilities. In addition, planners may take an initiative in providing technical assistance where it appears necessary and would be welcomed. Citizen groups who are clients of programs may in particular need technical assistance in order to monitor or influence the process of implementation. Planners' assistance to citizen groups effectively completes the responsibilities which planners accepted when they worked with citizen groups to identify and formulate problems at the beginning of the planning process. Planners' provision of technical assistance would be limited by their other responsibilities, but they could negotiate time for providing technical assistance in implementation as part of their regular responsibilities. Finally, planners may make referrals to others with expertise useful in implementation when the planners lack either the time or the expertise themselves.

This type of involvement in implementation would have two important effects. First, it would increase the likelihood that implementation corresponds to the principles in adopted proposals. Second, it would give planners a greater sense of connection between their efforts and outcomes. Planners' sense of competence and control over the products of their work would increase.

Consequences for Governance

Planners' adoption of this model is likely to have both short-range and long-range effects which contribute to the solution of governance problems. In the short run, more citizens will have information about planning issues, and more citizens will participate in various stages of decision-making with respect to these issues. This increase in information in the planning process will help to explicate conflicts of perception and interests which impede the formulation and solution of problems. Although intellectual understanding of conflicts does not inherently lead to their resolution, more informed participation in planning may contribute to effective problem-solving in two ways. First, increased communication among affected parties can facilitate the resolution of some conflicts where the parties have an interest in finding a mutually acceptable resolution. Here decisions may involve consensus about either the substance of a specific decision or about the procedure followed in resolving a conflict. Second, a reality of widespread informed participation is inherently a modification of governance procedures which is likely to lead parties to attribute legitimacy to a broad range of decision-making procedures. As a consequence, specific substantive solutions, even when they favor some interests and do harm to others, may acquire derivative legitimacy from the accepted ground rules.

The cumulative, long-run effects of this kind of participation are social learning and a heightened collective self-sonsciousness about planning. Each of the many participating actors will want the others to learn to understand its own perceptions and interests, and each will want the others to be conscious of the ways in which their actions are congruent with or in conflict with those perceptions and interests. Substantively, the cumulative effect of planners' directly or indirectly bringing citizen groups into the planning process is to begin to create explicitly political discussion about planning issues. These groups will watch planning decisions more carefully and raise political concerns in connection with them. Technical issues will have to be translated into clear formulations of the social, economic, and political interests which participating groups believe to be at stake. Technical issues will have to be identified more accurately as basic choices of policy direction.

Where self-consciousness about the political meaning of planning problems is accompanied by a commitment to finding solutions to these problems, procedural developments are also likely. Over time, planners and citizen groups will become increasingly conscious of the types of problem-solving procedures which prove effective in different situations. As more individuals and groups are involved in planning activities, they are likely to become increasingly conscious of themselves as people engaged in problem-solving. They are likely to attempt to develop a useful language and conceptual framework with which they can analyze their efforts to formulate and solve problems. They will become better able to identify effective procedures and, crucially, the characteristics of these procedures which make them effective under particular conditions. Planners and citizens can then begin to move more knowledgeably toward the development of governance procedures which may be broadly accepted and extensively effective.

This process of development is likely to be uneven for two reasons. First, actors who at any time perceive themselves to be more powerful than others are unlikely to see an incentive to collaborate with others in discovering new decision-making procedures, particularly when any such procedures hold out the risk of redistributing power. Powerful actors may be interested in learning about new procedures which will serve their interests but may seek to hinder the learning of others. Conversely, weaker actors who have been victimized by the more powerful actors may both mistrust collaborative learning with them and seek to learn strategies which may directly reverse power relationships while still avoiding collaboration. Probably only as a constellation of power shifts closer toward equality will disparate actors find such self-interested strategies to be self-defeating and, consequently, decide to engage in collaborative learning about problem-solving procedures. Subsequent interest in learning may fluctuate in relation to the social distribution of power.

A second source of uneven development is likely periodic "overloading" of prevailing procedures. As the number of interested actors who want to participate in planning decisions increase, normal decision-making processes are likely to become unable to accommodate widespread, explicitly political demands for participation.[18] Growing pressure on planning decision-making processes may force a recognition of the weaknesses of these procedures for governance in a society with so many broadly conflicting interests. Thus, whereas increased participation in contemporary decision-making processes may offer a temporary resolution of the problem of governance, longer-range solutions depend on the invention of other procedures. A period of increased participation may be followed by a period in which decision-making procedures are blocked. This blockage, in turn, should stimulate consideration of alternative procedures which may accommodate numerous conflicting interests. Thus perods of "overload" and innovation may alternate.[19]

EDUCATING PLANNERS FOR NEW ROLES

The study findings suggest that many planners prefer to work as purely intellectual problem-solvers because of their organizationless cognitive maps, their relatively concrete cognitive style, and their ambivalence about power. Accordingly, preparing planners to take roles corresponding to the proposed model will require significant changes in planning practitioners.

One strategy for increasing the number of planners taking roles consistent with the model is suggested by a pessimistic interpretation of the study findings in the context of the vocational choice literature. That literature suggests that people tend to select fields of study and occupations which they regard as congruent with their personality orientations. This study shows consistent modal personality orientations among planning practitioners at all ages and all stages of their careers. Significantly the personality orientations of planners and their feelings about power do not appear to be in any way related to the orientations of the planning programs in which they studied. Thus one might conclude that typical formal planning roles contribute to a public image of planning which tends to attract practitioners from a population which is relatively homogeneous with respect to personality orientation and which would practice planning similarly regardless of the nature of their formal planning education.[20]

If this interpretation is valid, then in order to increase the number of planners inclined to take roles corresponding to proposed model, it would be necessary to recruit different people into the field of planning in response to an alternative public image of planning built on this model. Thus reform in the formal roles which planners occupy, as well as changed expectations regarding responsibilities among planners, might attract practitioners with different cognitive styles and personality orientations. This strategy has been adopted by the Planners Network, an organization of politically activist planning academics and practitioners. Members of the network have formulated models of organizationally and politically sensitive planning practice and have presented these models to planning practitioners, planning students, and other interested citizens.[21] Insofar as planners and citizens find these alternative roles attractive, they may organize to persuade planning agencies to restructure the process of planning and permit planners and citizens to play new roles. In addition, practitioners who are attracted to these roles may attempt to enact them in their present settings and possibly effect some change in their discretion in their current roles. Finally, these alternative role models, along with whatever changes in the practice of planning they encourage, may attract a different population of students into planning education, and these people will be more likely to take these new roles than are those who presently enter planning.

Another strategy, not incompatible with the first, is suggested by an optimistic view of the potential of educational programs. This strategy would assume that, regardless of who might choose planning as an occupation, properly designed educational programs could affect students' cognitive style and personality orientation. This strategy would aim to design educational programs which would develop in students the cognitive style and personality orientation which would support taking the type of roles described here. Most programs in planning education focus on the presentation of specific cognitive knowledge. Implicitly they appear to reinforce a particular cognitive style and personality orientation.[22] The strategy for educational reform would explicitly confront issues of students' cognitive styles and feelings about power and would attempt to elicit characteristics most likely to contribute to practical effectiveness.

Such a strategy would entail supplementing current patterns of didactic education with active student involvement in experiential learning. There is evidence to suggest that this strategy is feasible. Kogan (1971) has observed that some empirical studies show successful educational efforts to modify cognitive style, although the balance of studies is inconclusive. Seidner (1976) has identified studies in which experiential exercises have affected organizational sensitivity, although this literature review is similarly inconclusive.

Student and teacher characteristics have differential effects on—and constrain—educational outcomes. The following examples from the empirical literature suggest potential effects of experiential education. Signell (1966) found that for learning complex concepts about the characteristics of other persons and relationships with other persons—the type of cognitive understanding required for organizational sensitivity—experiential learning appears to be superior to didactic learning. Livingston (1971) found that experiential education contributes to an ability to be empathic with actors in other social roles. Schild (1968) and McFarlane (1969) found that experiential education helps participants develop rational strategies for working with and influencing other persons. Other evidence comes from the observations of educators working with students in planning and related fields. For example, Beinstein (1976), although not directly concerned with cognition, reports that students placed in social agencies gained a noticeable sensitivity to the structure of complex organizations and a confidence in coping with novel situations. Heskin (1978), reporting on internships for planning students, emphasizes students' learning about the structures of groups, complex organizations, and political settings. These studies support more impressionistic observations by a number of educators (for example, Cook, 1970; Culbert, 1977; Kidron, 1977; Klein and Astrachan, 1971; and Kolb, 1976) that students being educated for professional practice learn best about the structure of organizations through structured direct experience in them.

Experiential Education for Planners

The remainder of this chapter focuses on ways of developing an educational strategy to increase the number of organizationally sensitive planners. As elements in an educational strategy, there are a number of experiential educational exercises, which may be arranged along a continuum from the relatively more didactic to the more purely experiential: case studies, simulation games, role playing, training groups, and supervised field instruction.[23]

Case Studies. Case studies permit vicarious participation in situations where the presence or absence of organizational sensitivity affected the outcomes of the planning process. Case studies may be most useful in alerting planners to the importance of this sensitivity and in pointing out some specific questions which planners have asked and some specific skills which planners have used in dealing with them. Case studies may have only a limited effect on feelings about power and other elements of personality orientation which keep planners from becoming conscious organizational actors.[24]

Simulation Games. Simulation games provide for direct participation in situations which comprise parts of a planner's role. For example, there are simulation games focusing on group decision-making and others concerned with the exercise of power. Two features of games are valuable in teaching organizational sensitivity. First, participants are placed in situations in which they are expected to take actions which have consequences for them. Hence they are required to pay attention to other participants and at least tacitly to identify incentive systems governing actions. Minimally, participants must involve themselves cognitively in the games. They are likely also to become involved emotionally. This involvement provides material with which participants may discuss the rules of their roles in the exercise and in planning organizations. The second important feature of simulation exercises is that teachers require participants to confront and analyze their actions in the games. Thus participants are encouraged to move beyond cognitive discussion of overt behavior to understanding the noncognitive and unconscious influences on their actions.[25]

Role Playing. Role playing involves simulation of an entire role substantially similar to one which a planner normally plays. The potential strengths of role playing include those of simulation games: participants are required to respond to others and take actions, and they are expected to analyze their behavior. Role playing's emphasis of whole "realistic" roles adds simultaneously a potential strength and a potential problem. Positively, participants who focus on cognitive, rational levels of experience will find their actions more plausible and, therefore, more meaningful. The transferability of the role playing experience to planning practice is evident. At the same time, the realism of the exercise may make it relatively easy for rationally oriented participants to analyze and dispose of issues in cognitive terms. Actions can be easily explained in terms of customary technical justifications, even though nonrational issues may affect choices.

The teacher plays a crucial role in helping participants to articulate and become self-conscious about their actions in the exercise. An effective teacher will block efforts by participants to use familiar jargon to talk about the exercise and, instead, will draw participants' attention to the interplay of conscious and unconscious issues which influence their actions. In this examination of behavior in roles in the exercise it is possible to identify patterns of behavior which may interfere with effectiveness in organizational settings. In addition to making participants sensitive to organizational issues which are implicit in their roles, teachers may introduce participants to organizational and political skills which may be useful in resolving issues which do arise. Whether participants change their behavior outside the exercise setting depends in part on their motivation and in part on the operative incentive system in work settings.[26]

Training Groups. Training groups immerse participants in making and responding to decisions about the use of power in group problem-solving. Both T groups and Tavistock groups require participants to be self-conscious about the behavior of the group of which they are a part and the ways in which group membership affects personal behavior. In a T group a consultant participates actively as a model of collaborative behavior. The trainer seeks to teach members to be self-conscious by providing observations about personal behavior. By example the trainer shows members how to communicate supportively as a means of creating trust and cooperation among group members.

The Tavistock human relations group focuses directly on studying the behavior of the group and members' feelings about that behavior. The consultant remains detached from the group and, following a psychoanalytic model, offers occasional observations about the behavior of the group. The minimal participation of the consultant tends to create frustration, anxiety, and, crucially, feelings and fantasies about authority, represented most significantly by the consultant. These powerful feelings about authority become material for group members to analyze. In examining these feelings, group members may become sensitive to the ways in which past experiences with authority figures tend to condition their responses to subsequent group situations and authority figures. Examining these feelings may make it possible to modify customary responses to organizational authority figures in order to be more realistic.

Both types of group experiences may make participants more sensitive to normal problems or conflicts which arise in the development and operation of any group or organization. They can develop a self-consciousness about the ways in which personal motives and needs contribute to processes and practices in groups and organizations. Additionally, participants may learn inter-personal skills which may contribute to effectiveness in both collaborative and conflictual organizational situations.

However, there is a potential lesson in the experience of Tavistock groups which T groups do not provide. The structure of human relations groups focuses participants' attention on their feelings about authority figures in particular and power generally. The powerful group experience may force participants to re-examine their assumptions about power and their feelings about their own relationships with power. Participants may directly confront an issue which is subsidiary in T groups: how to deal with power in ambiguous and conflictful settings. A new understanding of power may make participants more comfortable with it and more able to think about using it in organizations. As a consequence, they may become more sensitive to political issues which are implicit in the organizations in which they work. For those for whom obstacles to organizational sensitivity are unconscious, experiences in this type of group may be helpful in facilitating greater sensitivity to organizational issues. The carryover effect of group exercises depends on the incentive system of participants' regular organizational setting.[27]

Supervised Field Instruction. Supervised field instruction permits participants to work in positions in planning organizations under the joint direction of an agency employee and a faculty supervisor. The agency employee provides task direction and an orientation to the organization, and the faculty supervisor provides technical instruction and stimulation to develop a sensitivity to organizational issues in the placement. The quality of supervision is the crucial component of field instruction. "Real world" experience by itself has no inherent value in teaching organizational sensitivity or skills; otherwise, the practitioners interviewed in this study would think and act differently. A supervisor's consistent questioning of students can make them sensitive to certain types of concerns, such as organizational and political issues. In addition, a supervisor can help a student to develop skills to use in resolving these issues. Supervisors may meet with students individually and in group seminars. Supervisors may ask students to keep a journal as an aid to self-conscious thought about their actions.

A supervisor can raise questions about organizational issues in conjunction with typical sets of concerns which students experience in placements. For example, when a student first enters a placement, concerns center on getting a desk and telephone number, learning who has authority for supplies, and trying to understand who has authority over which parts of the placement assignment. At this point it is helpful simply to ask students questions about the formal organization of the placement setting, as a way of calling attention to the importance of organizational structure.

Frequently after the first few weeks in a placement students report that the people they work for are "crazy" or that the procedures at the agency generally are "crazy." At this point it is helpful to raise questions regarding differences between personal behavior and role behavior, as a way of indicating that people in organizations occupy formal roles and respond to incentives attached to their roles. It is helpful to indicate to students that they have instrumental role relationships with others in the organization, rather than personal or friendship relationships, even if some of their agency colleagues may become friends. Thus actions which may seem "crazy" when viewed as personal behavior may be understandable when viewed as role behavior. Questions about what different individuals in the agency really expect of the student and how they relate to others in the agency call attention to the nature of informal organizational relationships. Questions about how individuals in the agency may be responding to directions or pressures from others outside the agency begin to call students' attention to the presence of a political incentive system which will affect decision-making in the planning agency.

Once students have begun to overcome initial anxiety about their competence and to establish friendly working relationships with others, it is helpful to raise questions about how the student is working with others in getting tasks done. For example, it is likely that the student will have to spend time bargaining for information, or the student may be meeting with citizen groups to assess community needs or to develop planning priorities.

At the end of the placement it is useful to review the course of events in the placement in organizational and political terms. Questions should seek to clarify how the political context of the planning process influenced the course of work in the placement and the students' assignments. Students should be encouraged to discuss the ways in which the agency might be reorganized to facilitate any type of planning which they would prefer. In this context students should be urged to look at the ways in which the political environment of the planning agency may set constraints on the activities of the agency and to consider what types of changes in the political environment would be necessary to support the types of planning decisions which students would prefer.

These questions all help to sensitize students to interpreting their actions in the context of the organizational and political environment of their work. The similarity of placement positions to other planning positions contributes to the likelihood that sensitivities— and abilities—developed here will be carried over into other planning work.[28]

Different combinations of these exercises may be effective as an educational strategy to make more planners sensitive to the organizational issues and political interests implicated in planning issues. In addition, these educational experiences can help to teach organizational skills that can be strategically valuable in working with groups participating in the planning process. In the development of an educational strategy it is important to match the relative strengths of particular educational methods with the learning needs of specific groups of students.

CONCLUDING COMMENTS

This book has identified two reasons why it may be important that planners gain legitimacy in problem-solving. The first, which is most significant for practitioners themselves, is that planners would acquire a sense of effectiveness and social value. Feelings of powerlessness would be replaced by feelings of authority. The second reason, which is most significant for the larger society, is that, indeed, some group of "planners" would be effective in making progress toward solving major problems of governance. Citizens would bestow broad legitimacy on these practitioners as a result of their effectiveness.

What is required for planners to gain effectiveness in solving governance problems—and, with this effectiveness, social legitimacy—is an opening up of the practice of planning. Cognitively, planners need to open their thinking to new information about organizations. Socially, planners need to open the process of planning to include individuals and groups with whom they traditionally have had little contact.

This chapter has developed a model for planning practice which responds to the obstacles to effectiveness and legitimacy identified earlier. Advice-giving may continue to be ambiguous, with specific events remaining uncertain, but a planner who understands the nature of these ambiguities can bring to his or her practice the intellectual certainty of an overview which recognizes probable uncertainties. Anticipating likely ambiguities, this planner can work actively to bring about greater certainty in relations with clients, constituents, and others. Problem-solving may continue to involve fragmented responsibility, but a planner who understands the source of this fragmentation can view his or her actions within a framework which has intellectual coherence. Recognizing the sources of fragmented responsibility, this planner can work actively with others who are part of the problem-solving process in order to give their discrete activities greater coherence of effort and purpose. The intangibility of advisory problem-solving is likely to resist clear description for some time, but a planner who understands the sources of difficulty in describing planning can begin to develop language which increases the comprehensibility of this work. In general, as both planners and other citizens become self-conscious participants in the process of planning, their various interests will stimulate them to articulate more clearly what this process involves. A major theme of this study has been the difficulty which planners have experienced in describing what it is that they do day after day under the label of "planning." In articulating and analyzing that difficulty, this book has suggested a language which may provide a better understanding of "planning."

This book has examined planners' decisions about planning roles in a developmental framework, in which a sequence of influences shape individuals' choice of planning as a field and particular roles within it. Each of these influences affects the degree to which a more open practice of planning may be possible. First, for everyone there is a series of experiences in early childhood and youth which mold personality orientation, interests, and abilities. Apparently these experiences influence the choice of planning as an occupation, initial specific attractions to planning, and inclinations to particular roles in practice. Second, formal education in planning provides future practitioners with explicit instruction in practice methods and the use of particular bodies of knowledge. In addition, educational programs convey implicit messages concerning cognitive styles and feelings about power which may be appropriate for planning practice. It appears that either most planning programs convey a common tacit message regarding cognitive style and feelings about power, or else they fail to affect common predispositions of students entering the programs. Third, the agencies and firms in which planners practice have incentives and constraints which shape and limit the pattern of planners' work activities. Apparently, organizational roles affect planners' practical daily expectations and lead many planners to redefine their work roles.

This chapter has outlined strategies for increasing the likelihood that planners will adopt an organizationally sensitive role. For practical reasons these strategies focus on interventions in formal planning education and in the work setting. Although early life experiences may have considerable influence on people who subsequently choose to become planners, no intervention here is suggested because none is either feasible or proper. Rather, it is recommended that educators and employers recognize the significant ways in which these experiences may shape cognitive styles and feelings about power which will affect planners' expectations about and performance of work. Educators and employers may then act more selectively and deliberately in their recruitment and training efforts.

Considerable weight has been given to intervention into the structure of formal planning education. This emphasis stems from a conviction that the potentials of educational programs have been only superficially examined and that the opportunities for influence in planning programs are, at the least, more extensive than presently imagined. For example, whatever predispositions students may bring into these programs, the period of formal education in planning is one in which students anticipate being subjected to new knowledge and new experience. In addition, educators are only beginning to recognize what has been called the cognitive sensitivity to organization as something which they may attempt to teach. Further, the possibilities of experiential education in teaching this sensitivity and accompanying skills are only beginning to be explored and understood.

This chapter has identified two approaches for affecting the undeniable influence which formal work roles have on the expectations and actions of planners. First, planners graduating from educational programs with greater organizational sensitivity and skills are likely to expect to do more and to be able to exercise greater influence in organizational decision-making. Individually and collectively, a significant number of planners who seek to open the planning process to diverse groups of citizens and to work with citizens could, through their actions, make some changes in planning organizations and their relationships with clients and constituents. This approach is suggested in the belief that planners have not yet begun to test the limits to their discretion. Planners' ambivalence about exercising power is evidence that many planners have hitherto been reluctant to press apparent formal limits. A second, related approach to affecting formal work roles in planning organizations rests on planners' development of coalitions with citizen groups, in which they collectively attempt to reform planning roles and procedures to permit greater collaboration between planners and citizens in working on problems of societal governance.

It may be appropriate to conclude with a caveat. This book has emphasized the potential organizational change which more knowledgeable and more assertive planners could effect. However, it is important to avoid the trap of "blaming the victim."[29] It is important not to move simplistically from an accounting of gaps in planners' expertise to holding planners responsible for all limitations on their influence. It is essential not to overlook the ways in which elected officials may not want planners to take a more active role in decision-making. Further, it is crucial to understand the ways in which political or economic structures may set limits to planners' discretion. Study of these societal influences on planning organizations and the planning process will help to formulate a broad strategy for changing planners' roles, opening up the planning process, and directly confronting problems of societal governance. It should be assumed that planners would work with other practitioners and citizens in implementing such a far-ranging strategy.

NOTES

1. The questions described here really require two types of sensitivity. One is an organizational sensitivity, which is discussed here. The other is a temporal sensitivity, an appreciation of the ways in which social conditions may change and an ability to create mental scenarios which are extensive, differentiated, and realistic. The nature of the temporal sensitivity has frequently been discussed in connection with forecasting, which is an intrinsic part of planning. I have written elsewhere about the forecasting component of planning (Baum, 1976) and the ability to create useful images of the future (Baum, 1977a). Loye (1978) has examined the mental processes involved in contemplating the future.

2. The following presentation is an abridged version of a more extensive discussion in another paper (Baum, 1979b).

3. It may be recalled that Hudson (1966) found that people most likely to develop cognitive maps which are richly populated have cognitive styles which are "divergent." They see the world in general categories; they respond flexibly to cues; they tolerate ambiguity; and they reason by analogy. Cole (1975) found that planners most likely to think and act in political terms have cognitive styles which are abstract. They see the world in differentiated categories; they respond flexibly to cues; they tolerate ambiguity; they are sensitive to subtle cues; and they have the capacity to think hypothetically. There is evident consistency between Hudson's and Cole's findings. Hudson's reference to general categories and Cole's reference to differentiated categories reflect differences in the authors' emphasis, rather than differences in their subjects' cognitive styles. Hudson is referring to subjects' differentiation of information into relatively few general categories, whereas Cole is referring to subjects' integration of information into categories sufficiently differentiated to reflect the complexity of the world. For a discussion of this issue, see Kogan (1971, pp. 259-261, 271-277).

4. Accordingly, this section is not intended to review the literature on citizen participation or models for citizen participation in the planning process.

5. This approach to designing a model for citizen participation on the basis of cognitive requirements may be better understood by a comparison with earlier work by Faludi (1973). Faludi was interested in designing a structure for a planning agency based on a conceptualization of the planning agency as a brain. He asked what intellectual tasks a brain problem. To each task he assigned an organizational structure in specific working relationship with other structures. In the end, however, he succeeded in breaking down the "black box" of activities involved in planning into many smaller black boxes without shedding much light on the nature of the cognitive or emotional processes involved in planning. The approach here differs in two ways. First, whereas Faludi's black boxes are identified by the intellectual products which each should bring forth, this approach is concerned with the ways of thinking about the world—cognitive processes which are likely to produce those products. Second, it includes citizens in a more explicit and active role than Faludi's simply labelled "environment."

6. Each of these types of planner is described in detail in the source cited in the text. Here they are used as the basis for a composite role model.

7. To require that a technician be sensitive to political issues and that a plan-developer be sensitive to implementation considerations is not to imply that there will be no conflict among participants about which course to follow at any point. For example, technicians and political strategists may disagree vehemently about how problems should be formulated. Similarly, planners concerned about implementation feasibility may disagree with planners concerned about the economic rationality of recommendations. The requirement that these different planners attempt to understand others' concerns does not guarantee ultimate agreement, but the requirement does increase the likelihood that the course of action taken will incorporate a more comprehensive consideration of technical and political issues than is ordinarily the case. Moreover, more extensive consultation is likely to contribute to greater support for positions eventually taken.

8. Seeley (1967) has analyzed the ways in which the definition of a social problem is analogous to the delivery of a legal indictment.

9. I have written about problems in constitution-building in "Toward a Post-Industrial Planning Theory" (Baum, 1977b).

10. Argyris and Schon (1974 and 1978) have written about methods which may be used to help actors learn about their own and others' tacit assumptions which may interfere with agreement about working procedures. Michael (1973) has written as a social psychologist about organizational and individual tendencies which hinder this more open communication about assumptions. These books are helpful for the clinical insights which they offer, though they suffer from a tendency to

interpret perceived conflicts of interest as misperceptions which can be resolved by a simple commitment to candor. These books are less helpful in situations where not all parties share a commitment to learning about their differences. The literatures on community organization and group work offer much helpful guidance in the tasks of ground rule negotiation, as well as other, subsequent interpersonal and organizational tasks.

11. Several writers have observed that planners who want to be understood by decision-makers confront a cultural or linguistic problem, in which planners must attempt to understand the practical concerns of social actors and to translate their own technical concerns into terms which social actors can understand. Benne (1976) has delineated distinctions between the cognitive maps and concerns of planners and social practitioners. Other writers who have discussed cognitive problems in communication between planners and social actors include Churchman and Schainblatt (1965); Doktor and Hamilton (1973); Huysmans (1970); McKenney and Keen (1974); and Mintzberg (1976). I have reviewed these issues and this literature in "Educating Planners for Sensitivity to Organization" (Baum, 1979a). In addition to linguistic problems in communication between a planner and a decision-maker, nonrational psychological dynamics in the advising relationship may interfere with communication even when planners use language which decision-makers can understand. I have discussed these dynamics in "The Advisor as Invited Intruder" (Baum, forthcoming).

12. This approach to the adoption of a proposal is part of the conventional thinking of community organizers. In the planning literature, Bolan (1969) has provided a conceptualization of actors who should be considered at significant decision points. Kaufman (1976) has developed a guide to formulating strategies and tactics for influencing these decisions. Needleman and Needleman (1974) have provided case examples of ways in which community planners have organized political support for proposals.

13. Tennenbaum (1978) describes one kind of "entrepreneur-planner" who changes jobs in order to follow a plan from formulation and adoption through to implementation.

14. Meltsner (1972) has outlined the basic questions which a planner should consider in constructing such a scenario. Kaufman (1976) has provided a detailed discussion of strategic and tactical considerations which planners should take into account in developing proposals.

15. There is an extensive, though uneven, literature on the implementation of programs. Several books may be of particular interest to planners who are considering what to anticipate and how to structure appropriate incentives in developing proposals for solutions of planning problems. Michael (1973) has provided a broad-ranging survey of organizational and psychological issues which must be confronted in planning and implementing programs in a turbulent, uncertain social environment. He offers general guidelines for action. Sarason (1972) has described typical scenarios which take place when new programs are established without

consideration of the practicalities of implementation. Pressman and Wildavsky (1973) have provided a disturbingly graphic case study of the uncertainties which beset an implementation effort and offer some general suggestions about reducing some of the problems encountered.

16. Michael (1973) has argued clearly for the importance of acknowledging uncertainty in planning and implementation and of structuring organizational incentives so as to permit learning which reduces uncertainty. He contends that only tentative action in a spirit of experimentation can provide the learning necessary to improve the probability of effective action. This experimentation should improve the likelihood both that what is implemented resembles what is proposed and that program participants modify what is proposed when it appears inappropriate to the setting where implementation is attempted.

17. Bardach (1977) accompanies his discussion of expectable implementation games with a presentation of a method for constructing scenarios of likely responses to incentives built into proposals.

18. The problem of institutional overload is analyzed in readings collected by Rose (1980).

19. This alternation of overload and innovation resembles Kuhn's (1962) description of the change in scientific paradigms. What is involved here is the testing of social decision-making paradigms and a search for alternatives when existing paradigms become increasingly irreconcilable with the perceptions, actions, and demands of members of society. At the same time, the political character of overload should be noted, and the case of welfare rights organizations is illustrative. Convinced that existing social welfare policies are inherently inequitable, these organizations have explicitly advocated a strategy of overloading the welfare system in order to force reform. They seek to challenge existing social welfare policies by organizing citizens to make all legal claims on the welfare system in an effort to overload and break the system, in the hope that a crisis in the existing system would lead to a consideration of alternative policies. For a discussion of this strategy, see Piven and Cloward (1971).

20. This conclusion focuses on the perceptions of planners' roles by people who are considering vocational choices. Clearly, as this study shows, a majority of planners misperceive the reality of planners' roles. However, what is significant here is that most planners appear to misperceive this reality in ways which are similar and which appear to be based in elements of their personality orientation.

21. For examples of the views of Planners Network members, see Clavel, Forester, and Goldsmith (1980). This collection of readings, although not formally associated with the Network, includes writings by a number of people who have been active in the Network.

22. Clearly, not all programs are the same, and no program is monolithic. General tendencies are described here.

23. For an extensive discussion of all these types of exercises and their use in planning education, see Baum (1979a). The following discussion is a brief summary of that paper.

24. ICCH Public Policy and Management Program (1979) has compiled a broad range of case studies in planning and policy-making, including cases in organizational behavior and interpersonal relations. Charan (1976) has noted that the use of case studies in teaching has encompassed a range of practices from didactic pedagogy to active participation of students. He observes that there is no evaluative literature on the use of this method from which to draw any consistent conclusions. He suggests that methods for using case studies in teaching organizational understanding and skills must be clearly examined in order to learn how they may be most effective.

25. Johnson and Johnson (1975) and Kolb, Rubin, and McIntyre (1979) provide numerous simulation exercises in areas in which planners are involved in organizations and political settings. For example, they offer exercises in decision-making and the use of power. They discuss how these exercises may be structured in order to maximize the transfer of learning from the exercises to practice situations. At the same time, it should be noted that there is no systematic evaluation of the carryover effects of simulation game actions into practice settings.

26. Kidron (1977) has observed that role playing exercises encompass such a range of activities that evaluations of their lasting effects cannot be conclusive. Argyris and Schon's (1974) work with practitioners suggests that role playing exercises are likely to affect practitioners' subsequent actions to the degree that the exercises include systematic confrontation of practitioners' actions. In this way it may be possible to force the role players to articulate the "theories-in-use" actually governing their actions, which may be different from the "espoused theories" which rationally describe and justify actions. Uncovering "theories-in-use" makes it possible to identify obstacles to effectiveness inherent in customary ways of acting. Nevertheless, Argyris and Schon (1978) note, individual change is affected by organizational incentive systems.

27. Klein and Astrachan (1971) have systematically described and compared the Tavistock group and the T group as two theoretically well articulated approaches to understanding group process. They identify the ways in which these training groups may enable participants to learn about the dynamic meaning of group and organizational structures and about the use of power in affecting these structures. Astrachan and Flynn (1976) note that it is impossible to generalize about individual participants' responses to group exercises.

28. Beinstein (1976) and Heskin (1978) provide two accounts of field instruction experiences. Heskin is particularly helpful in indicating areas in which supervisors may be instructive to students in planning field placements by raising questions about practice issues. In addition, I have provided a narrative and conceptual description of a field instruction program with which I have worked in "From Practice to Theory: Using Field Work to Teach Planning Theory" (Baum, 1980). The discussion of field placements in this chapter is an abridgment of that paper.

29. This phrase is the title of an analysis of the War on Poverty by Ryan

(1976). Ryan contends that one shortcoming of the War on Poverty was an excessive clinical focus on poor persons as individuals, with the result that social structural causes for their poverty were overlooked—and acquitted. Consequently, many analysts erroneously tended to find the victims of these structural processes to be responsible for their own misery.

REFERENCES

Argyris, Chris, and Donald A. Schon. *Theory in Practice*. San Francisco: Jossey-Bass, 1974.

Argyris, Chris and Donald A. Schon. *Organizational Learning*. Reading: Addison-Wesley, 1978.

Astrachan, Boris M., and Hulda R. Flynn. "The Intergroup Exercise: A Paradigm for Learning about the Development of Organizational Structure." In Eric J. Miller, ed., *Task and Organization*. London: Tavistock Publications, 1976.

Bardach, Eugene J. *The Implementation Game*. Cambridge: MIT Press, 1977.

Baum, Howell S. "The Forecasting Component of Planning." Unpublished paper, University of Maryland, Baltimore, 1976.

Baum, Howell S. "Distribution of Ability to Imagine the Future: Implications for the Planning Process," *Plan Canada, 17*, 3-4 (September-December, 1977), pp. 218-236. (a)

Baum, Howell S. "Toward a Post-Industrial Planning Theory," *Policy Sciences, 8*, (1977), pp. 401-421. (b)

Baum, Howell S. "Educating Planners for Sensitivity to Organization." Unpublished paper, University of Maryland, Baltimore, 1979.

Baum, Howell B. "Policy Analysis: An Intellectual Attitude and a Cognitive Style." Paper presented at the conference on The Role of Policy Analysis in the Education of Planners, Massachusetts Institute of Technology, Cambridge, Massachusetts, October 11-12, 1979. (b)

Baum, Howell S. "From Practice to Theory: Using Field Work to Teach Planning Theory." Unpublished paper, University of Maryland, Baltimore, 1980.

Baum, Howell S. "The Advisor as Invited Intruder." *Public Administration Review* (forthcoming).

Beinstein, Judith. "Urban Field Education: An Opportunity Structure for Enhancing Students' Personal and Social Efficacy," *Human Relations, 23* (1976), pp. 677-685.

Benne, Kenneth D. "Educational Field Experience as the Negotiation of Different Cognitive Worlds." In Warren G. Bennis, Kenneth D. Benne, Robert Chin, and Kenneth E. Corey, eds., *The Planning of Change*, third edition, New York: Holt, Rinehart and Winston, 1976, pp. 164-171.

Bolan, Richard S. "Community Decision Behavior: The Culture of Planning," *Journal of the American Institute of Planners, 35* (September, 1969), pp. 301-310.

Boocock, Sarane S. "An Experimental Study of the Effects of Two Games with Simulated Environments." In Sarane Boocock and E. D. Schild, eds., *Simulation Games in Learning*. Beverly Hills: Sage Publications, 1968, pp. 107-134.

Charan, Ram. "Classroom Techniques in Teaching by the Case Method," *Academy of Management Review, 1* (1976), pp. 116-123.

Churchman, C. West, and A. H. Schainblatt. "The Researcher and the Manager: A Dialectic of Implementation," *Management Science, 11,* 4 (February, 1965), pp. B-69-B-87.

Clavel, Pierre, John Forester, and William Goldsmith, eds. *Urban and Regional Planning in an Age of Austerity*. New York: Pergamon Press, 1980.

Cole, David Bras. *The Role of Psychological Belief Systems in Urban Planning*. Doctoral dissertation, University of Colorado, Boulder, 1975.

Cook, S. L. "Purposes and Quality of Graduate Education in the Management Sciences," *Management Science, 17* (1970), pp. B-5-B-12.

Cox, Fred M. "A Suggestive Schema for Community Problem Solving." In Fred M. Cox, John L. Erlich, Jack Rothman, and John E. Tropman, eds., *Strategies of Community Organization*, second edition. Itasca: F. E. Peacock Publishers, 1974, pp. 425-444.

Culbert, Samuel A. "The Real World and the Management Classroom," *California Management Review, 19* (1977), pp. 65-78.

Doktor, Robert H., and William F. Hamilton. "Cognitive Style and the Acceptance of Management Science Recommendations," *Management Science, 19,* 8 (April, 1973), pp. 884-894.

Emery, F. E., and E. L. Trist. *Towards a Social Ecology*. London and New York: Plenum Press, 1973.

Etzioni, Amitai. *The Active Society*. New York: Free Press, 1968.

Faludi, Andreas. *Planning Theory*. Oxford: Pergamon Press, 1973.

Heskin, Allan David. "From Theory to Practice: Professional Development at UCLA," *Journal of the American Institute of Planners, 44* (1978), pp. 436-451.

Hudson, Liam, *Contrary Imaginations*. New York: Schocken, 1966.

Huysmans, Jan H. B. M. "The Effectiveness of the Cognitive-Style Constraint in Implementing Operations Research Proposals," *Management Science, 17,* 1 (September, 1970), pp. 92-104.

ICCH Public Policy and Management Program, compilers. *Cases in Public Policy and Management*. Boston: Intercollegiate Case Clearing House, 1979.

Johnson, David W., and Frank P. Johnson. *Joining Together*. Englewood Cliffs: Prentice-Hall, 1975.

Kaufman, Jerome. *Intervention: A Strategy to Increase Planning Effectiveness*. Madison: Department of City and Regional Planning, University of Wisconsin, 1976.

Kidron, Aryeh. "The Effectiveness of Experiential Methods in Training and Education: The Case of Role Playing," *Academy of Management Review, 2* (1977), pp. 490-495.

Klein, Edward B., and Boris M. Astrachan. "Learning in Groups: A Comparison of Study Groups and T. Groups," *Journal of Applied Behavioral Science,* 7 (1971), pp. 659-683.

Kogan, Nathan. "Educational Implications of Cognitive Styles." In Gerald S. Lesser, ed., *Psychology and Educational Practice.* Glenview: Scott, Foresman, and Company, 1971, pp. 242-292.

Kolb, David A. "Management and the Learning Process," *California Management Review, 18* (1976), pp. 21-31.

Kolb, David A., Irwin M. Rubin, and James M. McIntyre. *Organizational Psychology,* third edition. Englewood Cliffs: Prentice-Hall, 1979.

Kuhn, Thomas A. *The Structure of Scientific Revolutions.* Chicago: University of Chicago Press, 1962.

Livingston, Samuel A. *Simulation Games and Attitudes Toward the Poor: Three Questionnaire Studies,* Report No. 118, Baltimore: Center for the Social Organization of Schools, Johns Hopkins University, 1971.

Loye, David. *The Knowable Future.* New York: Wiley, 1978.

McFarlane, Paul T. *Pilot Studies of Role Behavior in a Parent-Child Simulation Game,* Report No. 39, Baltimore: Center for the Social Organization of Schools, Johns Hopkins University, 1969.

McKenney, James L., and Peter G. W. Keen. "How Managers' Minds Work," *Harvard Business Review,* 52 (May-June, 1974), pp. 79-90.

Meltsner, Arnold J. "Political Feasibility and Policy Analysis," *Public Administration Review, 32* (1972), pp. 859-867.

Meltsner, Arnold J. *Policy Analysts in the Bureaucracy.* Berkeley: University of California Press, 1976.

Michael, Donald N. *On Learning to Plan—and Planning to Learn.* San Francisco: Jossey Bass, 1973.

Mintzberg, Henry. "Planning on the Left Side and Managing on the Right," *Harvard Business Review, 54* (July-August, 1976), pp. 49-58.

Needleman, Martin, and Carolyn Emerson Needleman. *Guerillas in the Bureaucracy.* New York: Wiley, 1974.

Piven, Frances Fox, and Richard A. Cloward. *Regulating the Poor.* New York: Vintage Books, 1971.

Pressman, Jeffrey L., and Aaron B. Wildavsky. *Implementation.* Berkeley: University of California Press, 1973.

Rose, Richard, ed. *Challenge to Governance.* Beverly Hills: Sage Publications, 1980.

Ryan, William. *Blaming the Victim,* revised edition. New York: Vintage, 1976.

Sarason, Seymour B. *The Creation of Settings and the Future Societies.* San Francisco: Jossey-Bass, 1972.

Schild, E. O. "The Shaping of Strategies." In Sarane Boocock and E. O. Schild, eds., *Simulation Games in Learning.* Beverly Hills: Sage Publications, 1968, pp. 143-154.

Seeley, John R. "Social Science: Some Probative Problems." In John R. Seeley, *The Americanization of the Unconscious.* New York: International Science Press, 1967, pp. 149-165.

Seidner, Constance J. "Teaching with Simulations and Games." In N. L. Gage, ed., *The Psychology of Teaching Methods*, The Seventy-fifth Yearbook of the National Society for the Study of Education, Part I. Chicago: National Society for the Study of Education, 1976, pp. 217-251.

Signell, Karen A. "Cognitive Complexity in Person Perception and Nation Perception: A Developmental Approach," *Journal of Personality, 34* (1966), pp. 517-537.

Tennenbaum, Robert, "Try on a New Hat: It Might Suit You," *Planning, 44* (August, 1978), pp. 30-33.

Tolman, Edward Chase and Egon Brunswik. "The Organism and the Causal Texture of the Environment," *Psychological Review, 42* (1935), pp. 43-77.

APPENDIX: METHODOLOGICAL ISSUES

The Purpose of the Study

The discussion of planning and professions in the introduction refers to a number of questions for which there are not empirical answers in the planning literature. Although the stakes involved in planners' acquisition of professional status may be high, not even planners have a clear understanding of how planners as a group see their work or how these perceptions may influence public responses to planners' work.

In order to shed some light on some of these issues, this study interviewed a sample of planners about what they do and how they assess their work. Such direct study of planners is unusual, for two reasons. For one thing, planners comprise a small number of practitioners, and self-conscious curiosity about their work is a relatively recent development, stimulated primarily by the "identity crisis" and developments described in the introductory discussion. A second reason why planners have rarely written about other planners is also important. As the empirical material in the book shows, planners have tended to overlook the roles which they, as well as other people, actually play in the planning process. This bias is evident in the planning literature.

The planning literature may be divided into normative and empirical writings. The normative literature prescribes how planning should be done. This is by far the largest part of the planning literature, and almost all efforts at definition fall in this category. Part of the normative literature is concerned with policy issues. This literature identifies the types of questions which planners should ask in order to understand the political and economic implications of their actions. A far larger part of the normative literature is concerned with techniques which may be used in planning. Numerous books and articles describe various techniques for the collection, analysis, and presentation of information in describing planning problems and identifying their solutions. Both these types of normative literature share an emphasis on knowledge and intellectual activity.

What this literature may assume but rarely directly describes is discussed in a relatively small third type of normative literature. This is a literature which recognizes interpersonal and political components to planning activity. Writers here note that getting an assignment, acquiring information, and persuading others to receive and accept recommendations are all social processes, in which the necessary skills are organizational. This literature offers suggestions about how planners can negotiate some of the personal and political relationships which they encounter in order to influence decision-making on the problems with which they are concerned.

The empirical literature on planning, which describes ways in which planning has actually been carried out, is much smaller than the normative literature. Here there are a number of case studies, often explaining how the less-than-best-laid plans may go awry and occasionally identifying implementation successes for planners. Most case studies describe the ways in which the degree of planners' sensitivity to and willingness and ability to participate in political processes vitally affect the fate of their recommendations. These case studies are empirical accounts of specific planning projects and analyses of the political factors affecting their outcomes (for example, Altshuler, 1965; Jacobs, 1978; Meyerson and Banfield, 1975; and Rabinovitz, 1969).

These case studies, however, tell little about how the participating planners experience these projects or, for that matter, how they see planning generally. The studies reveal relatively little about whether planners like the roles they played in these cases, how the cases affected their views of planning, or how they feel about the political components of planning. A small number of studies in the empirical literature have attempted to describe the personal experiences of planners and how they make sense out of their work. For example, Catanese (1974) has summarized his impressions of planners from years of practice and has recorded the statements of a small number of planning directors invited to talk about their work (Catanese and Farmer, 1978).

Still, the perceptions and feelings of the large number of planning practitioners remain largely unrecorded. Some extensive surveys have asked planners' views on selected questions. Vasu (1979) interviewed planners about their political values in relation to planning issues. Howe and Kaufman (Howe, 1980; Howe and Kaufman, 1979; and Howe and Kaufman, 1981) asked planners about their ethical values, their conception of their roles, and their positions on some common planning issues. More intensive study of planners is rare. One exceptional study, by Needleman and Needleman (1974) is concerned with describing the daily experiences of planners in their own words. That study focuses on role conflicts which community planners experience as part of their dual responsibilities to public planning departments and neighborhood communities.

The present study builds on the latter tradition, focusing on the everyday experiences of planners and the meanings which they have for planners. In response to planners' "identity crisis" and the conflicts which accompany it, turns to planners' own statements about their work in order to make sense out of this work as planners see it. The study findings may help planners and their observers to understand what common tasks and concerns are shared by planners in diverse settings.

In particular, the study findings provide some empirical answers to questions about the professional status of planners. For example, the study helps identify what planners regard as their domain of practice and what type of expertise they believe they apply to this domain. The study helps make explicit planners' assessments of their effectiveness and their perceptions of their autonomy. The study helps describe the collective consciousness of planners, whether they do want professional status and autonomy, and how they represent themselves publicly.

The Method of the Study

The study was designed to elicit planners' descriptions of their work and their feelings about their work. The methods of collecting and analyzing information draw on the procedures of the qualitative research tradition. A semi-structured interview was selected as the format most likely to ensure coverage of basic issues related to planners' work while simultaneously permitting individual planners the opportunity to express their personal concerns. An interview questionnaire was constructed to cover the following topics: personal background, education, choice of planning as an occupation, work history, goals and sources of satisfaction in work, frustrations and recommendations for changes in the work setting, and current issues in planning (such as citizen participation, licensing, and advocacy planning). The questionnaire was pre-tested and modified to improve the validity of responses to questions.

This type of interview produced data which the methods of qualitative research are best suited to analyze.[1] A small number of closed-ended or forced-choice questions produced responses which could be readily summarized and analyzed quantitatively. However, both the form and the content of responses set limits to the possibilities of quantitative analysis. In form, most responses comprised brief or extended statements. These responses were analyzed in the following way. Individual responses to each question were examined for a dominant theme or themes. Then for any specific question the themes expressed in the responses for the total sample could be identified and summarized quantitatively. However, in order to give a more accurate representation of the sense, or meaning, of themes expressed, quotations have been excerpted from typical statements and presented.

In addition, the subtle content of the responses complicated analysis of the interview material. Much cognitive, or informational, content was straightforward and easily identifiable. In contrast, affective, or emotional, content might be expressed in the mood of an interview and in the connotations of selected words in responses. These emotional messages might add to the cognitive information, might express ambivalence with respect to overt statements in responses, or might even contradict those statements. Identification of affective content depended on a careful recollection of interview settings and reading of responses. Representation of this content was particularly difficult because it was rarely explicitly or succinctly expressed. Nevertheless, as with the .cognitive content, responses were examined for dominant themes, and quotations representing these themes have been excerpted and presented. Because of the elusiveness of the content, however, no quantitative summary or analysis of affective content was attempted.

For these reasons the presentation of the interview data includes a combination of quantitative and, primarily, qualitative analysis. Most discussions began with quantitative summaries of responses or themes. These summaries are then followed by qualitative elaboration on the themes and presentation of representative quotations. Because of the difficulty of quantifying responses, discussions frequently refer to "a few," "some," "many," or "most" planners. This imprecision is perhaps unsatisfying, but the data do not permit greater specificity, and these general adjectives have been selected in an effort to suggest at least the magnitude of a theme within the responses.

The Study Sample

The study sample was selected randomly from the membership of the Maryland Chapter of the American Institute of Planners, the professional association of planners. (This organization has since become the American Planning Association.) This sampling procedure was expected to include a large number of practitioners in diverse planning roles and settings. Further, it appeared that membership in the professional association involved some especially strong identification by individual practitioners of themselves as "planners." At the same time, it may be noted that some people join the professional association for pragmatic reasons related to the advancement of their careers. In addition, some planners with strong identification with "planning" decline to join the professional association because they cannot afford the dues or because they do not find membership useful to them. Nevertheless, the strengths of this sampling approach appear to outweigh possible shortcomings.

Because the study would consist of lengthy, intensive interviews conducted in person, a limited sample of 50 was selected. This represented 25 percent of the membership of the Maryland Chapter of the American Institute of Planners. The interviews were conducted between July, 1977, and July, 1978.

In contacting potential interviewees, I introduced myself as a planning faculty member of the University of Maryland who was interested in talking with planners about their perceptions of their work. Most people readily agreed to participate in the interview. The few who declined to participate included a small number of people who had left planning for other fields and a private consultant who said he could not afford the time needed for the interview. The interviews were conducted at the planners' offices unless they asked to talk elsewhere or convenience dictated a different meeting place. The interviews varied in length from 45 minutes to three hours; most lasted approximately an hour and a half.

As a planning educator and part-time planning practitioner, I was generally accepted as an "insider" by the people with whom I talked. Although some people tended to provide rhetorical or "public" responses to questions, most of the planners were remarkably candid in describing their goals, their work, and their frustrations. The consistent expressions of confusion were noteworthy. The affect of the interviews was itself significant. At the end of the interviews, people frequently made one or both of two statements. First, they thanked me profusely for listening to them, apologized for any comments which might have been boring, and expressed their hope that I had enjoyed the interview. They indicated that the issues which I raised were troubling to them and that they did not have much opportunity to discuss their uncertainties with other planners.

A second type of comment amounted to a request for a "grade." Some planners wanted to know how they stood in relation to other planners with whom I had talked. They indicated that they felt that they worked in isolation from a reference group of planners and that they felt like deviants in relation to this unknown reference group. They asked me to assure them in some way that they were doing work which was acceptably within the bounds of "planning." In responding to this request, I shared general impressions from other interviews and asked whether my impressions seemed reasonable to them. In this way the planners and I had an opportunity to interpret the material from the interviews together.

The basic characteristics of the sample of 50 planners are summarized in Table A-1, which also compares the sample population to the national membership of the American Institute of Planners and to planners enumerated in the 1970 Census. The table suggests that the sample resembles American planners in several major respects. The study sample is similar to the national membership of the AIP, as well as the American planners generally, with regard to sex, race, age, and income (with allowance made for inflation). The sample is similar to the national

AIP membership with respect to place of employment (public agency or private firm) and perhaps rank within the employing organization. In comparison with the national AIP membership the sample has more years of formal schooling in general and a higher proportion of engineers and social scientists in particular.

These characteristics suggest several observations about the generalizability of findings from this study. First, there are substantial similarities in the characteristics of the sample and planners nationally, with the implication that findings may be generalizable. Second, however, there are evident differences between the sample and planners nationally with regard to the level and type of education. For example, the sample has a higher proportion of social scientists in comparison with architects than the national sample. The implication of this difference is not clear, particularly insofar as some of the study findings appear counter-intuitive in this respect: despite the dominance of social scientists in the sample, the sample as a whole does not express a strong understanding of the social context of planning. The higher level of education in the sample may contribute to higher career expectations, although findings of frustration with limited influence are relatively consistent throughout the sample. Third, the geographic concentration of the sample in the Baltimore metropolitan area may contribute some uncertain biases to the findings. Finally, the size of the sample presents some limitations. It may prevent finding some groups and points-of-view which would be evident in a larger, more extensive sample. The size of the sample also requires generalizations from relatively small numbers of respondents and limits the ways in which the findings can be analyzed.

Limitations of the Study

This study is exploratory. It examines a small sample intensively. This intensive study permits the formulation of many questions, for which this book seeks to provide answers. However, the findings may be limited in two ways. The first concerns the small size of the sample on which findings are based. The second concerns the intangible, elusive character of the phenomena studied. Yet the findings are sufficiently provocative to suggest, where questions remain, that further study is appropriate and necessary.

TABLE A-1.   CHARACTERISTICS OF THE SAMPLE, WITH
COMPARISONS TO NATIONAL AIP MEMBERSHIP AND
PLANNERS ENUMERATED IN THE 1970 CENSUS

Characteristics	Sample (N = 50)	National AIP membership[a]	Planners in 1970 Census[b]
Sex			
Male	88.0%	90.9%	89.5%
Female	12.0%	9.1%	10.5%
Race			
White	94.0%	93.9%	91.0%
Black, other	6.0%	6.1%	9.0%
Age			
Range	26–78		
Median	37	35[c]	35.9[d]
Income			
Range	$10,000–$40,000+		
Median	$20,000–$24,999	$15,000-$20,000[c]	$11,544[e]
Employment			
Public agency	68%	63.3%[f]	79.8%
Private firm	32%	36.7%[f]	20.2%
Organizational rank			
"Public admin."[g]	34%		
Public agency directors		19.2% ⎫ 38.0%	72.6%
"Private admin."[h]	20%	18.8% ⎭	
Public staff	34%		⎫ 27.4%[c]
Private staff	12%		⎭
Undergraduate major			
Architecture	24%	27.2%[c]	
Engineering	20%	8.0%[c]	
Social Science	52%	36.7%[c]	
Other	4%	28.1%[c]	
Graduate education			
Master's, planning	74%	40%[c]	
Master's, other	26%[i]	12%[c]	
No master's	4%	48%[c]	
Law degree	6%		
Doctorate, planning	2%	3%[c]	
Doctorate, other		3%[c]	

[a] Unless otherwise noted, the source for all data on the national membership of the American Institute of Planners is American Institute of Planners (n.d.).

[b] All data from the 1970 Census are drawn from citations in Beauregard (1976).

[c] These data refer to a 1974 survey of AIP membership and come from American Institute of Planners (1974).

[d] This figure refers to male planners only. The median for female planners is 28.1 years.

[e] This figure refers to male planners only. The median for female planners is $6,726.

[f] These percentages are computed by including only those planners who do work in public agencies or private firms and by excluding all others, including those engaged in university work.

[g] The category of "public administrators" includes all persons in public agencies at or above the rank of section chief. When this category is used, "public staff" includes all persons below the rank of section chief.

[h] "Private administrators" includes principals of planning firms and freelance consultants.

[i] This number includes four persons, or eight percent of the sample, who have master's degrees in both planning and another field.

NOTES

1. For discussion of the methods of qualitative research and data analysis, see Bogdan and Taylor (1975); Filstead (1970); Glaser and Strauss (1967); Lofland (1971); Schatzman and Strauss (1973); and Zito (1975).

REFERENCES

Altshuler, Alan. *The City Planning Process*. Ithaca: Cornell University Press, 1965.

American Institute of Planners. "AIP membership has not changed much since 1965; average about the same but salaries and education higher," *AIP Newsletter, 9* (1974), pp. 1-3.

American Institute of Planners. "Membership Survey from 1976 Roster." Mimeographed, American Institute of Planners, Washington, no date.

Beauregard, Robert A. "The Occupation of Planning: A View from the Census," *Journal of the American Institute of Planners, 42* (1976), pp. 187-192.

Bogdan, Robert, and Steven J. Taylor. *Introduction to Qualitative Research Methods*. New York: John Wiley and Sons, 1975.

Catanese, Anthony James. *Planners and Local Politics*. Beverly Hills: Sage Publications, 1974.

Catanese, Anthony James and Paul Farmer. *Personality, Politics and Planning*. Beverly Hills: Sage Publications, 1978.

Filstead, William J. *Qualitative Methodology*. Chicago: Markham Publishing Company, 1970.

Glaser, Barney G., and Anselm L. Strauss. *The Discovery of Grounded Theory: Strategies for Qualitative Research*. Chicago: Aldine-Atherton, 1967.

Howe, Elizabeth. "Role Choices of Urban Planners," *Journal of the American Planning Association, 46* (1980), pp. 398-409.

Howe, Elizabeth, and Jerome Kaufman. "The Ethics of Contemporary American Planners," *Journal of the American Planning Association, 45* (1979), pp. 243-255.

Howe, Elizabeth, and Jerome Kaufman. "The Values of Contemporary American Planners," *Journal of the American Planning Association, 47* (1981), pp. 266-278.

Jacobs, Allan B. *Making City Planning Work*. Chicago: American Society of Planning Officials, 1978.

Lofland, John. *Analyzing Social Settings*. Belmont: Wadsworth Publishing Company, 1971.

Meyerson, Martin, and Edward C. Banfield. *Politics, Planning, and the Public Interest*. New York: The Free Press of Glencoe, 1955.

Needleman, Martin, and Carolyn Emerson Needleman. *Guerrillas in the Bureaucracy*. New York: John Wiley, 1974.

Rabinovitz, Francine F. *City Politics and Planning*. Chicago: Aldine, 1969.

Schatzman, Leonard, and Anselm L. Strauss. *Field Research*. Englewood Cliffs: Prentice-Hall, 1973.

Vasu, Michael Lee. *Politics and Planning: A National Study of American Planners*. Chapel Hill: University of North Carolina Press, 1979.

Zito, George V. *Methodology and Meaning*. New York: Praeger Publishers, 1975.

INDEX

305